A REPUBLIC, IF YOU CAN KEEP IT

THE FOUNDATION OF THE AMERICAN PRESIDENCY, 1700–1800

Michael P. Riccards

CONTRIBUTIONS IN POLITICAL SCIENCE, NUMBER 167

Greenwood Press

New York • Westport, Connecticut • London

Library of Congress Cataloging-in-Publication Data

Riccards, Michael P.
    A republic, if you can keep it.

    (Contributions in political science, ISSN 0147-1066 ;
no. 167)
    Bibliography: p.
    Includes index.
    1. Presidents—United States—History—
18th century.   2. Executive power—United States—
History—18th century.   3. United States—Politics
and government—1789-1797.   I. Title.   II. Series.
JK511.R53   1987   353.03′1′09   86-29595
ISBN 0-313-25462-1 (lib. bdg. : alk. paper)

Library of Congress Catalog Card Number: 86-29595
ISBN: 0-313-25462-1
ISSN: 0147-1066

First published in 1987

Greenwood Press, Inc.
88 Post Road West, Westport, Connecticut 06881

Printed in the United States of America

The paper used in this book complies with the
Permanent Paper Standard issued by the National
Information Standards Organization (Z39.48-1984).

10   9   8   7   6   5   4   3   2   1

TO MY CHILDREN
AND MY CHILDREN'S
CHILDREN

I have studied politics so that my children
would have the liberty to study mathematics
and philosophy, and in order that their children
will have the right to study painting, poetry,
music, architecture, statuary, tapestry,
and porcelain.

CONTENTS

Contents

ACKNOWLEDGMENTS

This study of the origins of executive authority and the Federalist presidencies owes much to the various librarians who have been so helpful to me at the University of Massachusetts/Boston, Princeton University, State University of New York College at Buffalo, Hunter College, and the Henry L. Huntington Research Library.

I am also grateful to the National Endowment for the Humanities, which awarded me a fellowship to Princeton University in 1977–78. With that opportunity and a sabbatical from the State University of New York, I had the time to work on this project and on another on religious socialization under the pleasant aegis of John F. Wilson.

My appreciation goes to James F. Brennan and Mildred Vasan who commented wisely on the first draft, and Margaret Foley, who has been almost as tolerant of this manuscript as she was of its demanding author. Diana Riccards has provided invaluable assistance and care for the second draft. As with my previous work and so much more in my life, I owe my deepest thanks to my wife, Barbara, and our children, Patrick, Catherine, and Abigail, to whom this volume is dedicated—in a paraphrase of John Adams, of course.

INTRODUCTION

In the past several years, many Americans have become critics of our most unique political invention—the presidency. Some have feared its strengths, and other have lamented its weaknesses. The debates about executive privilege, the power to wage war, the ability to conduct diplomacy, and the origins of impeachment are not merely dim historical episodes. Instead, they are the contemporary stuff of political controversy, disputes that are never permanently settled in a system of limited powers and overlapping ambitions.

Although the scope of the presidency has changed immensely since 1933, the office is, to a remarkable extent, deeply rooted in the past. This study chronicles the origins of the presidency and follows its development as the executive branch of the new government. As in so many aspects of early American culture, the presidency is best understood within the context of seventeenth-century British thought and political practices. The New World colonists were especially influenced by the controversies over the power of the Crown's ministers and the alleged corruption of parliamentary politics. They knew of executive authority from several sources—the Whig opposition in Britain, the great philosophical tomes of commentators such as Locke and Blackstone, the much discussed debates about the powers of the Crown, and the indigenous workings of the royal governors. From these experiences and upbringings, the colonist leaders marshaled their own opposition ideology, which was highly critical of executive authority as they knew or imagined it. In their battles, they relied on their own local assemblies to check the ambitions and pretensions of the Crown and its local agents, and consequently, they moved the British empire into war.

Yet the Patriots in rebellion saw the need to reestablish executive authority, at least at the state level, when they drew up the new constitutions after the war began. And despite all their animosity toward the executive branch, they came to admire the strong state governors who contributed to the Revolution. Foremost among them was George Clinton, the able governor of New York State, who showed, more than any other figure except George Washington, how a republican government could link up responsibility with authority.

When the Founding Fathers grew weary of the Articles of Confederation, they cast about for a more dynamic charter of government and a much enlarged executive branch. Not surprisingly, they looked to New York and Massachusetts, to the states with strong governors, as models for the new Constitution. On the floor of the Convention, the Fathers struggled with many of the same complex issues we face today in dealing with the presidency: the power to wage war, the lure of unbridled ambition, the meaning of executive responsibility, the relationship with the Congress. When they finished, the new Constitution was referred to state ratifying conventions, and once again controversy ensued.

The presidency in 1789 was a collection of phrases; it was Washington who lent his own immense prestige to this unformed office. More than anyone, he had symbolized the integrity of the republican experiment. He was not merely a Founding Father; he was the patriarch. He was not merely an occasional revolutionary agitator, but the great general who brought victory against incredible odds. In a short period, Washington went from being a discredited colonial officer in the British army to being a sober landowner, then a beleaguered commander, and finally a national and international hero. And in the midst of that heady glory, he resigned to go back to the simple virtues of republican farming.

His presidency began as an uncertain groping for the right gesture, the correct etiquette, the moderate exercise of executive authority. Early in his first term, the President suffered two major illnesses, and it seemed that Hamilton, and not the General, was the mainstay of the Administration. Opposition forces led by Madison and Secretary of State Jefferson began to question Hamilton's pre-eminence and his programs as well. An opposition press grew up and then opposition factions. Washington shied away from politics and partisan activity, but his second term was filled with rancor and division. The President became more the master of his administration and reasserted his authority, especially in crushing crude sedition in western Pennsylvania, dictating policy toward the Indian tribes, and insisting on neutrality in the great wars enveloping Europe.

Thus it is clear that the American presidency was a product of long and often tedious historical and constitutional debate, and it was reinterpreted and expanded in the bitter partisan controversies in the 1790s. Washington's consensus election in 1789 and later in 1793 may have retarded the natural development of political parties, but his approval of Hamilton's economic plans and his personal leadership in foreign policy provided the very issues that split the new republic.

In the process, the presidency expanded as Washington dealt with the rudimentary origins of executive privilege, personal diplomacy, undeclared frontier "police" actions, and legislative intrusion. The first president looked back for precedents and customs, but he also looked ahead at what he was leaving his successors and heirs. The Federalist era concluded with the passionate and vacillating presidency of John Adams. Adams, sometimes cautiously, at other times recklessly, led the nation in orchestrating its animosities to the British and the French assaults on American shipping and commerce. He wavered between war and diplomacy, with the latter winning out wisely but too late for his own political advantage.

This study examines the controversies and issues that provided the rich and heated contexts in which the early presidency grew up to be an established part of our system of government. Conceived in apprehension, viewed often as a chief magistrate, the presidency became the executive authority in a way that few could have envisioned. Aware of the abuses of the royal executives and appreciative of the sacrifices of the war governors, Washington himself directed the office away from the trappings of chief of state and the detailed work of clerkship. The presidency, from the beginning, engaged in leadership and generated controversy.

The central theme of this study, then, is that Washington created the Federalist model of the presidency—a model that fell into disrepute and disuse during most of the nineteenth century and that has been ironically rediscovered in the latter part of this century. The main elements of that model are mass appeal, often regardless of public policy positions; strong assertion of executive authority, especially in foreign affairs; general disregard of political parties; preoccupation with official pomp and protocol as a way of protecting and buttressing the incumbent; a conservative economic and social orientation; and an aloofness toward legislative controversies except where they infringe on the executive. Adams continued those orientations, having, though, a more difficult time than his popular predecessor. Jefferson and his followers posed a quite different approach: party government, cabinet leadership, democratic mores, and a partially hidden executive. Jackson later broke away from both traditions of the Founding Fathers, creating a populist presidency that delighted in confrontations with the Congress and with various elites. Lincoln's presidency is so unique that, even with his obligatory bow to Washington, he waged war in a nearly single-handed way, creating an office that temporarily bore little relationship to what went before and considerable kinship to what came about in the next century. And the terms after Lincoln were filled by custodians and by men of limited range and responsibility.

The Federalist model had to deal with a long tradition of ambivalence about power and authority in the new nation. Washington clearly reached back to the past in ruling the future—to the old Confederation executives, to the state wartime governors, and even to the royal traditions upon which American institutions both rested and rebelled against. The great controversies of his second term led Washington to assert even more the powers of his office and to focus more clearly on the central dimensions of the executive. There are, oddly enough, many similarities between the presidency of those limited times and the great executive of today. With the breakdown of the New Deal party system, the continued preoccupations with foreign danger, the yearning for presidential stewardship as an almost personal communication with the people, the Federalist model—the Washington model—may seem more appropriate than Franklin D. Roosevelt's partisanship, Wilson's prime ministership, or Lincoln's isolated agony. Washington, then, not only put together the office, but also created, by conscious design and pragmatic decisions, a specific style of executive leadership that has proven to be useful at other times in the republic's history. He did it both above the petty divisions of his day and within the vortex of its swirling controversies.

The presidency, as an office, has not been generally well received in our history, and its occupants have often been manhandled by their contemporaries and even by posterity. Washington left office still widely respected by the people but much criticized by elements of the capital elites. Adams was defeated and rode back to Quincy disgusted with his fickle countrymen. Jefferson's second term was a disaster, and he and the nation breathed a sigh of relief when he departed. Jackson remained a much abused figure until the late 1940s, when Arthur Schlesinger, Jr., convinced the historical community that Old Hickory was really FDR in frontier garb. The man chosen in nearly every current poll as our greatest president, Abraham Lincoln, was vilified unmercifully in his own time and nearly denied reelection in 1864. Wilson, too, ended up broken and repudiated, his name forever linked with the failure of the League treaty and not with the splendor of his first term. Still, four decades after his death, Franklin D. Roosevelt, certainly our most important modern president, is denied a simple monument in the city he so dominated, and the centennial anniversary of his birth was met with little homage and a much restrained recollection. And his true heir, Lyndon Johnson, the greatest of all legislative tacticians and the patron of contemporary domestic reform, left us the bitterness of war and deep disillusionment with the office he once occupied so ably.

This chronicle, then, examines, the origins of that office, and how controversy and bitter divisions have followed it and often been aroused by it since the beginnings of the republic. And yet, with all the rancor of the Federalist period, it is important to put the presidency and the new republic within the context of its times. Amid the wars of Europe, the grim autocracy of the princely states, and the dark despotisms of Asia and the Middle East, the contentious experiment of these New World republicans seems like a shaft of light, unique and perhaps enduring.

The Founding Fathers knew all too well the history of failed experiments in self-government. But they believed that America's true mission was to command other states to follow, not by power and influence, but by example and exhortation. They were cautious and suspicious, but not cynical. Sometimes, as one lives with the writings, the history, and the disgusted machinations of these men, it is easy to grow weary, for politics is too often pretension, broadsides, and contrived abuse. But one cannot, in the long run, leave their company without sharing a bit in the exhilaration of founding a new nation and of reaffirming the sweeping vision of a true civic order where political life was vibrant and important to its people.

This history of the early presidency is essential not only to those interested in understanding the complex roots and uneven development of that office. It is equally fascinating to watch the interplay of character and institution, of personality and history in the central definition of that unique political experience that once was our own.

Part One

THE ORIGINS OF EXECUTIVE AUTHORITY

1

THE UNCERTAIN HERITAGE

We are the last people in Europe to retain our ancient liberties.
                                                    Sir Robert Phelips, 1629

They were the sons and daughters of Englishmen, born in another land and cast on the virgin shores of a strange continent. Praying to a God of vengeance and not of love, confronted daily by the fierce quickness of death, and living in close communities for sheer survival, the new inhabitants tried to adjust their traditions to the seacoast frontiers they embraced. With their compacts, their charters, and their constitutions, they struggled to regulate the conflicts within themselves and work out a system of rational common action against the chaos that lived by their doorsteps.

In their adventure, these settlers stretched a fragile cord of memory and a broken line of sailboats across the sea from their mother country. They sought to impose on their experiments a standard far more exacting than ever existed before, and called on the Almighty to bless their righteousness and their sacrifice. Those settlers who came to this land had set sail for a variety of reasons. Many desired to acquire land and wealth, fearing that England was becoming overcrowded and prone to produce paupers. Others came to advance the causes of the English flag and contain the reach of the Catholic Spanish king. Still others braved the heartaches and the dangers to bring Christianity to the natives, and thus to further the spread of the Holy Gospel. And of course some of these noble ancestors were common criminals, social misfits, and political undesirables who were shipped to the New World, away from the decent peoples of the British Isles.[1]

Although an ocean separated the colonists from their ancestral homeland, they shared many of the ideas and habits of their previous compatriots. Their views of politics and government grew heavily on their experiences in England. Indeed anyone seeking to understand the origins of executive power in America must be aware of the general contours of the late seventeenth- and early eighteenth-century debates over the powers and pre-rogatives of the British king.

Those political controversies involved an ancient and uncertain tension between the monarch and the Parliament, a tension that was still unresolved at the time of the American Revolution. Supporters of a strong monarch reached back into medieval history, arguing that the Parliament existed by the grace of the Crown, and they relied on deference, divine right, and, later, patriarchal theory to support their view of the political world. The king was to the nation what the father was to the family, and by the nature of things, both ruled their realm, it was hoped, wisely and well. The ad-vocates of an independent Parliament, on the other hand, recalled to mind Anglo-Saxon myth, and argued that when their British forebears originally came out of the Germanic forests, they had already established traditions of self-government. In making their case, they relied on custom, common law, and crude notions of consent. Citing Tacitus' *Germania*, these theorists found the seeds of their representative body in the Saxon *Witan*. Saxon liberties were abridged in 1066, so that tale went, when William conquered the island and imposed Norman feudalism. Even the great jurist Edward Coke seemed to support this notion, when he argued that the Magna Carta was a reaffirmation of the common law and not merely a settlement of feudal rights.[2]

Many American colonists knew the outlines of this great historical debate. Indeed, aware Europeans everywhere knew of the contentious and violent history of the English nobility toward their monarchy and toward one another. The Americans, however, throughout most of the seventeenth century, had little to do with Parliament. Their colonies were sponsored either by proprietors or directly by the Crown, and colonial statements of rights and charters of limited self-rule came from the grace or the interests of the monarch and the royal circle.

When the Puritans ended the reign of Charles I, the colonial settlements outside New England refused to recognize Cromwell and his self-appointed protectors. Finally the new Parliament sent troops to remind the colonists that their loyalty to the Stuart line was misdirected and must cease im-mediately. Most important, though, is that during the preceding English Civil War, the American colonists were generally free of royal restraints, and they began to feel the first stirrings of self-determination. To combat these developments, Cromwell, and later Charles II, tried to restore British control over the colonists, resorting more to administrative regulation than to an assertion of abstract prerogatives.[3]

One of the major outcomes of the long Crown–Parliament rivalry was the creation of the nebulous, but powerful tradition called "the rights of Englishmen," a vaguely defined collection of personal and political liberties. Many British subjects, including the colonists, saw themselves as English-men who did not forfeit their heritage because of distance from the British

Isles. Both the Crown and the Parliament reinforced these colonial views by instituting local assemblies and allowing rudimentary representative governments to be established. The Crown and Privy Council were to argue later that these assemblies were not little parliaments with the British House of Commons' powers and prerogatives. Rather, they were consultative groups with a limited scope and subordinate to the provincial governors and the wishes of the London administration.

The role of these local assemblies was, however, a source of controversy in the eighteenth century and, as in England, the representative body began to assume ascendancy over the executive. As early as 1692, for example, England had to disallow a Massachusetts law that prohibited taxation without representation—a slogan that would later breed a revolution. As the colonists grew more assertive and less likely to bend quietly to British interests, they also focused their attentions on the nature of politics across the ocean. They began to ask, What was the balance of constitutional power in England? What were the roles of the Parliament and the monarch there and, by implication, in the colonies? Was the Britain they left being corrupted by avarice and exhibiting such a decline of civic virtue that the natural liberties of Englishmen were being destroyed at home and becoming undone abroad? These inquiries were not the product of idle speculation. For more than a generation before the Revolution began, they were the fierce stuff of political acrimony. Thus the natural strains of an acquisitive imperialist economy and the increasing confidence of the coastal colonies were accentuated by an ideology of personal liberty and a near paranoiac fear of conspiracy, enslavement, and political humiliation.[4]

The ultimate secession of the American colonists from the British empire was a transatlantic dispute that revolved around many points of contention, only one of which was the proper role of executive power. The American Revolution had many origins, but the most important cause was the simple process of political and economic maturation that was taking place in the British New World. The main reason for the creation of the colonies was to bring wealth and power to the mother country. But the hardy settlers who populated the coastlines and hinterlands developed their own assemblies and created economic opportunities for themselves and their progeny.

The Crown, for its own purposes, needed the patronage positions that the colonies provided. Consequently, local leaders were often excluded from the higher echelons of power and privilege, and they in turn moved to gain control of the local assemblies. Thus ambition, ideology, and idealism mixed into a volatile combination that spilled over and exploded into civil disobedience and revolution. The vocabulary the colonists used, the charges they enumerated in their resentment were similar to those of the old English Whigs, the "Commonwealthmen" who led the opposition back home to the Crown's control of Parliament through patronage and influence peddling.[5]

One of the most popular expressions of the Commonwealthmen ideology was a series of articles penned from 1720 to 1723 by John Trenchard and Thomas Gordon under the name of "Cato." These articles attacked the British ministry and warned of the destruction of liberty through political abuses and outright corruption. "Cato's" radical Whig letters were followed by those of the conservative Viscount Bolingbroke. In *The Craftsman*, Bolingbroke conducted a ten-year campaign attacking corruption, high taxation, and mercenary armies, and he boldly trumpeted the call for a "Patriot Prince" who would govern above petty interests and in harmony with a loyal and independent House of Commons. Thus the natural tensions between colonies and mother country, between representative assemblies and royal executives, between importing and exporting segments of an empire were aggravated by the heightening political anxiety in England. As the Crown moved to exert more authority after the French and Indian wars, the colonies began to assert their need for more leeway. The view of England that the colonists had was distorted then by geographical distance and by the political publications they read. As for the English leaders, their appreciation of colonial problems was limited and mostly unsympathetic.[6]

What was England like in the early eighteenth century? In one sense, the period from 1689 to 1725 was a time of relative political stability, and that stability was due ironically to some major social changes that had occurred. First, England experienced a rise in population and a growing diversification of economic life. Trade with America, the West Indies, and the Far East increased, and financial structures necessarily became more complex, embracing larger numbers of influential citizens both in the wealthier gentry and in the merchant class.

The growth of trade and the increasing danger of foreign wars led to shifts of power within the royal government. As the British entered into a network of alliances, they required naval, military, and diplomatic establishments to link the nation's interests together. All of these changes required more taxes, and these developments in turn helped to establish a strong cabinet system, with the Treasury in a pre-eminent role. More patronage flowed and more placemen found their way onto the royal payroll. The minor gentry, the backbone of the opposition element, strongly protested against the standing army, the rise in taxes, and what they found to be the corrupt environment in which politics was being conducted. In addition, there arose the beginnings of a party system protesting against what Bolingbroke in 1734 called "the ill-effects of that new Influence and Power which have gained strengths in every reign since the Revolution." But the opposition, in all its frenzy, was no match for the skillful minister Robert Walpole, who used patriotism, patronage, and a fear of radical Jacobinism to create a political system that gave strength and cohesion to the formal government.[7] Even to his enemies, Walpole was one of the most interesting figures of the period, and he emerged as the creator of a new, although frequently misunderstood, style of English politics.

Walpole was born in 1676 to a prosperous, well-established country family that had acquired wealth over the centuries but had produced few men of distinction. Although the family later abandoned their early allegiance to Catholicism, the most important figures in the Walpole history were Jesuits: the martyr, Henry Walpole, and two apologists, Richard and Michael Walpole. Robert was sent to Eton and then to King's College, Cambridge, but after two years in the university, his brother died and he was called home to manage the estate of his ailing father. Walpole soon entered Parliament and became a member of the Kit-Cat, the most fashionable Whig Club, where he came into contact with major literary figures of the time, including Addison, Steele, and Congreve. Through the influence of his friends, he was appointed to his first post in 1705, a seat in Prince George's Council. While the Duke of Marlborough waged war and his wife, Sarah, maneuvered in Queen Anne's court, Walpole attracted attention by his quiet confidence and cunning. By 1708 the Marlboroughs were out of her favor, but Walpole was raised to Secretary at War.

He loyally supported the war and managed its financial details so well that by 1710, Walpole was given the position of Treasurer of the Navy while he stayed as Secretary at War for a time. Increasing disenchantment with the war led to a Tory government, and consequently, Walpole was dismissed in January 1711 from his post as Treasurer. A year later his carelessness in handling one bill for payment led the Tories to try him, send him to the Tower, and expel him from the Commons. Portrayed as a persecuted Whig hero and a loyal ally of Marlborough, Walpole was released in six months and later returned to the House. The British finally signed the Treaty of Utrecht, ending the war and making a mockery of Marlborough's heroic exploits.

By 1714 Walpole was named Paymaster General, the most lucrative government post and a position in which he personally controlled a great deal of patronage. While he was Paymaster General, Walpole acquired a fortune that allowed him to entertain lavishly, and he became not just a major political figure, but a social luminary in high society as well. Back on the road to success, Walpole then went on to serve briefly as Chancellor of the Exchequer, and after once again being in disfavor, he returned as Paymaster General of the Forces and an advisor to the Prince, later George II. His skill in restoring financial stability and curtailing public panic after the South Sea speculation crash, along with his general knowledge of the House of Commons, led the King reluctantly to name him his first minister in April 1727. When George I died, his son continued to rely on Walpole's control of the Commons. Together with Queen Charlotte, Walpole effectively stayed in the monarch's favor and skillfully eliminated political rivals.

The genius of Walpole was not that he discovered that patronage and a desire for a pension were part of political life, but that he concentrated the disposition of these offices in his own hands and extracted maximum advantage. He extended his grasp to include the most meager position and created patterns of loyalty that supported a "Treasury party" in the Commons. Walpole even moved toward controlling the Church's patronage and filled its ranks with Whigs. Because only a minority of the seats in Parliament were contested, the government could concentrate on those closely fought boroughs. One can see the types of contests that took place by reading a letter from Walpole's agent in the southwest, John Wolrige, who wrote to him in 1727: "Every town has been tampered with, [for] which reasons the people who have always been bribed do now assemble and cabal to make their market, and this I believe, if you don't send money here beforehand, you may miss your views in more towns than one."

Walpole's role was enhanced because in eighteenth-century England the court was the center of politics, and the king controlled an immense amount of patronage, which allowed him to manage the government and direct foreign affairs. Civil servants were the king's own personal servants, and administration was carried out by the royal household. Patronage and court gossip were the standard currencies of the English government, and while cliques were commonplace, political disputes did not lead to stable parties. With the Glorious Revolution only a short time in the past, and with a Stuart Pretender still a threat to the House of Hanover in the early eighteenth century, the king's pre-eminence was a matter of grave concern to Whig and Tory alike.

As the years passed, Walpole seemed to be the master of both the court and the Commons. Except for a controversial excise bill that he backed away from, Walpole controlled both domestic and foreign affairs during his ministerial career. As the ferocity of the opposition's attacks grew, Walpole relied more on patronage and on the votes that his sycophants generated. In the public eye, Parliament became less important and the public read more about corruption, bribery, and influence peddling. English politics before this period had involved some venality, but no minister so unashamedly used the selfish impulses of men and so brilliantly celebrated the triumph of the vulgar in politics as did Walpole.

Yet Walpole had some redeeming qualities. Like so many conservative political figures, he disliked war, believing that it disrupted political allegiances, distorted personal alliances, and, above all, cost money. He was a brilliant administrator and a superb parliamentary manager; Walpole's strength in the House of Commons made him indispensable to the monarch, and his high esteem in court furthered his control in the Parliament.

The world before the American Revolution, though, was slipping away from Walpole and from the men who shared his concerns. By the 1760s England had a new monarch, George III, and a new hero, William Pitt the

Elder, who celebrated war as the mother of wealth and the precursor of empire. By the time of his retirement, the Great Commoner, as Pitt was known, saw French power swept from the seas, and in Asia, Africa, and especially North America, the British seemed ready to establish hegemony.[8] The England of the eighteenth century did indeed suffer from official corruption, and its politics could be seen as a crude debasement of representative government. Yet, compared with the rest of Europe, the British system was surely more praiseworthy than the assortments of tyrannies and unenlightened monarchies present elsewhere. But for the colonists, such imperfections were all too obvious and soon all too burdensome.

2

THE ROYAL
PREROGATIVE

The power to act according to discretion, for the publick good, without
the proscription of the Law, and sometimes even against it, *is* that which
is called *Prerogative*.

John Locke, 1689

For all of its capacity to embrace both the noble and the evil, politics is still
a contrived and often nonsensical exercise. Those standing outside the group
in time or in opinion can easily point to the seams and stitches of beliefs,
the tacit assumptions and half-acknowledged truths that so concern the
faithful. Now, more than three centuries later, we can recall only with great
difficulty the hallowed expositions about royal power and prerogative, and
these tenets all seem so alien to us. Indeed, they are alien, for history is a
cruel bard who tells us little about the blood and feelings of its players. It
should be equally humbling for us to realize that those who follow us will
be as confused and as disbelieving about what we now hold dear as well.

To the colonists in the New World, their experience with the noble myths
of executive authority revolved around two institutions: the king and the
Crown's provincial governor. In trying to ascertain what were the real
powers of the monarch during the early eighteenth century, the boundary
between royal theory and day-to-day political maneuvering remains unclear. For the colonists, without our perspective but with a storehouse of
experience, the question of royal authority was a topic of gossip, newspaper
debate, and scholarly disquisition. The educated among them were aware
of many important authorities on the matter, and some of the Americans
were familiar with the writings of Harrington, Hume, Bolingbroke, Sidney,
Ferguson, and others. But the two most important and popular writers
were Locke and Blackstone.[1]

John Locke (1632–1704), an Oxford don, was removed by the Crown
from his position at the University in 1684 because of his ties to the Earl

of Shaftesbury. Locke had, at one time, been a student of medicine and had supervised an abdominal operation that saved the Earl's life. In return, Shaftesbury promoted Locke's achievements and furthered his advancement until both fell out of favor with the Crown. Fortune, though, took a hand and the Glorious Revolution of 1688 ended the reign of the Stuart line. Locke in turn published his *Two Treatises on Government*, a work that later commentators saw as a grateful defense of the Revolution, although Locke had probably finished parts of his work before the actual upheaval took place.

In his *Second Treatise*, Locke dealt with the question of executive power. Although he stressed the need for popular consent in establishing a civil society, Locke still defended the notion of a royal prerogative. The executive, he argued, has by "the common law of Nature, a right to make use of it [the prerogative], for the good of the Society." In addition, "the Laws themselves should in some cases give way to the Executive Power, or rather to this Fundamental Law of Nature and Government, viz., that as much as may be, all Members of the Society are to be *preserved*." Thus the executive could rule counter to law but should always observe the public interest. If, to us, that notion seems quaint, a quick glance at American history will show that this precept, clad in different garbs, has been used by presidents as diverse as Abraham Lincoln, Franklin Roosevelt, and Richard Nixon to justify their public actions.

Locke insisted that the executive must use the prerogative only to promote desirable ends, that the prerogative "is nothing but the Power of doing publick good without a Rule." Yet he was wise enough in the ways of the world to concede that the reigns of good princes are always "the most dangerous to the Liberties of their People," for soon lesser leaders will recall the extraordinary use of power in the past and try to establish it as a new standard for the future.

Faced with the historical experience of a king committing grave abuses and being deposed by Parliament, Locke was unable to provide a method of settling disputes between the executive and legislative authorities. There is, he noted, no judge on earth who can settle such a conflict, and the people are left only "to appeal to Heaven." If abuses become severe enough, Locke seemed to allow for disobedience and, eventually, revolution.[2] In the American system, such intractable political disputes have generally gone to the Supreme Court for final arbitration, although why a co-equal branch of government has such authority has never been fully justified; nor is there a clear way of dealing with disputes between the high court and another branch of government. As Locke himself recognized, final judgments in politics, like first principles, are often vague; experience has shown that civility is preserved more by temporizing than by philosophizing.

In his time, though, Locke's philosophizing had a profound influence both in Europe and in the New World. His ideas on politics, as well as on epistemology and religion, were part of the Enlightenment spirit and eventually entered even the dark chambers of the legal profession through the influence of the great jurist William Blackstone (1723–1780). Blackstone's views became the paramount legal tradition for generations, and American leaders—many of them lawyers and judges—grew up on his Whig sentiments.

Blackstone started out as a lawyer whose brilliant lectures on the English law attracted wide attention and led to his election to an endowed chair at Oxford in 1758. Within a few years, he was further honored by being appointed the king's counsel, solicitor to the queen, and a bencher in the Middle Temple. In 1761 he was elected to Parliament, and four years later the first volume of his tetralogy, *Commentaries on the Laws of England* (1765–1769), was published. He was subsequently appointed to the Court of Common Pleas and then to the king's bench. Although Blackstone has been criticized for using historical sources too uncritically and for glossing over complex legal problems in arriving at his conclusions, his work was of immeasurable influence in the English-speaking world, even throughout the nineteenth century and on into the present.

Central to his erudite discussions of law and tradition is a detailed examination of the executive. For Blackstone, the king was vested by the general consent of the people with executive power, and he governed according to law. In the words of the great coronation oath, the monarch must "govern the people of this Kingdom of England, and the dominions thereto belonging, according to the statutes in parliament agreed on, and the laws and customs of the same." Blackstone defined the prerogative in much more specific terms than did Locke, calling it "that special pre-eminence, which the King hath, over and above all other persons, and out of the ordinary course of the common law, in right of regal dignity." Blackstone began his treatment of the topic by dividing the prerogative into direct and incidental types. The first type is rooted in the king's political person and included such important powers as the right to send ambassadors, to create peers, and to make war or peace. Incidental prerogatives are distinct from the king's person and are usually exceptions to the general rules of the community, such as the dictum that no costs can be recovered against the king. Under English tradition, no one could sue the sovereign without his permission, although an individual could petition the king's court of chancery, which would examine the claim as a matter of grace but not of right.

In keeping with the sovereign majesty of the king, the monarch can do no wrong, and if acts of oppression occur within the realm, the wicked ministers and evil counselors could be indicted and impeached. The law, Blackstone maintained, ascribes to the king not only great powers and emoluments, but also "certain attributes of a great and transcendent nature; by which, the people are led to consider him in the light of a superior being, and to pay him that awful respect, which may enable him with greater ease to carry on the business of government."

If the king is induced to grant a franchise or privilege that turns out to be unreasonable or injurious, then he must have been deceived. The king is not only incapable of doing wrongly, but even of thinking wrongly, for he "can never mean to do an improper thing: in him is no folly or weakness." The king is always biased toward the public good; he is never negligent; and on taking the throne, a person is purged of any stain of corruption, including treason or a felony. In the eyes of the law, the king is never a minor or under age and the monarchy does not die, for the royal power passes on in perpetuity from one person to another. Having said this, Blackstone also had to deal with some nasty historical episodes, such as the deposing of lawfully crowned kings. His uneasy response was that when a monarch violates the fundamental law of the constitution, the Parliament can rule that he has "abdicated" and that the throne is therefore vacant. Thus Blackstone, with all of his praise of the royal prerogative and its grandeur, had to acknowledge, as a good Whig, the bloody and bitter history of English political life that led to the development of a strong Parliament.

With a lawyer's love of examples and a professor's tendency toward tedious specifics, Blackstone expanded in great detail on his notion of the prerogative. The king is the sole magistrate of the nation, and unless the constitution expressly or "by evident consequence" prohibits it, he can reject bills, make treaties, coin money, create peers, and pardon offenders. Blackstone, though, partially accepted the notion that the executive may exercise discretionary power when acting for the public good in cases where the laws are silent. When such a prerogative is exercised in an unconstitutional manner, then the ministers advocating and enforcing such actions may be impeached.

The king has extensive powers in dealing with matters of war and foreign affairs. He can make treaties, wage war, declare peace, issue letters of marque and reprisal, and grant safe conduct to foreigners in the realm. The monarch is generalissimo and has the sole power to raise and regulate fleets and armies, erect and maintain forts, prohibit the exportation of arms and ammunition out of the kingdom, and, within some limits, both curtail travel abroad and demand a particular person's return. In the areas of judicial administration, the king is portrayed as being "the fountain of justice and general conservator of the peace of the Kingdom." He can erect courts of judicature, nominate judges, and pardon offenders, except in cases of probationary impeachments. The king can issue proclamations that, when they are based on the law, have binding force. In addition, the king has some discretion as to the manner, time, and circumstances of executing parliamentary acts.

As the monarch, the king has the right to confer honors and titles and control commerce by constructing public markets, regulating weights and measures, and establishing standards for the coining of money. Being also the head of the Church of England, the king has authority over all ecclesiastical synods and convocations, can fill all vacant bishoprics, and is the ultimate appeal in cases involving ecclesiastical courts.[3]

Of central concern to any monarch was control over revenue. This is where Blackstone's list ranges far and wide. The king receives money from the custody of some church property, from tithes and ecclesiastical taxes, from rents and profits of royal lands and arbitrary tenures, from fees for wine licenses, and from judicial court revenues. The king can even insist that one of his chaplains be supported by a bishop and have a pension paid to a chaplain of his choosing. In addition, the monarch's sway includes the rights to "royal fish" (whale or sturgeon) that were caught or came ashore, remains of shipwrecked merchandise, treasures found buried in the earth (but not on it or in the sea), recovered stolen goods that went unclaimed, stray animals, forfeited lands or goods taken for offenses, and copyrights for royal proclamations, acts of Parliament, church liturgies, bibles, almanacs, and several other published works. The king could buy precious metals at the value of the base metal, control lands where the line of inheritance is defective, and maintain custody over the possessions of certified lunatics and idiots.

To administer the government, the king, through his ministers, must rely on the various levies laid on the people by Parliament, and Blackstone goes on to enumerate each one. In a sanguine mood, he notes how, in the past century, some of the more odious aspects of the royal prerogative—the Star Chamber, high commission courts, arbitrary tenure, purveyance, and pre-emption—have been curtailed and civil liberties protected.

In understanding the full majesty of the monarch, one must realize how the definition of treason in Britain was broadened beyond the narrow view of giving aid and comfort to the enemy. At times, the law of treason included a whole host of activities that might harm or defame the king or interfere with the royal line of succession. The following activities at one time or another were proscribed: to kill the king; to attempt to imprison him; to speak critically of the monarch; to have sexual relations with his wife, eldest daughter, or the wife of the king's eldest son; to make or pass counterfeit money; or to kill a high-ranking royal officer of justice.

In the reign of Henry VIII, a person could be found guilty of treason if he refused to renounce the pope, believed that the king lawfully married Anne of Cleves, or was involved in any of the following: "deflowering or marrying without the royal license any of the King's children, sisters, aunts, nephews, or nieces; base solicitation of the chastity of the queen or princesses, or advances made by themselves; marrying with the King by a woman not a virgin without previously disclosing to him such her unchaste life."

The expanded list of activities was later dropped, but the punishment for treason remained rather brutal: the offender was hanged, his entrails taken out and burned while he was alive, his head cut off, and his body finally quartered. The conviction for treason apparently overrode the traditional Christian admonition for a decent burial. Women were treated somewhat less severely—they were only taken to the gallows and burned alive. Blackstone summarized the punishments as "very solemn and terrible," although he concurred with jurist Edward Coke that such brutal accountings are also found in the Scriptures.[4]

Thus these prerogatives, and the dignity they were supposed to confer on the monarch, were compiled by Blackstone into an overreaching theory of royal power. He fully supported a strong monarch but yet accepted the obvious realities that came from Parliament's ascendancy after the Glorious Revolution of 1688. If today these historical lessons seem less obvious or the theory rather fanciful, we should, nonetheless, realize that the English form of government was at this time greatly celebrated by enlightened thinkers outside the realm as the best in the world. Voltaire praised the British system, and Montesquieu, in his *Spirit of the Laws*, called attention to what he discerned as the delicate political balance through the separation of powers that helped to assure responsible government.[5] Some American political thinkers and leaders were greatly influenced by Montesquieu's analysis, and yet the very system they were reading about was gone—if it ever existed—by the time they were becoming aware of it. By then the House of Hanover ruled England and the reign of the three Georges led to major changes in the English political structure. The heralded separation of authority was being eclipsed by the dynamics of coalition building; learned statements on prerogative and a balanced constitution gave way to a calculated marriage of royal patronage and parliamentary ambition that was to govern the new British imperial world.[6]

As for Locke and Blackstone, their ideas made their way across the ocean and became part of the American mind. The notion of prerogative, in the narrow sense of being executive action without full legislative approval, is not a simple historical artifact. Presidents have claimed, and still do claim, a prerogative-type power, especially in times of crisis, and free people must grapple with the proper line that separates legitimate necessity from gross abuse.

3

THE PROVINCIAL
GOVERNORS

I must freely own, that I think [my salary is] . . . much below the dignity
of the station of His Majesty's governor of this province. . . .
                                                    William Shirley, 1742

Although the ideas and philosophies are important, people learn most
quickly from experience, for the lessons of life are often stark and clear
even to the dullest pupil. So it was with the colonists, who, although they
heard discussions of the royal prerogative, often came to make their judgments about English politics based on their sad experiences with the provincial governors and with the decrees promulgated in London that these
officials had to enforce.

The great British experiment in colonization grew markedly in the first
three-quarters of the seventeenth century. These settlements were usually
founded, not by the Crown, but by private initiatives, and these colonies
often took on the appearance of vast private estates, owned by adventuresome proprietors who held broad powers and extensive privileges granted
under the seal of royal charters.

Fearful of the growing power of the Catholic French monarchy and wary
of its aggressive policies, the British government soon began to express
more of an interest in the Western hemisphere. By the 1670s a committee
of the Privy Council, the Lords of Trade, took over direct supervision of
these plantation activities and the influence of the king and his circle began
to expand. Charters were revoked, private properties were converted into
royal provinces, and all of the territory from Kennebec to the Delaware
was designated as the Dominion of New England. Faced almost at once
with strong opposition in the colonies and political problems at home, the
advocates of the Dominion concept made a tactical retreat. Yet the Crown
continued its general policies aimed at bringing the New World under the
control of the Old.[1]

When Parliament, after 1706, expressed its unwillingness to end the rights of the proprietary colonies, the Crown moved to increase in other ways its authority in America. By mid-century every British colony except Maryland, Pennsylvania, Connecticut, and Rhode Island fell under the king's direct control, and the Crown's influence in the first two of these holdouts was significant.

The Crown originally had sent over companies of troops to settle colonial disputes and support the latest change in English policy. These garrison governments, as they have been called, provided royal provincial officers with rather effective support and kept the local elites in check. But the gruesome days of large standing armies were not yet a standard part of the English government. Men were often only sometime soldiers, and the taxes necessary to support armies at home and then abroad were too burdensome for even the most adventuresome administration.[2]

The focal point of royal authority in the colonies then was the provincial governor, who reported directly to the Board of Trade. The provincial governor was assisted by local assemblies that were created at the pleasure of the Crown and had powers enumerated in the royal instructions to the governor. In the eyes of the British authorities, these assemblies were not legislative bodies, but simply consultative groups established by the grace and favor of the Crown. But as so often happens in history, intention and consequence do not run in tandem. To the colonists, anxious about their security and their status, these modest assemblies of often pompous and selfish local leaders became great bodies designed to protect their rights as Englishmen. Just as the haughty nobles at Runnymede, in asserting their dated feudal rights, gave the world the Magna Carta, so now their frontier descendants created representative government on these shores. The Crown and its partisans had tried by mighty design to contain and control the Parliament in Britain; yet, by their grace and favor, the monarchs had created a host of little parliaments across the ocean, fertile plots in which the seeds of resistance and rebellion were inadvertently planted generations before Lexington or Concord. In the center of this developing controversy was the royal governor. On arriving in the colony, he was usually welcomed by a stream of visitors, addressed as "his Excellency," entertained with congratulatory odes, feasted at elegant dinners, and given a seventeen-gun salute. As the colony's executive, he was its "captain general and commander-in-chief." Sitting with him was the provincial council, usually twelve persons, appointed by the Crown and composed of merchants and lawyers. The council, and not the assembly, was the main group of advisors to the governor, and most of his specific powers could be executed only with its advice and consent. With the council's approval, the governor could create and regulate the lower courts and appoint judges, commissioners, and ministers; the governor and the council sat together as the highest court of appeals in the province. The governor usually needed the advice and consent of the council also to summon the assembly, appoint officers, issue money, and establish martial law in time of war. He had to have the approval of a majority of that body to suspend any member of the council, with the Board of Trade having the final say on the matter.

The Crown usually allowed the governor to exercise some control over the provincial militia. The governor could require inhabitants to serve in the militia, transport them into other provinces, create ports and harbors, set up customs and warehouses, and examine rates and shipping duties. With the council's advice, he could establish forts and provide the troops with equipment and supplies. The governor was the vice admiral of the province, although he had no authority over the royal navy in his area and had only oversight powers concerning the vice admiralty courts.

Governors, as keepers of the Great Seal, were the officials who authenticated public documents. They also were often charged with overseeing the moral life of the colonial people under their care. After 1700 a governor was subject to trial before the court of the king's bench, or before royal commissioners and a jury, if he violated the laws of the realm or oppressed his subjects. In general, a governor served at the pleasure of the Crown and was not permitted to leave America without specific permission.[3]

The provincial governor was given some opportunity to fill local offices, but that power gradually was eroded as the patronage needs of London grew insatiable. By the early part of the eighteenth century, the secretary of state in England took over more control of appointments; from 1748 to the 1770s, the number of positions at the disposal of the secretary increased from 85 to 226. The Board of Trade became, in reality, a committee of the Privy Council, and it ended up competing with merchant groups, colonial agents, and patronage seekers in making policy in the overseas areas. The Walpole ministry eagerly filled the posts that became available, and the ability of a provincial governor to form a strong coalition at home by using the appointment power was severely undercut. Thus the greed of the London court partly helped to further the gap between the Crown and the local provincial leadership.[4]

After 1756 provincial governors were faced with another political problem—the presence in London of American agents hired by the colonists. All too often political leaders are swayed by those nearest them, and weigh gossip and intrigue as heavily as more substantiated judgments. Repetitions, often carefully contrived, become truth, and those not near the courtiers easily fall from favor without cause or merit. Many provincial governors in this situation did not know until it was too late what was being said about them in London, and their ability to deal with court intrigue was limited.

In the crucial period between 1752 and 1766, the governors further found that they had to correspond not with one of the secretaries of state, but with the weakened Board of Trade. Also, after 1756, the British military forces arriving in the colonies were no longer under the governors' control.

But the real nemesis of the provincial governors was the local assemblies. Although the Crown and the Parliament did not recognize these bodies as representative forms of government, with the power to tax and make laws, the assemblies charted a different course. As the assemblies matured, they began to develop a view of themselves that remarkably paralleled the parliamentary assertion of power against the Stuart monarchs. The local bodies insisted on the sole right to raise revenues, dispense funds, and pay the salaries of the governors and other local officials. In New York, New Jersey, New Hampshire, and the Massachusetts Bay colonies, assemblies frequently withheld or delayed governors' salaries as a way of expressing disapproval. Although the councils tried first to share in the appropriations process, the assemblies recognized the central significance of this power and managed generally to fend off the other body.

A governor, when he was sent to a post, received a list of the types of laws that required prior consent from England, those that were to be postponed until approved by royal consent, and those that were outside the scope of permissible local action. But the governor's instructions frequently carried little weight with the brashly assertive local leaders. Even in establishing courts, the popular assemblies bitterly opposed the right of the governors to create special courts, especially chancery courts, although on that issue the Crown stood firm.[5]

The provincial governor was the symbol of authority on the ragged edges of the frontier, a creature of a king and a court that constricted his powers and resources at the same time they were demanding more control over the maturing colonies. The perils of being a provincial governor can be seen most graphically in the tragic career of Thomas Hutchinson (1711–1780), the last royal civilian executive of Massachusetts. Born into a respectable family that had come to the colony in 1634, Hutchinson was chosen at the age of twenty-six to be a selectman in Boston and was also elected to the colonial House of Representatives. He established his reputation as an advocate of "hard money" and as a defender of his colony's boundaries against the claim of neighboring New Hampshire. Gradually but sure-footedly, Hutchinson made his way up the colonial *causus honorium*, serving on the council, as a judge of probate, as a justice of common pleas, and as a representative of the province in 1754 to the Albany Congress, where he supported Franklin's premature plan for a union of colonies. By 1750 he became lieutenant governor and was also appointed chief justice by Governor Bernard, who, in the process, passed over the elder James Otis.

Otis' son threatened that if his father were denied the position, he would stir up the whole province, which indeed he did with the assistance of

Samuel Adams, whose own father had been injured economically by Hutchinson's monetary policies. Despite the historical legends that would link the Otis and Adams names to the noble defense of colonial rights, the initial anger of these two firebrands was due more to personal envy and jealousy. The political leadership of colonial America was often in the hands of only a few individuals, and family alliances, personal cliques, and local loyalties played a major role in fueling the forces of acrimony. Solitary misunderstandings among onetime friends tend to be more long-lived than the most protracted hatred among recognized enemies. And a politics that mixed kinship, close acquaintances, and neighborhood divisions often left little room for forgetting or forgiving.

As for the younger Otis, he was a brilliant and vitriolic agitator whose personality seemed at times unstable. As with many other self-proclaimed revolutionaries across the centuries, the turmoils of his era helped to destabilize even further whatever delicate balance he was struggling to maintain in himself from time to time. The questioning of traditional values, the upsetting of established assumptions, the reformulation or rejection of basic beliefs can be a liberating experience, one that is necessary for change. But for some types of people, the loss of certainties unleashes forces of hostility and rage that are best left repressed. Such was the case with Otis, who led the attack on Hutchinson and the entire upper ministerial establishment. Otis focused on his opponent's propensity to hold multiple offices, a not uncommon practice in those days, which Otis claimed was clear evidence of Hutchinson's overwhelmingly dangerous ambition and insatiable greed.

Although Hutchinson had opposed the Sugar and Stamp Acts, he never denied that Parliament had the legal right to lay such taxes. Thus he found himself increasingly separated from the prominent Patriot sentiment and subject to Otis' tirades. As relations between the colonies and England worsened, the attacks on Hutchinson grew more personal. Finally, on August 26, 1765, an angry mob, in an attack of extraordinary ferocity for that period, destroyed Hutchinson's splendid mansion and nearly killed him. The agitation continued throughout the 1760s, and Hutchinson had the unfortunate fate to be named acting governor in 1769 and then governor three years later. He was no longer just another misguided supporter of the Crown's policies; he now became the center of frenzied criticism. Unfortunately for him, Hutchinson's opponents obtained some of his confidential letters in which he urged that the British government exert more authority over the provinces. Meanwhile Hutchinson developed an interest in his sons' tea business and became involved in the dispute that led to the Patriots' dumping of British tea into the harbor. Finally, by 1774, the Governor went to England and General Gage was appointed to replace him. Stranded in a land not of his birth and pledged to a monarch whom his countrymen despised, Hutchinson died in England during the height of the War for Independence.[6]

The post of royal governor became an easy target of opportunity for the Patriot leaders, with their sense of organization and their propensity for direct action. Isolated from the people, far from the British Crown, the governors became symbols of an increasingly objectionable set of policies— policies that they often had little influence on and that they had to carry out. As for the Americans, these royal governors were the first real executives they had encountered, and discussions of tyranny were often linked with the notion of executive authority. Later it fell to the new war governors in the states to recast somewhat the link between popular sovereignty and executive responsibility in ways both familiar and acceptable to the fiercely independent American provincials.

One such governor who was especially adept in this regard was Jonathan Trumbull (1710–1785), the only person to be royal governor in Connecticut and, later, to be reelected state governor throughout the American Revolution. Trumbull was born in Connecticut and educated at Harvard College, where he was in fact a classmate of Hutchinson. After graduation he decided to enter the ministry, and in 1730 he had completed his studies and was preparing to take over a Congregational pulpit. The press of family problems, however, forced him to join his father in managing the farm, and Trumbull never went back to the ministry.

Prospering as a merchant and as a farmer, he was elected to the General Assembly and commissioned as an officer in the colony's regiment. In 1740 he became a trusted member of the governor's council and later served as a judge while he was still in the Assembly. By the time of his election as governor in 1769, Trumbull had been a member of the council, Speaker of the House, and Chief Justice of the Superior Court. Unlike Hutchinson, though, Trumbull vigorously opposed the Stamp Act and refused to take part in an oath-swearing ceremony before the council. As the colony moved farther away from the orbit of British politics, Trumbull became more critical of the Crown and its policies. Because of different political traditions in Connecticut and the colony's lesser importance compared with Massachusetts, Trumbull was able to place some salutary distance between himself and the British government, a step that Hutchinson could not take even if he had wanted to.[7]

By most reliable accounts, Hutchinson and Trumbull were honorable and honest individuals who represented the best traditions of their generation's view of public service. But like so many loyalists, Hutchinson was caught between a vacillating Crown policy and an assertive Assembly, and he had the particular misfortune to be in the one colony where agitation was fiercest. His story is the tragic tale of one of the many high British officeholders in the colonies, men who shouldered the burdens of being royal governors in the most difficult times at the center of the Patriot storm.

4

THE WAR GOVERNORS

The history of the violations of the Virginia constitution extends from the year 1776 to the present time—violations made by formal acts of the legislature: everything has been drawn within the legislative vortex.
Edmund Randolph, 1788

As more British troops arrived, the American response in the early stages of the conflict seemed timid and disjointed. Quick to anger, slow to revolution, the Patriots began to recognize the full impact of leading a divided people. At one point John Adams confessed that no more than a third of the colonists supported the war effort, with an equal number opposed and another third neutral. As is so often the case in human affairs, the views of a highly mobilized and committed minority carried more weight than their numbers alone would have allowed. Under their leadership, the diffident and sporadic rebellion blossomed into a revolution—the first modern anti-colonist war, marked by a series of inchoate battles that somehow resulted in the defeat of the greatest imperial power in recent history. In that process of war and upheaval, the Patriots, in the years between 1775 and 1777, forced out all of the provincial royal governors, except for the durable Trumbull, who was annually elected from 1769 to 1784.

During the early phase of the American Revolution, some internal disorders occurred, owing in part to the absence of political authority. Although the patriot leaders were revolutionaries against the British Crown, most were, nonetheless, respectable men of means and social position. They countenanced violence against a foreign enemy; they did not propose to support the aspirations of the lower classes within their own cities and regions. In the midst of this revolutionary fervor, some Americans proceeded rather cautiously in dealing even with royal governors. For example, in early 1776, the Maryland Council of Safety refused to arrest their governor, Sir Robert Eden. The Council argued that they wished to preserve the peace and warned ardent followers of the cause that if the governor were treated with "ignominy," then one could not tell "what will be the consequence."[1]

As the war progressed, the states were advised to write new constitutions, republican documents purged of references to the Crown and its once recognized favors and graces. To guide such discussions, George Wythe, in early 1776, wrote John Adams for advice on how to proceed. Adams put forth a constitutional blueprint, which he later published in a pamphlet entitled "Thoughts on Government." He warned his fellow countrymen against concentrating all powers in a revolutionary congress or committee, and he reminded them that "governors and councils we have always had as well as representatives." Yet, with all his avowed sympathy for the executive, Adams recommended substantial curtailment of most of the powers that might be assigned to that position. In this cautious approach, he reflected the pronounced concerns of other American leaders as well.

Because of the obvious association of the royal governors with unpopular British policies, the executive power was generally restricted during the Revolution. As James Wilson explained, before the war the executive and the judicial powers were "placed neither in the people, nor in those who professed to receive them under the authority of the people. They were derived from a different and a foreign source: they were regulated by foreign maxims: they were directed by a foreign purpose." Partially in reaction to this history, many new state constitutions transferred executive powers to the legislature and restrained the governor in several ways. These documents usually limited the term of office to one year, denied re-eligibility, established a strong council, and provided for election by the legislature. In Jefferson's words, "Before the Revolution we were all good English Whigs, cordial in their free principles and in their jealousies of their executive Magistrates. These jealousies are very apparent in all our state constitutions."[2]

Yet, despite the apparent movement away from executive authority, most of the state constitutions provided some recognition of the role of the governor, even if many of the powers had to be shared with a council or the legislature. Most significant, two major states, Massachusetts and New York, departed from the general temper of the times and provided for strong executives. Their constitutions were to influence greatly the Founding Fathers as they gathered in Philadelphia to write the new federal document with its strong executive article.

Article II, which contains most of the language in the Constitution on the presidency, enumerates the powers of the office and provides for the election process. The president is given "the executive power"; is commander-in-chief; can grant reprieves and pardons (except for impeachments); has the authority to make treaties, which have to be ratified by two-thirds of the Senate; names major appointments with the advice and consent of a majority of the Senate; and is allowed to fill vacancies during Senate recesses. The executive can also require written opinions from the heads of departments, address Congress on the state of the Union, recommend measures for its consideration, and convene the Congress and adjourn it if the two houses disagree on the date. He can veto bills subject to two-thirds override by both houses, receive foreign ministers, and commission all officers of the United States, and he is instructed to "take care that the laws be faithfully executed." The president is guaranteed a fixed salary during his term, can be reelected indefinitely every four years, and can be removed only for high crimes and misdemeanors after indictment by the House and conviction by the Senate. Brief and succinct, Article II is the basic constitutional foundation on which is built the most powerful elective office in the world.

Some of these phrases, like "executive power" and the faithful execution of the laws clause, have provided important constitutional justification for the great and grave use of presidential power. Scholars have frequently asked from what source do these phrases arise and are they really innovative interpretations of executive authority.

Actually, the phraseology of Article II is similar, but not identical, to some of the major state constitutions. The New York Constitution of 1777, for example, provided for a popularly elected governor with a three-year term, who was general and commander-in-chief of the state militia and admiral of the navy. He was empowered to convene the legislature; prorogue or discontinue it for up to sixty days on extraordinary occasions; grant reprieves and pardons, except in cases of treason or murder; recommend measures he deemed important; and inform the legislature about the condition of the state. In words similar to Article II, this governor was required to "take care that the laws are faithfully executed to the best of his ability." Unlike the president, though, the governor shared the veto power with a council made up of the chancellor and judges of the state supreme court. In terms of appointments, the constitution provided for the assembly to nominate a group of senators who in turn would give their advice and consent to the governor's nominees. The assembly also had the power to begin impeachment charges against officials for "mal and corrupt conduct," with a court of select senators and state judges pronouncing the final verdict.

The second major constitution that was well known to the Founding Fathers was the 1780 Massachusetts charter. In *The Federalist*, Hamilton noted on several occasions that this document was the model from which the federal Constitution was copied.[3] The Massachusetts Constitution provided for a "supreme executive magistrate" who was chosen yearly by popular vote. He retained the veto power, which could be overridden only by two-thirds of both houses; he could, in some cases, with the advice of the council, adjourn or prorogue the legislature and pardon offenders, except in impeachment cases.

There has been considerable discussion over the years about what are the "war powers" that various presidents have claimed to exercise in times of crisis. The Massachusetts Constitution gives an interesting elaboration of the powers of the governor in this regard:

The governor of this commonwealth, for the time being, shall be the commander-in-chief of the army and navy, and of all the military forces of the state, by sea and land; and shall have full power, by himself, or by any commander, or other officer or officers, from time to time, to train, instruct, exercise and govern the militia and navy; and for the special defense and safety of the commonwealth, to assemble in martial array, and put in warlike posture, the inhabitants thereof, and to lead and conduct them, and with them to encounter, repel, resist, expel, and pursue, by force of arms, as well by sea as by land, within or without the limits of this common-wealth, and also to kill, slay, and destroy, if necessary, and conquer, by all fitting ways, enterprises, and means whatsoever, all and every such person and persons as shall, at any time hereafter, in a hostile manner, attempt or enterprise the destruction, invasion, detriment, or annoyance of this commonwealth; and to use and exercise over the army and navy, and over the militia in actual service, the law-martial, in time of war or invasion, and also in time of rebellion, declared by the legislature to exist, as occasion shall necessarily require; and to take and surprise, by all ways and means whatsoever, all and every such person or persons, with their ships, arms, ammunition, and other goods, as shall in a hostile manner, invade, or attempt the invading, conquering or annoying this commonwealth; and that the governor be intrusted with all these and other powers, incident to the office of captain-general and commander-in-chief, and admiral, to be exercised agreeably to the rules and regulations of the constitution, and the laws of the land, and not otherwise.

In other states the executive powers varied in differing degrees from those in Massachusetts and New York. In New Hampshire the 1784 document called the state executive "the President," possibly because he presided over the Senate, and gave him powers similar to those of the Massachusetts governor. In New Jersey the 1776 constitution provided for a governor who would be "the supreme executive power, the Chancellor of the Colony, and act as captain-general and commander-in-chief. . . . " The North Carolina constitution, passed in the same year, also used the expression "captain-general and commander-in-chief" and gave the executive the power to lay embargoes; call up the militia; fill, with the advice and consent of the Council of State, vacant positions; and, when the state assembly was in recess, grant pardons and reprieves. In general, the governor was instructed to "exercise all the other executive powers of government, limited and restrained by this Constitution. . . . "

Maryland used similar language in its 1777 charter and added the warning that "the governor should not, under any pretense, exercise any power or prerogative by virtue of any law, statute, or custom of England or Great Britain." Virginia, the year before, had included the same sort of admonition and allowed for impeachment proceedings against a governor even after he had left office. Georgia gave its governor, with the advice of the council, the right to use the "executive powers of government," except for the pardoning power. Its 1777 constitution, as other state charters, provided for an oath of office requiring that the governor promise to "execute the said office faithfully and conscientiously, according to law, without favor, affection, or partiality; that I will, to the utmost of my power, support, maintain and defend the State. . . . " Other constitutions gave even fewer powers to the governor: Delaware had its state president elected by joint ballot in the legislature and denied him the veto power. Pennsylvania, in the midst of a democratic upheaval in 1776, created collective leadership with a president and a council of twelve that made appointments, granted pardons, remitted fines (except in impeachment cases), laid embargoes when the legislature was in recess, heard and judged impeachment cases, and was responsible as a group to take care that "the laws be faithfully executed." The president was given the title commander-in-chief but could not personally lead the troops.

Lastly, South Carolina, in 1778, provided for a governor and commander-in-chief who must be a Protestant, be a resident of the state for ten years, and be worth £10,000 currency. Other states besides South Carolina had residency requirements, minimum wealth criteria, and minimum age levels, and four others had a religious qualification or oath. When the Founding Fathers came to write the federal Constitution, they, too, added a residency requirement of fourteen years in the country and a statement that one had to be a "natural-born citizen, or a citizen of the United States, at the time of the adoption of this constitution." The presidential oath made no mention of religious orthodoxy, but required that the individual promise faithfully to execute the office and to preserve, protect, and defend the Constitution.[4]

Thus, despite all the bitter criticisms of royal government, of its prerogatives, and of the abuses of power perpetrated by energetic ministers and unsympathetic agents, the American political leadership showed a fairly general consensus about what properly constituted executive authority in a rather narrow sense. What the war years provided was the experience of some successful republican executives who could be admired and held up favorably to public scrutiny. Energy and dispatch were once again prized attributes in government, and as more influential men looked at a weak government run by congressional committees, they began to rethink the value of executive authority.

Article II of the federal Constitution was not a brilliant innovation, but like most of the American system of government, it was an adaptation of the familiar to the novel, a blending of tradition and experience to the uncertain world that demanded both authority and restraint. Of course paper constitutions are not the same as political history and a collection of clauses do not an office make. The true tale of executive power in that period can best be related by looking at the actual wartime governors in order to comprehend how they dealt with the problems of leading their states during the confusing and demanding War of Independence.

Overall, the men who served in these positions were not only experienced in local politics, but had a special understanding of the national war effort as well. They were not provincial lawyers and merchants who knew only success in the neighborhood and the friendships of the local folk. In fact, about half of the governors had at one time or another served in the Congress and were familiar with the delegates from other states in the new Union. Delegates corresponded regularly with the governors, and Congress actively sought out the views of the governors and usually supported them in disputes with Continental army officers. Many of the governors could draw warrants on the national treasury to pay for supplies and bounties and for expenses incurred in defending the frontiers. The governors also could remove recruiting officers and appoint Continental agents and Indian affairs commissioners.

As a group, the governors were strong supporters of General Washington and, unlike some congressional leaders, they were generally unimpressed with his rivals in the military ranks. Washington in turn kept in close contact with the executives, especially in the war zone, and after 1779 he communicated more frequently with them than with the Congress, to which he nominally reported. Like the governors, the General was also faced with the dire consequences resulting from a lack of funds and the short duration of enlistments. In trying to understand the larger war effort and in calling men to arms, the state governors admired Washington, the one leader who epitomized the noble nature of the long struggle and embodied the type of civic virtue that even the most opportunistic of these men recognized as the driving force of the new republican experiment.[5]

These governors, then, were important figures in the Revolution, and their performances as executives were often closely and carefully evaluated by their fellow citizens. One of the most powerful and popular of these figures was George Clinton, who exercised a major influence in this critical period. Clinton had grown up in Ulster County, New York, then the state's frontier. He served as a privateer in the French and Indian War and later became a lieutenant in the state militia, assigned for a while to Lord Jeffrey Amherst, who captured Montreal. Clinton then studied law, like Washington became a surveyor, and in 1768 was elected to the state assembly. In the early phase of the Revolution, he became a brigadier general in the militia and was involved in the defense of the Hudson Valley. In 1777, aided by the soldier vote, he was elected governor and was later reelected seven times and chosen twice as vice-president of the United States.

Clinton dominated his state council for nearly fifteen years of his long tenure and worked closely with Washington, the Continental Congress, and patriot leaders in other states. He adopted the custom of personally reading his messages to the legislature—a practice Washington and Adams adhered to as presidents—and he was able to convince the state legislators to sustain about half of his vetoes of their bills. During the war, the Governor mobilized troops, provided supplies, and actively quelled signs of discontent. He moved quickly to curtail Loyalists, controlled disgruntled Indians on the New York frontiers, and supported the end of the states' claims in the West, a position that led to the ratification of the Articles of Confederation in 1781. Yet Clinton could press New York's interests when he so desired; for nearly ten years he convinced the state legislature to reject the petitions of Vermont settlers who wanted to split off from New York and apply for admission as a separate state.[6]

Clinton's record as an energetic and successful governor was extraordinary and unique. Other governors lacked his abilities or were severely limited by their state constitutions or the impact of circumstances. One of the most unfortunate in this regard was Thomas Jefferson, who served as governor of Virginia. Jefferson's term is important because it was an episode that haunted him during his great career, and because it shows that Americans of that generation knew what effective executive leadership was and expected it to be exercised. The Revolution was not, as is so often repeated, a flight from authority or a battle against executive power.

At the age of thirty-six, Jefferson succeeded Patrick Henry as Governor of the Commonwealth, a post that was considerably weaker than the New York position. Jefferson was not particularly imposing in his dealings with the legislature, although, by all accounts, he was conscientious and as supportive of Washington's efforts in the field as he was able to be. Then, in 1780, Virginia was invaded by the British, who seized the capital, Richmond, forcing the governor and legislature to flee. Jefferson's opponents blamed the governor for not having prepared for the obvious invasion, and after he left office, the Assembly conducted an inquiry into his conduct. Although Jefferson was fully vindicated, he remained embarrassed by the charges, and implications of cowardice and ineptitude followed him throughout his later career. Regardless of the record of his tenure, it is clear that Jefferson's contemporaries did not welcome a weak governor, despite their often expressed reservations about possible abuses of executive power. In fact, some Virginian leaders, at several points during the Revolution, considered the need for a "dictator" to protect their troubled state.[7]

Americans then were more pragmatic in their philosophical discourses on government than is generally recognized, and many came to understand the need for executive authority. In the real seats of government, then the state capitals, many of them recast their concepts of political power and made them fit into the new order of things. America had both strong governors and weak ones during this revolutionary period, but when it came time to reframe the national government, the Founding Fathers looked more toward New York and Massachusetts for guidance than toward Pennsylvania and Virginia.

5

CREATING THE
PRESIDENCY

We must follow the example of Solon who gave the Athenians not the
best government he could devise; but the best they would receive.
                                                    Pierce Butler, 1787

In many nations the post-revolutionary period is often a time of further
bloodshed, purges, and frantic centralization. For the Americans, though,
many patriots seemed content to stay with the loose collection of states that
lined the Atlantic seaboard, each separate and unique, and joined together
by strong ties of language and custom and only the barest thread of confederation. Despite the prevalent historical view that the Articles of Confederation were a failure, the truth is that for about six years, they proved
to be a modest but still significant step toward national unity. Indeed, under
the Confederation, the colonies had, with some luck and considerable
French assistance, won a war against the greatest power on earth.

Some signs of strain and weakness were becoming increasingly evident,
though, in the confederation. To men of commerce, the separate states
posed major obstacles to free trade; to men of affairs, the American nation
lacked a firm diplomatic presence and financial stability; and to ambitious
patriots, their confederation had no vigor or authority. Did not Shays'
Rebellion in 1786 show all too well the weaknesses of state governments
and how strong the spirit of anarchy was that characterized some of the
baser elements of society?

In that same year the state of Virginia organized a general trade convention
in Annapolis that was attended by five states. From that session a report
was circulated that urged the state legislatures to call a national convention
for "the special and sole purpose" of putting forth a plan to rectify the
serious defects in the then federal system. Twelve state legislatures, led by
Virginia, responded positively, and the Congress concurred on February

21, 1787. Only Rhode Island, as usual, was unwilling to join in the common convention.

When the delegates arrived in Philadelphia, it soon became obvious that some of them wanted not to modify the Articles, but to create a new document. After Washington was chosen presiding officer and some procedures were established, Edmund Randolph presented, on May 29, the Virginia delegation's sweeping proposal. In a long speech he enumerated the defects of the Articles of Confederation, charging that the federal government could provide no security against foreign invasion, lacked overall authority, offered little direction in the way of regulating commerce, and could not defend itself from encroachments by the more aggressive states.[1]

In place of the current system of government, Randolph proposed a bicameral legislature, with one branch to be elected by the "free inhabitants" of the states and the second branch to be chosen by the first from a list of people nominated by the state legislatures. The national legislature was to have broad powers to pass laws, void state acts contravening the Constitution, and use force against recalcitrant states. The executive—whether it was a single or a plural one was not specified—would be elected by the legislature for only one term, guaranteed a fixed salary, and given "the executive rights vested in Congress by the Confederation." A council of revision, made up of the executive and "a convenient number of judges," was to exercise a qualified veto. Other provisions in the plan provided for a national judiciary, the admission of new states, and steps for ratifying and amending the document.

At first, the Virginia Plan seemed to command quick assent, and a majority of state delegations went on record supporting the bold nationalistic position. But majorities are often deceiving and their true impact must be carefully weighed if decisions are to make more than vague assents to temporary leanings. The Founding Fathers knew that any new constitution required a broad consensus in which the smaller state delegations and the more moderate reform leaders had to be satisfied with the outcome. Some of the nationalists in the small state delegations may have agreed with the Virginia Plan, but they candidly reminded their more eager counterparts that they could not get support back home for such a radical departure. The Constitutional Convention is often seen as a remarkable coup for the nationalists, like Madison, when in fact it was a cautious compromise for a limited federal government.

During the first week of June, the debate focused on the executive article. Charles Pinckney of South Carolina argued that, although he personally favored a vigorous executive, he felt that to give that position the power of war and peace would lead to "a monarchy, of the worst kind . . . to wit an elective one." Randolph, who had introduced the Virginia Plan, now argued that he feared having only one person assume all the executive powers, for that was "the foetus of monarchy." James Wilson, a distinguished Pennsylvania jurist and one of the strongest defenders of a powerful executive, responded that holding one individual responsible was the "best safeguard against tyranny."[2] He went further and supported, at least in theory, popular election of the executive and cited the experience of New York and Massachusetts. Later he would propose that the people choose the electors for the presidency, a procedure that was not fully adopted in the early years of the republic.

Then, for some reason, Benjamin Franklin insisted on having a long letter read in which he opposed granting the executive any salary. Wilson obliged and read the letter for the aged philosopher. Finally, as Madison notes, Hamilton kindly seconded the motion and the proposal "was treated with great respect, but rather for the author of it, than from any apparent conviction of its expediency or practicability."[3]

As the debate continued from one day to another, the delegates, by a vote of six to three, agreed to a single executive and began to consider the nature of a veto or, as they were to term it, the "negative." Wilson again stressed the need for a strong executive who would be given either an absolute veto or one jointly shared with the judiciary as a way to protect those two branches of government from legislative intrusion. But opposition to the veto proposal developed. Franklin interjected that one governor in his state had used the veto as a way of extorting money from the legislature. George Mason raised the chilling specter of "a hereditary monarchy" developing on these republican shores. But in the end the Convention approved, eight to two, the veto, with an override by two-thirds of both houses. Wilson and Madison then tried to reintroduce the idea that the veto power be exercised by the executive and some judges sitting as a council of revision, but the Convention, by a vote of eight to three, rejected the council proposal, arguing that it was an inappropriate use of the judiciary. The delegates were becoming increasingly sensitive to the need for a separation of power among the branches, as well as to the need for checks and balances.[4]

Several days later the focus of the debate on the floor quickly shifted. William Paterson of New Jersey introduced a proposal to reform, in a modest way, the Articles of Confederation. With the support of his state delegation, Connecticut, Delaware, New York, and one delegate from Maryland, Paterson outlined an alternative to the nationalist Virginia Plan. He asked instead that Congress be granted some new powers to raise revenue and regulate commerce, and that an executive be created (the number of people was undesignated) who could "call forth the powers of the confederated states" to enforce national laws and treaties. The executive would also choose a supreme court to hear cases of impeachment of federal officers and appeals in cases arising from enemy captives, felons on the high seas, the collection of federal revenue, national regulation of commerce, and proceedings involving ambassadors and foreigners. Although the New Jersey Plan never commanded majority support, the message to the Convention was clear. The broad outlines incorporated in the Virginia Plan would not satisfy important delegates, in part because those representatives, even if they were so disposed to support the nationalist position, could not guarantee ratification of the new document back in their states. The grand vision of the Virginia Plan suddenly grew clouded, and the impetus for quick and decisive action was spent. Now the Convention moved on to the long, grinding process of building a consensus as well as writing a document.

Strangely, on June 18, Alexander Hamilton of New York rose and for more than four hours laid out an even more radical nationalist plan. Madison commented in his notes that Hamilton "had been hitherto silent on the business before the Convention, partly from respect to others whose superior abilities of age and experience rendered him unwilling to bring forward ideas dissimilar to theirs, and partly from his delicate situation with respect to his own state, to whose sentiments, as expressed by his colleagues, he could by no means accede." When he did speak, he proposed a national legislature with the power to pass any laws necessary to govern the country, and an executive who could be chosen by popularly elected electors, would serve for life, and could exercise an absolute veto. That executive would direct war when it was authorized or begun, make treaties with the approval of the Senate, have sole appointment powers in choosing the chief administrators of major departments with the Senate's approval, nominate all other officers, and pardon all offenses except treason. The Senators were also to be chosen for life, and the state governors were to be appointed by the national government and given a veto that could void acts of the state legislatures. As he argued later in defending his proposal, "Whatever is the Virginia Plan but pork still with a little change of the sauce?" The implications of Hamilton's plan were surely breathtaking, but in a convention that had just resisted the more moderate nationalism of the Virginia Plan, his speech was rather ill-timed. The delegates listened and went on to the business at hand. Hamilton left the Convention in late June, returning home. He came back periodically and finally signed the document in early September. As for the Convention, it did without his great gifts, and the delegates plodded through the issues seeking solutions that to Hamilton seemed so clear.[5]

Two major controversies divided the Convention: the basis for representation of the states in the new government and, to a considerably lesser extent, the question of slavery. Some moderate delegates and delegates from several of the smaller states were unwilling to accept a legislative branch based only on population. After lengthy debate, the Convention created a

Congress with one house based on population and one house with equal representation from each state. The solution, called later the Great Compromise, settled what Madison called the main dispute before the delegates.[6]

Less important at the time, but equally far-reaching for the new nation was the issue of slavery. As the hot, humid summer wore on and took its toll on the tempers and patience of the debaters, the ugly issue emerged. As if waiting in the shadows of stately Independence Hall, the form of slavery sulked forth, giving lie to the rhetoric of republican virtue and the sanctity of a revolution based on human rights. Being men of practical designs, the main critics of slavery, the New England delegates, did not press their true feelings at first, for they sought an agreement on the structure of government. The Southern delegates, even those who held slaves, refrained on their part from celebrating the virtues of their "peculiar institution," a sensitivity that the next generation of leaders in that region would lack.

The personal exchanges were, in the beginning, guarded and circumspect, but then they became more pointed. Gouverneur Morris called slavery "a nefarious institution, the curse of heaven on the states where it prevailed." He compared the prosperity of the North with the supposed wastelands of the slaveholding states and boldly exclaimed, "The vassalage of the poor has ever been the favorite offspring of the aristocracy." John Rutledge of South Carolina countered that the issue was not one of morality, but one of self-interest and that the South could not join the Union if its interests were threatened. Oliver Ellsworth of Connecticut pleaded that each state should be left to decide its own best solution to the issue, and Roger Sherman sanguinely observed that the abolition of slavery seemed to be progressing gradually.[7]

But the most telling remarks came from George Mason, one of the great liberal figures from Virginia and yet the owner of some 200 slaves whom he had tried unsuccessfully to free. Mason reiterated Jefferson's attack in 1776 on the British for their role in having brought slavery to the New World and then in having prevented attempts to check it. Mason declared that every slave master "was born a petty tyrant," and that slavery had discouraged honest labor and retarded the salutary growth of the arts and manufacturing. He went on to support the general government's having the power to prevent the increase of slavery and lamented that "some of our Eastern brethren have from a lust of gain embarked on this nefarious traffic." New Englanders shuddered at the obvious reference to their region's part in the slave trade.[8]

In the end, though, this was a gathering of pragmatic delegates whose aim was to create a new government for free white men. The Constitution made no mention of slavery by name, but it contained provisions that protected and fostered the institution. The slave trade was guaranteed until 1808, and a fugitive slave clause was written in general terms. For the

purposes of representation and taxation, the delegates adopted the congressional formula used in 1783 that counted a slave as three-fifths of a free
person.

Thus the two major divisive issues were resolved during the summer
session of 1787. The first solution is still incorporated in our law, the
centerpiece of the federal system of states and diverse peoples. The second
decision is still imbedded in our national soul, a compromise that tore the
nation apart, led to the bloodiest war of the nineteenth century, and left a
legacy of hatred that still will not wear away.

In one obvious sense, the creation of the presidency was not a problem
of such magnitude; it did not pit section against section or threaten to divide
the Convention on the basic issue of state representation. The debate on
Article II brought forth a great deal of intense rhetoric and confusing rancor;
it was not the most explosive issue, but as best one can tell, it surely must
have been the most continually complicated one.

Part of our uncertainty about how the presidency came into being may
be due to the extant accounts we have of those debates. The Convention
was held under the strictest secrecy, and the summaries of the deliberations
mainly come from Madison's notes, a diary that was not made public until
a generation after the Constitution's passage. From this work we probably
have a fairly accurate account of what happened on the floor of the Convention. Surely some of the stops and starts, the sudden changes and persistent tedium, come through in reading Madison's notes and the fragments
left by other delegates. But at several crucial junctures, the delegates were
unable to accommodate their honest differences, and unsettled and previously settled issues were referred to committees on detail, on style, or on
postponed matters for review. While we can understand the floor debates,
how or why the Founding Fathers ended up where they did in writing each
article, let alone each phrase, is often unclear. It was in these committees,
bodies made up of sensible men who were not great constitutional scholars
or profound political theorists, that the presidency was finally created.

The Convention avoided any quick settlements of the differences, and
from July 17 to July 26, a variety of issues were discussed, including the
executive. On July 17 the delegates wrestled once again with the method
of electing the executive. Gouverneur Morris repeated the separation of
powers argument, warning that if the legislature controlled the election
process, the executive would end up being its "mere creature." Citing the
New York and Connecticut experiences, he praised popular elections because the people would "never fail to prefer some man of distinguished
character or services." Wilson picked up Morris' proposal and added his
own support once again, but Charles Pinckney responded that the most
populous states would end up choosing the executive who in turn would
"carry their points." George Mason sarcastically added that popular election
in this case was as unnatural as referring "a trail of colors to a blind man."

The Convention then refused to support either popular election or the choice of electors by state legislatures. Instead, the delegations were unanimous in supporting election by the Congress.[9]

By so deciding, the delegates had created a formidable problem for themselves. They believed that the separation of powers was, in Madison's words, "essential to the preservation of liberty," and yet they gave the legislature the power to elect the executive. Now they wondered whether he should be eligible to be reelected and if so, how the executive could be "independent of the legislature, if dependent upon the pleasure of that branch for a reappointment." Continuing the debate, Madison commented that the state governors were "in general little more than cyphers," and that legislative dominance led to revolution and the destruction of republican institutions.

The next day the Convention laid aside the question of reeligibility and voted to give the executive a veto subject to an override by two-thirds of both houses. Having given that power to the executive, the Convention turned around and voted down allowing the executive, instead of the Senate, to appoint judges.

By Thursday, July 19, the delegates seemed ready to discuss the question of reeligibility, and Gouverneur Morris opened with a long defense of the importance of a strong executive to a republican government. In his eyes the legislature would seek to aggrandize itself and the "Executive Magistrate should be the guardian of the people, even of the lower classes, against legislative tyranny, against the great and the wealthy who in the course of things will necessarily compose the legislative body. Wealth tends to corrupt the mind and to nourish its love of power, and to stimulate it to oppression. History proves this to be the spirit of the opulent."[10]

He went on to support reeligibility because without it, the reward of reappointment would be eliminated. "The love of power is the great spring to noble and illustrious actions. Shut the Civil Road to glory and he may be compelled to seek it by the sword." Thus Morris countered the ancient adage that power led to corruption and stood it on its head: leaders in a republican society hope to gain fame and glory, and realize that in order to achieve those distinctions, "they had to be reelected and thus accountable to the people."[11]

Morris, too, swept aside the need for a provision allowing the executive to be impeached; instead, that remedy should be reserved for the "great offices of State," the cabinet officials who do his business. The Convention moved on, continuing the debate over election and eligibility, and finally voted eight to two for election by electors chosen by the state legislatures. The executive would serve a six-year term and would indeed, as Morris advocated, be eligible for reelection.[12]

By Friday, July 20, the Convention had decided to discuss the number of electors and the question of impeachment. Morris and Pinckney argued against impeachment, but other delegates saw this guarantee as necessary to ensure "good behavior." As Mason asked, "Shall any man be above justice? Above all shall that man be above it, who can commit the most extensive injustice?" Franklin, listening to the debate, interjected that without impeachment, the only other way to get rid of an objectionable executive was assassination. Madison, too, added his support: how else could the citizens defend "the community against the incapacity, negligence or perfidy of the Chief Magistrate." Even Morris wavered and came to support an impeachment provision; it passed eight states to two. The Convention then went on to reject still once again a council of revision and continued to give the judicial appointment power to the Senate. The presidency, at best, had a mixed day.[13]

During the next week, on Tuesday, July 24, a rehashing of the basic issues concerning the executive began anew. Hugh Williamson of North Carolina challenged the whole idea of a single magistrate and proposed a three-person office, with each section having one representative. The Convention voted seven to four for an executive to be chosen by the national legislature and then reopened the whole length-of-term question. Should it be eleven years, fifteen years, twenty years, or eight years? Unable to reach an agreement, the Convention postponed the matter for later debate. The next day Madison reopened the election issue, and finally the whole executive article (except the stipulation that it would be a single person) was referred to the Committee on Detail. The Convention had reached some tentative conclusions but could not finally agree from one day to the next on some basic provisions.

On August 6 John Rutledge gave the committee's draft report, which included a much strengthened executive article. The executive power was vested in a single person, called "The President of the United States of America" and addressed as "His Excellency." He was elected by the legislature for only one seven-year term and could be removed after impeachment by the House of Representatives and conviction by the Supreme Court for treason, bribery, or corruption. The president was to see that the laws were faithfully executed, commission officers, receive ambassadors, grant pardons and reprieves (except for impeachments), appoint most officers, veto legislation subject to an override of two-thirds majority in both houses, give information to the legislature on the state of the Union, and convene the legislature on extraordinary occasions. He was also commander-in-chief of the armed forces and the militia of the several states. On his death, resignation, or disability, the president of the Senate exercised his powers and duties. When the debate over the committee report began, Pinckney tried to add a stipulation that a prospective president must have $100,000 in property, but Franklin bitterly opposed the change, noting that he had a personal "dislike of everything that tended to debase the spirit of the common people."

As the delegates discussed at length the basic provisions of the committee's draft, they rejected the clause giving the legislature the power to "make" war. Instead, that body would "declare" war, with the understanding that the executive would have the power to repel sudden attacks. The Convention accepted the change in language by a vote of seven to two and then unanimously voted down an attempt by Pierce Butler of South Carolina to give the legislature also "the power of peace."

The Convention's deliberations on the war powers, an issue so important to posterity, appear disjointed and confused in the records that are available. What seems probable is that although the executive did retain the power to repel invasions, no prolonged military action would be undertaken without congressional approval and oversight. The delegates surely must have realized that undeclared war was the norm in eighteenth-century Europe, a reality brought close to home by the Seven Years' War between Britain and France. The delegates, though, allocated to Congress important parts of what could be termed the war powers. They gave to the legislative branch the power to provide for the common defense; to define and punish piracies and felonies committed on the high seas, and offenses against the law of nations; to declare war, grant letters of marque and reprisal, and make rules concerning captures on land or water; to raise and support armies; to provide and maintain a navy; to make rules for the government and regulation of the land and naval forces; to provide for calling forth the militia to execute the laws of the Union, suppress insurrections, and repel invasions; to provide for organizing, arming, and disciplining the militia, and for governing such part of them as may be employed in the service of the United States, reserving to the states, respectively, the appointment of the officers and the authority of training the militia according to the discipline prescribed by Congress. States are prohibited from entering into any treaty, alliance, or confederation and from granting letters of marque and reprisal. In addition, no state, without the consent of Congress, could keep troops or ships of war in time of peace, or enter into any agreement or compact with another state or with a foreign power, or engage in war unless actually invaded or in imminent danger. Lastly, the power to suspend the writ of habeas corpus is specified in Article I dealing with Congress, and not in Article II, which outlines the power of the executive.

Indeed, until the last two weeks of the session, the Senate even held the sole responsibility for making treaties and approving ambassadors. Several years later, in 1789, Madison wrote to Jefferson that the power to loose the "Dog of War" was transferred from the executive to the legislature, from those "who are to spend to those who are to pay." At the Convention, Madison even wanted to require that peace treaties needed only the approval of a majority of the members in the Senate, rather than the two-thirds present being proposed. In that way the executive's tendency to aggrandize his power during war could be more easily checked. The Convention agreed at first to Madison's proposal by a vote of eight to three, and then the next day rejected that view by the same margin.

On a matter of lesser importance, the Convention discussed the proper length of time an immigrant should have to wait before becoming a citizen. In a new nation with fairly flexible requirements about residence and nationality, the issue was of concern, especially to some of the Founding Fathers who were not native born. Regarding eligibility for "the great offices of Government," however, Gouverneur Morris was insistent in wanting to extend the probationary period. When a proposal for four years' citizenship before election to the Senate was suggested, he insisted on fourteen instead. He sarcastically noted that "some tribes of Indians carried their hospitality so far as to offer strangers their wives and daughters. Was this a proper model for us?" He would allow the foreign born to "worship at the same altar, but did not choose to make priests of them." As for the so-called philosophical citizens of the world, he frankly "did not trust them. The men who shake off their attachments to their own country can never love any other."[14] The Convention finally required that a person wishing to become a senator would have to be a citizen for nine years, and to become a representative, seven years; the president was to be a resident for fourteen years and a natural-born citizen or a citizen at the time of the adoption of the new Constitution. Except, then, for the founding generation, which included some prominent immigrants, such as Wilson and Hamilton, all future presidents had to be born Americans, a requirement that presumably meant that they were to be free of foreign attachments.

The Convention later considered Morris' proposal for a council of state made up of the chief justice and the secretaries of domestic affairs, commerce, foreign affairs, war, marine, and state. The delegates also debated the proposal that the Senate, not the president, make treaties and appoint ambassadors and Supreme Court justices. Again they pondered how the executive should be chosen; by the end of the month, the Convention accepted Morris' motion to strike out of the draft the clause giving the national legislature the power to elect the president. The Convention once again was left with some difficult contradictions, and it resolved to delegate the matters to another committee.

The "Committee on Postponed Matters," as it was termed, was given these and other unresolved differences. When the group returned with a new draft, it contained major changes in the executive article. The draft now had age, residence, and citizenship requirements, transferred the trial of an impeached president to the Senate, and mandated a four-year term with unlimited reeligibility. In dealing with the difficult issue of election procedures, the committee had the president chosen by electors who were selected by the states in a manner each state legislature directed. Thus the delegates neatly sidestepped a point of endless contention and allowed each state to choose how much popular control would be permitted. The electors had to vote for two candidates, at least one of whom had to be a resident from outside their respective states. If no candidate received a majority, the Senate would choose the president. The delegates later changed this provision and substituted the House of Representatives for the Senate, another concession to the smaller states. In the House, each state delegation could cast only one vote in choosing the executive.

The president was also given the right to make appointments if a majority of the Senate gave its advice and consent, and he could finalize treaties with the concurrence of two-thirds of that chamber. Up to two weeks before the end of the Convention, the Senate had been designated as the body to both appoint ambassadors and judges and make treaties. Now this draft shifted these important responsibilities to the executive. Wilson tried to give the president even more power by proposing that he should need only the approval of a majority of the Senators in order to ratify a treaty, but the delegates refused to support the proposal. Then Madison pushed again for a council of review and Hamilton, who had returned from New York, argued for life-time tenure and an absolute veto. But the majority of the delegates had decided to accept overall the draft that came out of committee.

With most of the outstanding issues on the executive and on other areas being settled, the Convention sent the full draft to a "Committee on Style," which, in the process of rewriting the document, decided to drop the provision allowing Congress to appoint the treasurer, an item quickly accepted by the delegates. The president thus ended up with the authority to appoint major officers, cast a qualified veto, receive a fixed salary, and appoint inferior officers if the legislature so approved. Pinckney, on seeing the final draft, felt that it still was deficient and criticized the "contemptible weakness and dependence of the executive." But another delegate, Pierce Butler, wrote that the powers of the president were great, and that the executive article would not have been so broad "had not many of the members cast their eyes toward General Washington as President, and shaped their ideas of the powers to be given a president by their opinions of his virtue."[15]

As the delegates filed forward to sign the Constitution, the outcome of a difficult summer's work, Madison concluded his account of the deliberations:

Dr. Franklin, looking toward the President's chair, at the back of which a rising sun happened to be painted, observed to a few members near him, that painters had found it difficult to distinguish in their art a rising from a setting sun. I have, said he, often and often in the course of the Session, and the vicissitudes of my hopes and fears as to its issue, looked at that behind the President without being able to tell whether it was rising or setting: But now at length I have the happiness to know that it is a rising and not a setting Sun.[16]

So it was that the American presidency was created, a product of intense debate, committee compromises, historical precedents—all influenced by a long-held suspicion of power and yet infused with the confidence that only the first generation of nation builders can bring. Perhaps once again it was Benjamin Franklin who best summed up the Founders' deep ambiguity about their experiment. Legend has it that as the aged statesman shuffled down the streets of Philadelphia, an inquisitive woman stopped him and asked, "What have you given us?" And Franklin is supposed to have responded, "A Republic, Madam, if you can keep it."

6

THE RATIFICATION CONTROVERSY

The only real security of liberty in any country, is the jealousy and circumspection of the people themselves.

James Iredell,
North Carolina Ratifying Convention, 1788

Agreement was reached in Philadelphia; now it was necessary to convince a far more skeptical people about the wisdom of this new Constitution. The delegates forwarded their document to the Confederation Congress, and on September 29, over the opposition of some of the New York representatives, the Constitution was "transmitted to the several legislatures in order to be submitted to a convention of delegates chosen in each state, by the people thereof."[1] The theater of action shifted to the states, and during 1787 and 1788, an extraordinary political dialogue took place, unique in even the brief annals of free republics. The newspapers were filled with commentaries, aimed at influencing the state conventions and molding the opinions of merchant and yeoman alike. Other partisans wrote long pamphlets that were widely circulated during this period.

The most effective defense of the new Constitution came from "Publius," the joint pen name of Hamilton, Madison, and John Jay. As if trying to make up for his lackluster performance at the Convention, Hamilton carried the burden of authoring most of these newspaper pieces written under the collective title *The Federalist*. Some eighty-five essays were printed in various newspapers between October 27, 1787, and August 16, 1788. Jay wrote only a few of the pieces and only one deals with the presidency. In November 1787 Jay reminded his readers that secrecy and dispatch are often essential in negotiating treaties and that the executive alone epitomizes such attributes. Jay found that, while the proposed Constitution required that "the President must, in forming [treaties], act by the advice and consent of the Senate, yet, he will be able to manage the business of intelligence in such a manner as prudence may suggest."

Madison's role in defending the Constitution was more substantial, and he drew on his vast learning in political theory and on his practical sense to deal with the task at hand. Much of his effort was devoted to various discussions of the causes of ruination in other republican experiments and to the nature of power and the workings of political factions. In examining the executive, he reassured readers that the method of election by state electors showed that the proposed government was a federal and not a national structure. Furthermore, while "the executive department is very justly regarded as the source of danger and watched with all the jealousy which a zeal for liberty ought to inspire," nonetheless the Constitution contained careful limits on the executive's powers.

In one sense, it is ironic to see Madison defending the new government as a federal and not a national one, since he was the driving force behind the original Virginia Plan. Even more interesting are Hamilton's labors with regard to the new Constitution, a document for which Madison privately expressed no real admiration. Yet in 1787 and 1788 the only choice was between the Articles and the proposed new Constitution, and Hamilton surely supported the latter. In his analysis of the presidency, he candidly noted that no article has been as difficult to write and no part of the document was so unjustly criticized. He swept aside the hollow accusation that the presidency would become a monarchy and remarked in passing "that the executive's powers were in few instances greater, in some less than those of the governor of New York."

He insisted that the method of election had been accepted by nearly all, and that even some of the critics of the Constitution had found that provision praiseworthy. Hamilton predicted that "the office of President will never fall to the lot of any man who is not in an eminent degree endowed with the requisite qualifications." Hamilton clearly rejected the idea that the presidency was patterned after the British monarchy and instead cited the governors as the most likely models, noting in one instance that the veto power in the proposed document was the same as that of "the Governor of Massachusetts, whose constitution, as to this article, seems to have been the original from which this Convention have copied." In discussing the commander-in-chief provision, Hamilton moved closer to home and reminded his readers that those clauses resembled the powers granted to the governor of New York, at least as much as the prerogatives of the British king, and that in fact the executives of both New Hampshire and Massachusetts may have greater authority in their spheres than the president has in his.

Hamilton went on to observe that while the president can pardon all offenses except impeachment, the governor of New York can pardon such crimes but not treason or murder. The same state governor, like the king in Parliament, can prorogue the legislature, while the president can only adjourn the Congress when the two houses disagree about the time for adjournment. Unlike the king, the president has limited constitutional power, grants no titles, establishes no currency, heads no church, and needs the Senate's advice and consent to make treaties. Even his power to receive ambassadors and foreign ministers is "more a matter of dignity than authority."

Hoping to have laid to rest fears of a new monarchy, Hamilton then affirmed the advantages of having a vigorous executive, an argument more to his temperament and liking. "Energy in the executive is a leading characteristic in the definition of good government," he asserted. Such energy is derived from a unity of authority, duration in office, an adequate provision for its support, and competent powers. Hamilton strongly supported a single executive and maintained that duration in office rested on personal firmness and administrative stability. Like some of the other Founding Fathers, he argued that the possibility of reelection was an inducement to a balanced government and proper zeal in the public's service. With heavy irony, he lamented the plight of one state that had a dozen former magistrates who were "wandering among the people like discontented ghosts, and sighing for a place which they were destined nevermore to possess." A constitutional requirement for periodic turnover would seriously upset the need for stability and presumably increase the number of discontented ghosts in the republic.

In addition to these observations, Hamilton went on to defend other provisions, including a guaranteed salary, a qualified veto, the commander-in-chief clause, the pardon, and the ability to appoint officers. Hamilton's efforts were instrumental in lending support to the executive office and the entire new Constitution. Looking back, *The Federalist* is truly one of the most impressive statements of American political theory, rivaled only by John C. Calhoun's discourses on concurrent majorities. But in 1788 these essays, appearing under the noble Roman pseudonym of Publius, were only one contribution to a long and sometimes acrimonious debate that was occurring.[2]

The proposed Constitution came in for its share of criticism, and in terms of the executive article, no section of the document raised more fears than the relationships between the president and the Senate. Seeking to provide some check on the president, the delegates had insisted that the Senate be granted a part in the ratification of treaties and in approving major appointments. Elbridge Gerry, who was at that convention, warned later that the executive and legislative branches were "so dangerously blended as to give just cause of alarm."[3] George Mason, also back from the Philadelphia meeting, pressed publicly for a six-man council of state, made up of two representatives from each section. In this way a more effective check could be provided against the possibility of executive abuse; also, his region, the South, could protect its navigational interests from precipitous action by the new government. Still another critic, Jonathan Jackson, argued just the opposite: the president should be independent of the Senate so that he could be held personally responsible for actions done in his administration.[4]

Another area of controversy was the method of election and the length of term—two topics that had so divided the delegates themselves. Although Hamilton had sanguinely observed that this section had drawn little criticism, he seems to have overlooked some rather influential dissenters, including Jefferson and, more important, his own governor. Still in Europe, Jefferson expressed to some of his friends his objection to the reeligibility provision. However, his distance from the national scene and his personal reluctance to attack the work of the Convention, a group he earlier had respectfully called an assembly of demigods, meant that he would have no real influence on the ratification debates. Governor George Clinton, however, took up his pen and under the name of "Cato" severely judged the new executive article and found the full Constitution lacking. Citing Montesquieu, Clinton maintained that a term longer than one year would be dangerous. He foresaw the possible development of a despot surrounded by a court of flatterers and sycophants. In charged language, the powerful governor recited the familiar litany of horrors that power might incur:

The deposit of vast trusts in the hands of a single magistrate enables him in their exercise to create a numerous train of dependents. This tempts his *ambition*, which in a republican magistrate is also remarked, *to be pernicious*, and the duration of his office for any considerable time favors his views, gives the means and time to perfect and execute his designs; he *therefore fancies that he may be great and glorious by oppressing his fellow citizens, and raising himself to permanent grandeur on the ruins of his country*.

Instead of lamenting the lack of a council of state, Clinton derided the cabinet as being "the most dangerous council in a free country. The language and the manners of this court will be what disguises them from the rest of the community, not what assimilates them to it; and in being remarked for a behavior that shows they are not *meanly born*, and in adulation to people of future and power." With some knowledge, Clinton criticized those who said that there are few differences between the governorship of New York and the proposed presidency. He concluded that "this government is no more like a true picture of your own than an Angel of Darkness resembles an Angel of Light."[5]

Clinton's reservations were not isolated sentiments. There was a broad, but not well-organized group of Americans who opposed the Constitution and who focused their attacks on, among other points, the possible abuses of executive power. Other critics pointed to the pardoning power and speculated on how a president's political associates might be absolved from paying for their crimes; still others attacked the veto as a violation of the separation of powers doctrine, and one pamphleteer, Benjamin Workman, saw the commander-in-chief clause as leading to an elected kingship. The president, he insisted, would be surrounded by "a standing army, officered by his sycophants, the starvelings of the Cincinnati, and an autocratical Congress of the well-born."[6] Even the Founding Fathers' token nod to the spirit of the Enlightenment—the absence of religious qualification—was objected to by one pamphleteer, John Sullivan. Under the proposed Constitution, he remarked, "A Turk, a Jew, or Rom[an] Catholic, and what is worse than all, a Universal[ist], may be President of the United States."[7]

The pro-Constitution pamphleteers joined Hamilton and Madison by brushing aside this iliad of fears and by trying to remind their readers that in a republic of honest citizens, venial and grossly criminal acts are less likely to occur because of the strength of public opinion. Alexander Conte Hanson predicted that as regards the president, "every citizen in the Union will be a censor of his conduct. Not even his person is particularly protected; and the means of oppression are little in his power." Another supporter of the Constitution, Tench Coxe, reminded his readers that although the monarch cannot be removed from his position, the president "is one of the people at the end of his short term, so will he and his fellow citizens remember, that he was originally one of the people; and he is created by their breath."[8]

Although these and other polemical debates were vigorously carried on in the newspapers and through pamphlets, they generally lacked vigor and depth. More systematic discussions of the proposed Constitution took place at the state ratifying conventions, where Federalist and Anti-Federalist factions went through the new document section by section. There, in the states, many of the more prominent delegates at the Philadelphia Convention were obliged to answer the questions and counter the criticisms of their fellow citizens. And it was at these conventions that the presidency was being discussed at some length and often in passionate and fearful terms.

The conventions in the important eastern states of New York and Pennsylvania were more measured and moderate in tone than in some of the southern regions. In New York many of the delegates had reservations, but the Federalists convinced them first to approve unconditionally the document and then to recommend a series of proposed amendments. In terms of the presidency, the amendments included provisions that the executive be limited to one seven-year appointment, that he not command the armed forces without the consent of Congress, that there be a congressionally selected council to advise the executive on appointments, that Congress must approve pardoning convicted traitors, and that the executive be able to establish, with the consent of Congress, commissions to review Supreme Court decisions. The delegates also expressed concern both that the Senate was too powerful and that the executive's control over appointments would lead to corruption. When the state convention ended, the New York delegation had narrowly approved the proposed Constitution without conditions. The Federalist cause received a major boost throughout the nation.

In Pennsylvania many of the same concerns were raised. The criticisms of the executive article were adroitly answered once again by James Wilson, who had played such a major role in creating the language of Article II. Wilson dismissed the charge that the presidency was a weak office, "a tool of the Senate," as one dissenting voice objected. He informed the state convention that he had favored the direct election of the president but that most of his fellow delegates at Philadelphia thought that the size of the new nation made that design impractical. Wilson then pointed out the major powers that the president had: he was commander-in-chief, controlled the departments of government, possessed the right to grant pardons, and was entrusted with the faithful execution of the laws. Taken together, these provisions created a powerful national executive with great responsibility and considerable independence from the legislature.[9] In the end, the Pennsylvania convention, too, approved the new Constitution.

The Federalists, better mobilized and more informed about the document, were able to repeat their successes in a variety of states that year. The most intense battle, though, was waged in Virginia, where many of the major heroes of the Revolution ended up on opposite sides. The leader of the opposition was the frontier Demosthenes, Patrick Henry, whose rhetoric quickened the hearts of all patriots and whose words were legendary exclamations in the vocabulary of liberty.

The Federalists soon felt his scorn as he attacked the proposed presidency. Looking over the state convention and seeing many familiar faces, Henry began: "This Constitution is said to have beautiful features: but when I come to examine these features, sir, they appear to me horribly frightful. Among other deformities, it has an awful squinting, it squints toward monarchy; and does not this raise indignation in the breast of every true American?" The aged patriot continued, arguing that the president could easily become a king. "Where are the checks in this new government? How easy it is for a man of ambition to become absolute with the army at his disposal." Then the one individual who had done more than anyone before the Revolution to challenge the abuses of the king denounced the proposed presidency by exclaiming, "I would rather infinitely—and I am sure that most of the convention are of the same opinion—have a king, lords and commons, than a government so replete with such insupportable evils." The king, Henry observed, "rules within certain bounds, this president with his army will have none." Swept up in the raw emotions of old, Henry went on, "Away with your president! We shall have a king: the army will salute him monarch: your militia will leave you, and assist in making him king, and fight against you: and what have you to oppose this force? What then will become of you and your rights? Will not absolute despotism ensue?"

Suddenly the record we have of this debate breaks off; the stenographer simply summarized, "Here Mr. Henry strongly and pathetically expiated on the probability of the President's enslaving America, and the horrid consequences that must result." We do have the reaction of another observer, who found Henry's description so frightening that he "involuntarily felt his wrists to assure himself that the fetters were not already pressing his flesh and that the gallery in which he sat seemed to become as dark as a dungeon."

The Federalists sought to counter Henry with rhetoric and reasoning of their own, but he quickly came back to the perils of this new executive. First, he acknowledged the glorious and magnanimous "dictator" we had who led the American army to victory, but then he went on, "we gave a dictatorial power to hands that used it gloriously; and which were rendered more glorious by surrendering it up. Where is there a breed of such dictators? Shall we find a set of American presidents of such a breed? Will the American president come and lay prostrate at the feet of Congress his laurels? I fear that there are few men who can be trusted on that hand." And then he summarized in a single sentence the core of the Anti-Federalist objection: "Cannot people be happy under a mild as under an energetic government?"[10]

Pointedly, he was to respond to the strong nationalist vision with another admonition: "You are not to inquire how your trade may be increased, nor how you are to become a great and powerful people, but how your liberties can be secured." No one matched the linguistic flights and dark imagery of the master wordsmith Patrick Henry. But the Federalists had carefully mobilized their supporters, knowing full well the likely impact of his assault. When Patrick Henry finished, when the great passions had run their course, and men ceased admiring the magnificent display, the vote was taken. The Constitution received the support of the powerful state of Virginia. The most formidable challenges were over—only North Carolina and Rhode Island still had not ratified the new document by the end of the year.

So it was that in the context of revolutionary memories and legalistic exercises the early presidency was born. Men who had fought the abuses of a foreign king and his local ministers now came to accept the necessity for a new national executive. From one end of the seaboard to the other, the partisan pamphleteers and the political classes carried on a public debate unparalleled in the history of their time. Fresh from the unifying common experience of war, they were now divided on the future of the very republic they had created. What was at stake were not only matters of self-interest, power, and privilege; the Federalists and Anti-Federalists subscribed to different dreams of that future. The opposition would repeatedly rephrase Patrick Henry's simple question, "Cannot people be as happy under a mild as under an energetic government?" The answer of the more ambitious nation builders was clear: they wanted not just liberty, but also grandeur, not just republican virtue, but also a place in the sun. For those purposes they created a set of strong national institutions and later buttressed them with an alliance of finance and privilege. Yet, during this long and tortuous debate, the Federalists acknowledged and perhaps even shared in some of the Anti-Federalists' misgivings. Their first order of business in the new Congress would be a Bill of Rights, and in looking for a national executive, they chose essentially a figure of the past, a man who symbolized the revolutionary struggle to his three million fellow countrymen. His choice was obvious. Throughout the rancor of the ratification debates, both factions agreed on one thing—they knew that their Cincinnatus could never become a Caesar.[11]

Part Two

THE WASHINGTON ADMINISTRATION

7

THE AUTHENTIC
AMERICAN

I have heard the bullets whistle and believe me there is something charming in the sound.

George Washington, May 29, 1754

It is not unusual for a newly independent nation, freed from the bonds of colonialism, to turn to its revolutionary heroes for continuing leadership. The same phenomenon is clear today in the emerging states of Africa and Asia, and it held true as well for the United States. The single most important hero of the American Revolution was, of course, General George Washington, and the basic outlines of his distinguished career were well known to every schoolchild in his native land.

Although Washington was, in Light-Horse Harry Lee's words, "first in war, first in peace, and first in the hearts of his countrymen," his record as president is vague and often forgotten. Some historians maintain that Washington's contribution to the presidency is simply that he was our first national executive. Others see Washington as a decorative backdrop for the brilliant Hamilton on center stage. Indeed, even Hamilton, who should have known better, concluded that the President's importance was that "he was an aegis to me."[1]

Yet a closer examination of the early presidency leads to quite a different picture of Washington's role and contributions. First, the presence of Washington served several important symbolic functions. By linking up the spirit of the Revolution with the new national experiment, an aura of legitimacy was lent to the Constitution. The Progressive historians, writing in the early twentieth century, concluded that the Constitution was a retreat from the democratic impulses that emerged in the Revolutionary period. Whether that stark interpretation is correct is open to serious question, but surely Washington's presence made it easier for most Anti-Federalists to accept whatever political transformation was occurring.

Second, Washington's pre-eminence tended to retard the growth of political parties. His election was so expected and acceptable that no national division took place, and personal coalitions were not sharply defined by the only national race that took place. Modern proponents of a strong party system regard this postponement as unfortunate, but in many new nations, a period of contrived unity is often a benevolent respite from major conflicts while fragile institutions are being established.[2]

Third, Washington, as a leader, had enough personal credibility that he could make that collection of vague constitutional clauses into a political office. Even at the lowest point of his popularity, during the Neutrality Proclamation and the Jay Treaty, Washington was able to fend off challenges to his office and prevail over the opposition largely because of the continuing goodwill he drew on. The most bitter of his foes could not counter the popular predisposition that although the General might on occasion err, he was still the epitome of the selfless, honorable patriot.

But even leaving aside all of those symbolic and practical aspects, Washington's presidency was important for other reasons as well. For eight difficult years he led the loosely constituted nation through a series of major conflicts and intense political disputes. The Washington administration was not a prolonged honeymoon, but a period that demanded prudent judgment, political acumen, and a thick skin against criticism. As for the man himself, Washington was careful in his use of power and concerned about the future of the executive branch of government. He created precedents not as an exercise in statecraft, but as a response to particular crises. Indeed, he found an office and left it an institution.

Yet, for all his contributions and our popular knowledge about the man, Washington seems to us, like most figures in mythology, a distant and aloof character, a person far removed from our contemporary experience. The outlines of his career were generally well known. Washington was born on February 22, 1732 (February 11, Old Style Calendar), in Pope's Creek, Westmoreland County, Virginia. He was the first child of the marriage of Augustine Washington and his second wife, Mary Ball. Despite their modest status in the New World, the roots of the Washington line went back deeply into English history and the family was at one time closely aligned with the Stuarts. When the Puritan Revolution came, part of the family left for Virginia in order to begin a new life. Despite ambition and energy, Washington's forebears were unable to move up into the innermost circle of power in the colony. Young Washington grew up in a household where his father was frequently absent and his older brothers were off on their own. His mother was extremely protective and seldom exhibited pride in the achievements of any of her children, even though she lived to see her eldest son lead his country to independence and then be elected its first president. In the midst of the Revolution, she unfairly chastised George publicly for not providing for her proper upkeep, and much to his embarrassment, she even petitioned the Virginia legislature for relief.

As he grew up, Washington became withdrawn, restrained, and rather self-reliant. When his father died, Washington was only eleven and fell under the care of his elder half-brothers, Lawrence and Augustine, who became somewhat surrogate fathers. Quite understandably he followed their example, left his mother's influence, and joined their circle of friends. The developing, awkward Washington began to frequent the company of the politically powerful Fairfax family, where he developed an attachment for Sally Cary Fairfax. Under the patronage of that family, Washington became a surveyor and worked for a land development company. In the drawing room of the Fairfax family, he discovered Joseph Addison's play *Cato*, a work that glorified civility, reason, and public service. Whether the play molded his values or complemented them, Washington began a concerted effort to master his explosive temper and form his own character. He drew up more than 100 "Rules of Conduct"—an impressive milestone in the attempt to transform a frontier fellow into a country gentleman.[3]

Washington's career as a surveyor was modestly successful, but on September 19, 1751, he decided to travel with his brother Lawrence to Barbados, hoping that a change of climate would help cure the latter's tuberculosis. While on the island, George contracted smallpox, a fortuitous setback that led to his inoculation against future and even graver attacks of the disease that was to so plague his contemporaries. On July 25, 1752, his brother died, and when Lawrence's last surviving child passed away two years later, George inherited the estate of Mount Vernon. Washington, then in his early twenties, was once again forced back on his own personal inner resources. For him and for so many others, the eighteenth-century world of pestilence and hardship did not easily lend itself to close and lasting personal ties.

Washington, with his knowledge of the topography of the frontier, retained a love of the land around him and an interest in the growing development of the colony. When the Governor of Virginia had to have an important message from the English king delivered to the French forces near the Ohio River, he accepted William Fairfax's recommendation that his young surveyor be sent.

This onetime errand was a major turning point in Washington's life. He soon perceived that war was in the wind, and after returning home, Washington asked his friends to help him get a military promotion. They were soon successful, and Washington was commissioned a lieutenant colonel and sent to Alexandria, Virginia, to recruit, supply, and train 300 soldiers in order to reinforce a company at the strategic fork of the Ohio and Monongahela rivers. Unfortunately for Washington, his apprenticeship was rather short and too eventful. On moving through the wilderness, he and his troops grew anxious that a French attack was impending, and they ended up confronting a nearby French force, leaving ten soldiers dead. A second battle ensued and the colonists were defeated by the French, who demanded that they destroy their arms, withdraw from the Ohio area, and confess to the previous "killings." In a written cease-fire statement, the colonists agreed to sign a document that contained the French word "assassinat" without understanding what it implied.[4] Thus the young Washington had turned the French–British war of nerves into a series of battles, in which he had been humiliated in defeat, and had then mistakenly agreed that he and his troops had treacherously "assassinated" men whom the French later claimed were ambassadors. The obscure Virginian was soon a major figure of controversy. The British criticized his imprudence, and even the king was supposedly annoyed over the young man's impetuous actions. The great Voltaire is also recorded as having commented on this American's barbarity. Washington struggled to defend himself and clear his name, but it seemed that his dream of honor and public respect had turned into a nightmare. Gone was the cockiness of the young hopeful, who in 1755 wrote his mother that he could not refuse to lead the Virginia regiment lest it "would reflect eternal dishonor upon me."[5]

By the spring of 1758, Washington, sick with dysentery and exasperated with the English command, resigned and decided to run for the Virginia House of Burgesses. Aided by a growing coterie of friends and by his willingness to buy forty gallons of Madeira and a hogshead of fine Barbardos rum to woo voters, he was elected. Washington, though, retained a fascination for the military and organized a group of Virginians at Fort Cumberland, Maryland, leading them on some expeditions during the French and Indian War. But in terms of the British, they ignored his views and one of his superiors remarked that the Virginian's behavior was insufferable and ridiculous and "in no ways like a soldier."[6] Finally, after five years of dedicated service, an angry Washington found himself held in low esteem by some of the very people for whom he had fought so bravely. Several months later, Washington made another important decision: he decided to marry a young widow with two children and extensive property holdings. Although still infatuated with the charms of his neighbor's wife, Sally Fairfax, Washington nonetheless proposed to Martha Dandridge Custis. Once again the maturing Washington had attempted to direct his varied and strong impulses into the accepted, conventional channels of society. A prosperous marriage changed a modest colonel of a provincial militia into a major landowner in the colony. By the age of twenty-seven, Washington decided to retire from the glamour and the proven anxieties of military regimen in order to take up family life.

As might be expected, he grew somewhat bored with the ease of the plantation and resumed his seat in the House of Burgesses. For the next nine years, Washington worked on its obscure committees, sponsoring such landmark bills as a measure to keep pigs out of the watering troughs of Alexandria and, more important, learning the rules and idiosyncrasies of representative bodies.

By 1769 Washington's role in the colony was greatly enhanced. The relationships between Britain and its North American empire were deteriorating and the forces of opposition began to mount. With the assistance of the highly respected George Mason, Washington sponsored a series of proposals to establish a colonywide network of associations of planters and merchants aimed at restricting the importation of British goods.

As the conflicts mounted, Washington increasingly cast his lot with the patriot cause. The British moved to control the resistance and began to mobilize troops and close the port of Boston. By September 1774 delegates from all over the colonies met to consider what should be done to counter the British. One delegate, Silas Deane, recorded that Washington said little in the floor debates, and that when he did, he "speaks very modestly, and in cool, but determined style and accent."[7]

Once again Washington sensed the coming war, positioning himself as before, in the midst of the conflict. Back in Virginia he and Mason used their own money to drill and train a militia. Washington's role was clear: in a letter to his brother John, he confirmed that "it is my full intention to devote my Life and Fortune in the causes we are engaged in, if need be."[8] And he was indeed correct about the flow of events.

The British and the colonists clashed openly in Boston, and in May 1775 the Second Continental Congress met in Philadelphia. Washington appeared not as another delegate, but clad now in a military uniform that he himself had created for his local troops. John Adams, obviously impressed, wrote: "Colonel Washington appears at Congress in his uniform, and by his great Experience and Abilities in military Matters, is of much Service to us."[9]

Washington's contemporaries noted that even then he cut an impressive figure. Nearly six feet two inches in height, he towered over the men of his time. Although he had rather narrow shoulders and chest, he gave an impression of great physical strength. Usually tanned, his skin was only slightly scarred by the smallpox he had contracted in Barbados. His eyes were gray blue, his hair reddish brown, and he was rather graceful both on horseback and on the dance floor. Jefferson once commented that his fellow Virginian was "the best horseman of his age and the most graceful figure that could be seen on horseback." And scores of ladies throughout the years recorded in their diaries how flattered they were by his invitation to join in the stylized dances of that period.

The Continental Congress, led by Adams, looked for a Southerner to assume command of its armed forces. The conflict against the British had to become more than a New England affair, and Washington was now the available man. Congress, though, did not vote specifically for war, but rather it chose Washington to manage its military affairs and help preserve

American liberty. As one of his modern biographers has observed, Washington was not, in 1775, supposed to fight for independence as much as be the standard around which the cause was to rally. Faced with that troubling ambiguity and his own realization that he was more of a frontiersman than a field commander, Washington modestly responded to the Congress, "I do not think myself equal to the command I am honored with."[10]

The armies in New England embraced about 18,000 to 20,000 soldiers, being about fifteen times larger than any group Washington had ever commanded. In addition, he knew few of the patriot leaders outside his own state, and Congress itself was unsure of the future of the rebellion it was encouraging. As for the new commander of the armies, he bravely wrote: "to struggle with misfortune, to combat difficulties with intrepidity and finally to surmount the obstacles which oppose us, are stronger proofs of merit and give a fairer title to reputation than the brightest scenes of tranquility or sunshine of prosperity could ever have afforded."[11]

Washington, despite his hunger for glory and military renown, understood well the immense problems he would find. He wrote his brother John: "No man perhaps since the first institution of armies ever commanded one under more difficult circumstances than I have done." And after a year in command, he could at least take solace in the observation, "I am happy, however, to find and hear from other quarters that my reputation stands fair, that my conduct has hitherto given universal satisfaction."[12]

But the war did not go well from the beginning. A substantial segment of the population opposed the Revolution, and Washington's army lacked experienced officers, adequate supplies, and strong discipline. Addressing a group of new recruits, he exhorted and threatened, "If I see any man turn his back today, I will shoot him through. I have two pistols loaded. But I will not ask any man to go further than I do, I will fight as long as I have a leg or an arm."[13]

Despite his efforts, support for Washington was not as widespread as he would have imagined or liked. Early in the war, he even considered resigning, explaining to a friend, "I see the impossibility of surviving with reputation."[14] After the loss of New York in 1776, there was some talk of replacing him with General Lee, and Lee himself had written to General Gates, "*Entre nous*, a certain great man is most damnably deficient." Then, as luck would have it, Lee was captured by the British while he was engaging in a romantic liaison with an obliging widow. By the end of the year, Washington dragged his tattered army through New Jersey and over the Delaware River. Then, in an incredible gamble, he turned his forces around and crossed the icy river early on Christmas morning. After some brief hostilities in Trenton, the army moved on toward Princeton, where Washington won his first major battle since the "Jumonville massacre" against the French some twenty years before.

News of his victories swept across the dispirited colonies. Even Frederick the Great, in reviewing the marches, proclaimed them "the most brilliant of any recorded in the annals of military achievement."[15] But one great victory was not enough; supplies were short, the troops came and went, and Washington soon lost Philadelphia. Then political pressures mounted: General Thomas Conway was appointed Inspector General by a newly constituted Board of War, and he, Thomas Mifflin, and General Gates formed the core of an anti-Washington alliance. But the Conway Cabal, as it became known, was unable to gather enough support to dismiss the commander, and he stubbornly refused to retire. Faced with intrigue and the pathetic sight of hungry, half-naked men at Valley Forge, a bitter Washington held on throughout the discontented winter of 1777–1778. Much to the displeasure of some Americans, Washington continued his Fabian strategy of circumspect delay and careful temporizing. He had little choice— the army was disorganized and poorly supplied and the Continental money he received was so inflated that it was nearly worthless. Then one of his more trusted comrades in arms, Benedict Arnold, betrayed the cause. The only encouragement Washington had was the arrival of French forces to fight with the patriots against their age-old enemy, the British.[16]

While Washington was insisting that New York was his main concern, he found out that a French fleet from the Indies was moving up the Chesapeake but would not come as far as Sandy Hook, New Jersey. The French expected that Washington would concentrate his forces in the South, and the hesitant American commander was left with little choice about the next theater of action. To use effectively the forces of the French navy, Washington mobilized his troops in Virginia and eventually forced Cornwallis into an untenable position. The British finally surrendered on September 19, 1781, and in one fell swoop they lost nearly a quarter of their North American army. The victorious Americans watched the formal ceremonies of surrender and listened to the melody of a prophetic tune—"The World Turned Upside Down." Thus Washington's greatest climactic victory came about in a reluctant campaign that the French had forced on him. The cautious and harried general became a living legend, and the aura of success quieted his persistent critics and stunned the faint of heart.[17]

The war was in effect over, and the negotiators worked out a final treaty of parting. But for Washington, the Continental army—still denied proper wages and adequate supplies—became a center of discontent. Foolishly, some members of the Congress, including Hamilton and Robert Morris, seemed to welcome the growth of a martial spirit, hoping that it would lead to a strong national government. The tensions reached a flash point on March 15, 1783, when officers led by General Gates organized a meeting at Newburgh, New York, to consider methods of redressing their grievances.

As the meeting began, an uninvited guest arrived and strode over to the dais. Washington looked over the hostile military officers, many of whom were considering force against their own weak government. He started slowly, speaking of their common sacrifices, and urged them to "express your utmost horror and detestation of the man who wishes, under any specious pretenses, to overturn the liberties of our country, and who wickedly attempts to open the flood-gates of civil discord and deluge our rising empire in blood." His audience remained unmoved by the all-too-familiar call for restraint. Then he reached for a letter from a member of Congress in order to show the legislature's concern for their plight. He paused, unable to make out the lines, and fumbled for his wire-framed glasses. Spontaneously he murmured, "Gentlemen, will you permit me to put on my spectacles, for I have not only grown gray but almost blind in the service of my country." The hardness of the crowd turned to sympathy and some war-weary veterans cried at the sight of their commander, who had shared their often thankless sacrifices. Washington read the letter, left the hall, and rode out of sight. The Newburgh meeting dissolved that night.[18]

8

CINCINNATUS RETURNS

I have no wish which aspires beyond the humble and happy lot of living
and dying a private citizen on my own farm.

George Washington, 1788

Despite the uncertain fate of the proposed Constitution in 1788, one political
fact was clear: General Washington commanded the respect of his fellow
countrymen and would obviously be elected president if he so consented.
To the loose string of republics along the eastern seacoast, Washington was
a national hero and a true international figure. Of all the leaders who
emerged from the crucible of the Revolution, no one combined better the
attributes of experience, sagacity, and "gravitas" that so captivated the
imaginations of those frontier republicans. In trying to appreciate his unique
historical role, many educated Americans regarded Washington as their
Cincinnatus, the noble Roman who has left his plow, saved his country,
and then returned to his farm, personally uncorrupted by the lure of power.

With a tint of jealousy, John Adams once said that Washington's main
assets were that he was tall and a Virginian. Indeed he was both. But
Washington was also a man of considerable means who had risked his life
and future in a seemingly hopeless gamble. While not one of the signers of
the Declaration of Independence served in the Continental army, Washington shared in the soldiers' misery and despair and went on to reap quite
rightfully the compelling glory that only military victory can bring. Like
so many of the Founding Fathers, he sought fame and desired to have
posterity remember him for his patriotic services. To many Americans of
his time, Washington was already the embodiment of republican virtue, a
testament that men raised by proper breeding might very well be able to
handle honestly the lure and trappings of power.[1]

As the long debates on the Constitution continued, there was near universal agreement that Washington should be the first president. There were

some isolated voices of opposition, especially in New York, to Washington's strong Federalist leanings and the names of George Clinton, John Hancock, and the elderly Dr. Franklin were brought up. But none of these figures had strong, popular support, and Washington's choice was a foregone conclusion if he would agree to serve. In February 1788 his fifty-sixth birthday was celebrated throughout the nation, and on the Fourth of July, many citizens called for his election. In one toast at Wilmington, Delaware, he was hailed "Farmer Washington—may he like a second Cincinnatus, be called from the plow to rule a great people."[2]

Observing from a respectable distance the spontaneous public display of affection and confidence, Washington seemed to hesitate on what he should do. Having already established his reputation, he was, in his own words, reluctant to risk it. Besides he felt that his candidacy had several drawbacks. He was too old to take on another public position, his views were not acceptable to the Anti-Federalists, and he was not particularly inclined to assume new and unfamiliar duties once again. Then, too, his return to public life might be viewed as evidence of rashness, or even rank ambition.

Yet he also wondered if his fellow citizens would criticize him for refusing to discharge his duty and answer the call to service. Might it not be possible, he wondered, to hold the office briefly and then, once the government was established, return to the solitude of Mount Vernon? Finally in his own mind he worked out his position: " . . . nothing in the world can ever draw me from [retirement] unless it be a *conviction* that the partiality of my countrymen had made my services absolutely necessary, joined to a *fear* that my refusal might induce a belief that I preferred the conservation of my own reputation and private ease to the good of my country."[3] So it seemed that Washington was indeed willing to accept the office if it were thrust upon him, which he knew in all likelihood would happen.

While the General was debating his own fate, some of his associates were already deciding whom to support for the vice-presidency. Most of the Federalist leadership wanted John Adams, but Adams, during the war, had sought to curtail the General's power, citing the ever present dangers of a standing army. Recognizing the difficulty, an old friend of Washington, Benjamin Lincoln, volunteered to write to the General and warn that those who opposed Adams really wanted to elect an opponent of the Constitution as vice-president. Washington, picking up the cue, responded tactfully that he would support any true Federalist and would trust such a person "with perfect sincerity and the greatest candor."[4] Later he followed up his remarks with a suggestion that perhaps it might be wise for the nation's electors to choose a vice-president from Massachusetts. Privately he let it be known to friends in Virginia and Massachusetts that he favored Adams over Governor Clinton, who had opposed the new Constitution and challenged the very system being created. In an age of differential politics—even in areas where the franchise was comparatively widespread—citizens tended to vote for and follow the advice of men of wealth and standing.[5] Many of the friends of the Constitution were in close contact by either letter or personal visits and the wishes of Washington were quickly conveyed with some discretion.

By the end of January 1789, the electors had been chosen by a variety of methods, and in February they cast their ballots. Ten states had sent sixty-nine electors; North Carolina and Rhode Island had still not ratified the Constitution, and New York had not yet chosen its electors. As the Founding Fathers expected, no one election process was acceptable to all the states. Five state legislatures chose their electors, three states held popular elections, Massachusetts combined popular election and legislative selection, and a divided New Hampshire started out with a popular election, but since none of the electors received majority support, the state senate ended up naming the electors. Each elector voted for two men for president, with Washington receiving 69 of the 138 votes cast—the unanimous choice for president—Adams receiving 34 votes—enough to be elected to the second spot. A proud, sensitive man, Adams was somewhat angry that he had not received more votes and was to blame Hamilton for allegedly working to keep the total down.[6]

While he patiently waited for official confirmation, Washington began to lay down certain rules of conduct that would guide his early appointments. In general, he would make no commitments and avoid appointing those related to him or who were close friends in the past. He would, though, favor those who had fought in the Revolution and would take into account geographical considerations in distributing offices. With these principles in mind, he turned to more immediate matters. First, Washington, with all of his land holdings, lacked a cash reserve and was in debt. He tried to borrow about £1,000 to pay off some of his outstanding notes, but at first he could not find a person willing to loan him the money. Finally Richard Conway of Alexandria gave Washington a £500 loan at 6 percent interest and an additional £100 to cover the new President's costs to travel to his own inauguration. With that problem solved, Washington paid one last visit to his bitter, eighty-one-year-old mother, who was dying of cancer. They had never been close, and Washington went forth to complete a duty, one that he knew would be his last concerning his mother.[7]

News of the election traveled throughout the new republic and Washington waited to be summoned to the Capitol. On April 14, at noontime, he greeted an old acquaintance, Charles Thomson, the new Secretary of the Congress. They exchanged greetings and moved into the high-ceilinged banquet room of Mount Vernon. Thomson formally announced that Washington was elected president and that he had been commanded by Congress to accompany the President-elect to New York City. Thomson then read a letter from John Langdon, the president pro tempore of the Senate, transmitting again the news and wishing Washington well. Washington in turn reached for a written statement addressed more to history than to the audience of one before him:

Sir, I have been long accustomed to entertain so great a respect for the opinion of my fellow-citizens, that the knowledge of their unanimous suffrages having been given in my favor, scarcely leaves me the alternative for an option. Whatever may have been my private feelings and sentiments, I believe I cannot give a greater evidence of my sensibility for the honor they have done me, than by accepting the appointment.

I am so much affected by this fresh proof of my country's esteem and confidence, that silence can best explain my gratitude—while I realize the arduous nature of the task which is conferred on me, and feel my inability to perform it, I wish there may not be reason for regretting the choice. All I can promise is, only that which can be accomplished by an honest zeal.

Upon considering how long time some of the gentlemen of both Houses of Congress have been at New York, how anxiously desirous they must be to proceed to business, and how deeply the public mind appears to be impressed with the necessity of doing it immediately, I cannot find myself at liberty to delay my journey. I shall therefore be in readiness to set out the day after tomorrow, and shall be happy in the pleasure of your company; for you will permit me to say that it was a peculiar gratification to have received the communication from you.[8]

Later Washington was to write to Langdon that he "concluded to obey the important and flattering call of my country."

Two days later, flanked by Thomson and his personal aide, Colonel David Humphreys, Washington entered his carriage and left his estate. In his diary he added: "I bade adieu to Mount Vernon, to private life, and to domestic felicity, and with a mind oppressed with more anxious and painful sensations than I have words to express, set out for New York... with the best disposition to render service to my country in obedience to its will, but with less hope of answering its expectations."[9] So after five years of retirement, the General of the Revolution was to emerge once again on center stage in the new experiment of national self-government. Reputation intact, wearing heavily the burdens of being a living legend, George Washington traveled on toward New York City, the scene of some of his worst military defeats and the temporary capital of an unformed government.

9

THE GRAND
PROCESSION

And behold a white horse; and he that sat on him had a bow, and a crown was given unto him, and he went forth conquering, and to conquer.

Revelation 6:2

In our own times, racked by turmoil and genocidal war, we may understandably agree with Bertolt Brecht's wistful observation: fortunate is the nation that has no need for heroes. Our larger-than-life figures are usually political men, prophets who turn plowshares into swords and send the young into wars of undefined purposes. It is difficult to appreciate the heroic image and the hold it had on the popular imagination; for us, the early American attachment to Washington seems a bit overdone, surely a misreading by historians far away from the events they so inaccurately describe.

Yet in an age of kings, even republican partisans understood the importance of personality in leading a nation. And in an age of limited war and brief skirmishes, the dread of annihilation and wanton destruction did not so infest the general population. To recoin a cliché, it was a more modest time in which some veils of innocence were still left hanging. Enthusiasm was possible, and the world viewed with lofty admiration personages called great. In the new America, such feelings were all so apparent as Washington began his week-long journey from Mount Vernon to New York City. A multitude of references support the judgment that this journey was the occasion of one of the most remarkable outpourings of public goodwill and affection ever shown to one man in his lifetime.

Not far from home, the local citizens at Alexandria, Virginia, gave Washington a testimonial dinner and the Mayor, Dennis Ramsey, toasted the guest and, when the public business was completed, asked God "to restore to us again the best of men and the most beloved fellow citizen."[1] Washington responded with a statement that made public some of his apprehensions, as well as joys:

Gentlemen: Although I ought not to conceal, yet I cannot describe, the painful emotions which I felt in being called upon to determine whether I would accept or refuse the Presidency of the United States.

The unanimity of choice, the opinions of my friends, communicated from different parts of Europe, as well as of America, the apparent wish of those, who were not altogether satisfied with the Constitution in its present form, and an ardent desire on my own part, to be instrumental in conciliating the good will of my countrymen towards each other have induced an acceptance.

Those who have known me best (and you, my fellow citizens, are from your situation, in that number) know better than any others that my love of retirement is so great, that no earthly consideration, short of a conviction of duty, could have prevailed upon me to depart from my resolution, *"never more to take any share in transactions of a public nature."* For at my age, and in my circumstances, what possible advantages could I propose to myself, from embarking again on the tempestuous and uncertain ocean of public-life? I do not feel myself under the necessity of making public declarations, in order to convince you, Gentlemen, of my attachment to yourselves, and regard for your interests. The whole tenor of my life has been open to your inspection; and my past actions, rather than my present declarations, must be the pledge of my future conduct.

In the meantime, I thank you most sincerely for the expressions of kindness contained in your valedictory address. It is true, just after having bade adieu to my domestic connexions, this tender proof of our friendship is but too well calculated still farther to awaken my sensibility, and encrease my regret at parting from the enjoyments of private life.

All that now remains for me is to commit myself and you to the protection of that beneficent Being who, on a former occasion has happily brought us together, after a long and distressing separation. Perhaps the same gracious Providence will again indulge us with the same heartfelt felicity. But words, my fellow-citizens, fail me: *Unutterable sensations must then be left to more expressive silence: while, from an aching heart, I bid you all, my affectionate friends and kind neighbors, farewell!*[2]

From Alexandria onward, Washington's welcome increased in intensity. Delegations of local dignitaries awaited him at each town and relays of horsemen relieved one another every dozen miles or so in order to form a continuous honor guard. Washington's carriage sped along in a cloud of dust that covered the carriage and soiled the General's clothes. At the Potomac, he crossed by ferryboat and was greeted near Spurier's Tavern by a Maryland escort, and on April 17 Washington was in Baltimore and the guest at a supper at the Fountain Inn. After dinner, Washington was presented with an address containing the names of former Revolutionary War associates, which read: "We behold, too, an extraordinary thing in the annals of mankind; a free and enlightened people, choosing, by a free election, without one dissenting voice, the late Commander-in-Chief of their armies, to watch over and guard their civil rights and privileges."[3]

Washington retired at ten o'clock and left at half past five the next morning. Despite the early hour, he was greeted by a company of leading citizens on horseback and cannons roared as he departed. For seven miles the escort traveled with his carriage until Washington insisted that they turn back. Then for two days he moved through the sparsely populated countryside, where he could distinguish in the small crowds that awaited him in little towns the faces of some of the men he had last seen years ago in the war.

On the morning of the twentieth, the Burgesses and Common Council of Wilmington, Delaware, presented the General with an address thanking him for his willingness to give up retirement and return to his country's service. More horsemen accompanied him to the Pennsylvania border, where Washington was greeted by many well-known veterans of the war. By the time he made his way to Chester, it was morning, and most of the spectators lined the streets or tried to go into the inn where the general had breakfast and was listening to another brief welcoming. Washington then mounted a white steed and marched at the lead of a column of well-wishers as it moved toward Philadelphia. As he rode on, his view caught the familiar pontoon bridge across the Schuylkill River at Gray's Ferry. There the owners of the bridge, with the help of the gifted artist Charles Willson Peale, had adorned the structure with large arches of laurel roses and green boughs hidden in the woodwork. The approach was graced with a large banner that proclaimed the birth of a "New Era"; another had a rising sun; still another had the motto "May Commerce Flourish" and a fourth, the familiar "Don't Tread on Me." The banners of the eleven ratifying states and the flag of the new American Union fluttered in the breeze.[4]

As he rode under the first laurel arch, a pretty, fifteen-year-old girl appeared and Washington bowed to her. Suddenly the arch opened up, and a laurel crown descended above the General's head. Tradition has it that the crown landed directly on the startled hero's head and, in true Roman fashion, he brushed it aside, pausing to kiss the young girl as he rose over the swaying bridge. Between the bridge and the city, some 20,000 citizens lined "every fence, field, and avenue." Cannons thundered, church bells rang, colored flags waved gloriously as the General rode on his white horse down Market and Second streets to the City Tavern. After dinner, fourteen toasts, and a display of fireworks, Washington returned to the home of his old friend Robert Morris to spend the night. The next morning Washington, anxious to travel more quickly than he had been able to thus far, requested that the troops of horsemen not accompany him out of town because of the rain. How like the modest republican leader, noted one editor, that he could not think of "traveling under cover while others get wet."[5]

Washington's carriage left by ten o'clock, and in the afternoon he approached the Delaware River near Colvin's Ferry. There he was met by a large body of citizens and horsemen who were ready to escort him to Trenton, and once again Washington mounted a handsome horse and rode toward Assunpink Creek, where a dozen years before his army had taken refuge from the British. On the bridge was another triumphal arch, some twelve feet long and twenty feet high, covered with evergreens. On top of it was a dome of flowers, with the dates of previous battles fought there marked out in blossoms: "December 26, 1776—January 2, 1777," and the words "The Defender of the Mothers will also Defend the Daughters" spelled out. As Washington rode on alone, thirteen young ladies, dressed in white and decked with wreaths and flowers, threw blossoms under the feet of his horse and sang:

> Virgins fair, and Matrons grave
> Those thy conquering arms did save,
> Build for thee triumphant bowers.
> Strew, ye fair, his way with flowers—
> Strew your Hero's way with flowers.[6]

Washington, remembering the difficulties he had suffered at this spot before, was dazzled by the full impact of his welcome. Deeply moved, he thanked the crowd and later personally copied down the song the young girls had sung in his honor.

The next morning Washington, with an escort, was off for Princeton, where he was formally received by the president of the college before he proceeded up the road to New Brunswick. Greeted first outside that city by the mayor and some leading citizens, Washington heard the familiar cannon fire and pealing church bells as he entered the center. Companies of infantry and artillery with a detachment of cavalry formed a line and Washington rode by them to the cheers of the crowd and the sound of military music. By five o'clock in the afternoon Washington left New Brunswick, probably slept in a tavern on the way, and then moved on toward Woodbridge. The next day, with detachments from nearby Bridge-town and Rahway, Washington made his way to Elizabethtown, where in the morning he entered the city and was greeted by a vast throng of people. There he received again a variety of officials, including a delegation from Congress, that were to take him to the new capital. A new barge, costing £200 to £300, carried Washington on the last part of the trip, and the public reception he received was no less awesome than elsewhere. As the barge made its way, ships with flags followed and salutes rang out along the shore. By the time the barge reached Bedloe's Island, a fine sloop came up near the barge and, to the tune of "God Save the King," a group of singers began their praises. Another craft pulled up, and one passenger handed out copies of an ode that was rendered in four parts, written in honor of the General. Then, to add to the confusion, porpoises were attracted by the commotion and began to play near the prow of the barge. As Washington looked out on all this incredible spectacle, he saw another vessel approaching, featuring "Dr. King's South African orangutans," which had come out supposedly in his honor.

As the barge entered the landing, scores of foreign vessels displayed their colors, and at the pier the President-elect saw thousands of people. On shore cannons rang out and church bells clanged for a half hour as Washington, dressed in a cocked hat, blue suit, and buff underdress, stepped off the barge. Up the carpeted steps flanked with crimson upholstery he went and was greeted by Governor Clinton and a host of dignitaries. An officer stepped up, smartly saluted, and announced that he commanded the honor guard that awaited the General's orders. Washington's reply was the type of republican gesture that stirred the hearts of American yeomen: "As to the present arrangement, I shall proceed as is directed, but after this is over, I hope you will give yourself no further trouble, as the affection of my fellow-citizens is all the guard I want."[7]

Washington declined to ride in the elegant carriage that had been held for him; instead, he walked through the cheering, pushing crowd toward his new Cherry Street residence. It took the General a half hour to walk the half mile, and at each point the crowd shouted its approval of their newly elected leader. At his residence, wine and punch were served, and Clinton soon arrived to take Washington to the dinner and fireworks given later in his honor.

Physically and emotionally exhausted, Washington finally went back to his Cherry Street home and there, in the dark hours of the night, probably relived in his mind the magnificent day he had just finished. Washington had experienced a staggering display of public confidence and affection. The public image he had created for himself as a noble republican freeman had captivated the mixed peoples of his difficult land, and they responded with a loyalty kings would have envied. He indeed was their Cincinnatus, the father of their country, the General of their glorious revolution. But beyond the laurel and the cheers lay the slow, confusing day-to-day process of governing. As Washington himself must have acknowledged that first marvelous night in New York City, there were expectations that even he could not fulfill.

10

THE FIRST
INAUGURATION

This is a great, important day. Goddess of etiquette, assist me while I describe it.

William Maclay, April 30, 1789

The New York City that Washington entered in 1789 was quite different from the Virginia estate he was used to. The city contained 30,000 persons at the time, making it second only to Philadelphia in size. Despite migrations of German, French, English, and black inhabitants, the city was still heavily influenced by the Dutch. Few of the streets were paved, and Franklin once sarcastically observed that one could always spot a New Yorker by the way he shuffled. Livestock roamed the streets and thousands of pigs feasted on the garbage that people threw into the gutters. The poet Philip Freneau looked at the streets and penned the conclusion:

Our streets that were just in a way to look clever
Will now be neglected and nasty as ever
Again we must fret at the Dutchified gutters
And pebble-stone pavements that wear out our trotters.

The best residential area was near Wall and Queen streets, and there most of the government leaders lived. Manhattan at that time was heavily wooded, and in language so alien to New Yorkers today, Abigail Adams described her house on Richmond Hill, near what is now MacDougal and Charlton streets:

In natural beauty it might vie with the most delicious spot I ever saw. In front of the house, one could see the clear Hudson River. And on the right were pastures full of cattle and on the left a view of the city partially concealed by trees. In the background was a large flower garden with groves of pines and oaks. The songs of birds filled the air and the partridge, woodcock, and pigeon darted through the forests.

Not all accommodations were as pleasant. Near the fields, today's City Hall Park, were an almshouse, bridewell, debtors' jail, and the gallows. In 1789 ten persons were executed on the Chinese pagoda-style gallows, none for a crime more serious than burglary. Close to the gallows were the whipping posts and the stocks.

New York was the center of commerce and transportation at the time of the formation of the new government. By stagewagon, it took two days to reach Philadelphia, three to get to Albany, and at least six days to make Boston. The trip by boat to Boston took half the time—if the winds blew in the right direction—but to Philadelphia the trip took twelve hours longer. Travel was somewhat of an ordeal even for the hardiest rider. A passenger arrived at three or four o'clock in the morning and continued on the stage until ten o'clock in the evening. Wagons usually had no springs because of the rough, winding roads, and some had no brakes because of the slow pace, often dictated by the rock-strewn roadways.

The value of the currencies one carried varied enormously. In a trip from Philadelphia to New York, a traveler's pennies changed value four times. In Philadelphia it was fifteen to a shilling; in Trenton, thirty; in nearby Princeton, twenty-four; up the road in New Brunswick it was twenty; and in New York the rate changed to twenty-one to a shilling and later the rate became forty to one. At some stops a dinner cost two shillings, with an extra beefsteak adding one shilling six pence to the bill, and a bottle of champagne was ten shillings.

In New York prices then as now seemed to travelers generally high. Washington paid $80 a month just to livery his horses; a skilled worker earned 50¢ a day and an unskilled one about half that amount. A loaf of bread sold for 3¢ and it cost a workingman a week's wages to buy a ticket to Philadelphia and two days' wages to see a theater performance, if he were so inclined. Doctors charged $1 for a visit and medicine, $5 for advice, $4 for cupping, $50 to $100 for an amputation, $125 for a hernia operation. Those in search of other types of comfort could avail themselves of the various brothels and nearly 330 licensed drinking places—or more than one for every hundred inhabitants. Also, the records show that New Yorkers at the time were reading sentimental romances and historical and travel books, and there was little interest in books on religion and philosophy—tastes in literature that are somewhat similar to those of today.[1]

The New York City that Washington arrived in then was the closest approximation to a cosmopolitan center that existed in the American nation. For the first couple of months, though, the President-elect was interested in his own inauguration and then in the selection of officers to head up the major executive departments. Although Washington arrived at the capital on April 23, he was not inaugurated until a week later. During that time, much of the public debate revolved around questions of etiquette and ceremony. Unfortunately for most of the participants in these discussions, the main source we have is the journal of William Maclay, a frontier lawyer elected senator from Pennsylvania, who considered the whole business pretentious nonsense. No figure drew his scorn as much as John Adams. It seems that Adams, certainly one of the major figures of the Revolution, had acquired an interest in titles and court etiquette. Perhaps he felt that the fabric of a stable government rested on deference and ceremony, or it may be that his years of service in the courts of Europe had weakened his firm commitment to republican simplicity.

On April 25, in one of his least memorable speeches, Adams asked the Senate what was he to do when Washington came to address that body. As he put it, although he was the vice-president of the United States, and thus subordinate to the president, he was also the president of the Senate and presiding officer of that body. He explained it in terms that even today seem a bit overwrought:

Gentlemen, I do not know whether the framers of the Constitution had in view the two kings of Sparta or the two consuls of Rome when they formed it; one to have all the power while he held it, and the other to be nothing. Nor do I know whether the architect that formed our room and the wide chair in it (to hold two, I suppose) had the Constitution before him. Gentlemen, I feel great difficulty how to act. I am possessed of two separate powers; the one in esse and the other in posse. I am Vice-President. In this I am nothing, but I may be everything. But I am president also of the Senate. When the President comes into the Senate, what shall I be? I can not be [president] then. No, gentlemen, I can not, I can not. I wish, gentlemen, to think what I shall be.[2]

Then Adams, with a distressed air, threw himself back in his chair, waiting for the Senate to discuss the monumental problem that he had posed. The next Thursday, before Washington was due to arrive, Adams again raised the grave question of etiquette, "How shall I behave? How shall we receive him? Shall it be standing or sitting?" There followed considerable discussion as to how the House of Commons and the House of Lords dealt with the king's arrival. One senator noted sagaciously that the reason the members of the House of Commons stood was because there were no seats. Then, in the midst of this discussion, the secretary of the Senate whispered to Adams that the clerk of the House was at the door with a message. How was he to be received? Once again, Adams asked the Senate, and there ensued a discussion of the ways the House of Commons handled similar situations. In the midst of this confusion, Senators got up, left their chairs, milled around, talking and waiting for the entrance of the Speaker of the House and the Representatives. Finally the Vice-President restored order and Congress sent a delegation, headed by Senator Ralph Izard, to bring the President from his residence to the chamber.[3]

At home, Washington had been ready for some time. He had dressed in a Hartford-made brown broadcloth suit with buttons decorated with the impression of a spread-winged eagle. His stockings were white silk, the shoe buckles silver, and to add to his appearance, he fastened on a dress-sword in a steel scabbard. For several weeks Washington had been working on his inaugural address. Originally, in February, he had completed a seventy-three-page statement, which he laid aside, and then, with Madison's assistance, he had composed a shorter statement in its place. Anxiously he tucked the final text in his brown coat pocket and watched as the crowd grew outside his residence.

Then, at noon, he greeted Izard and the rest of the committee. At their bidding, he stepped into a grand coach drawn by four horses especially bought for his inauguration. The Senate members of the committee and the troops led the way; behind Washington's carriage were the President's secretaries, the Representatives on the committee, Chancellor Robert Livingston, who was to administer the oath, the heads of the federal departments, and other illustrious citizens. Down Cherry Street and into Queen and then to Great Dock Street the procession went, turning westward at Great Dock and moving down Broad toward Wall Street. Washington and his entourage stopped and walked up Broad Street toward the newly decorated Federal Hall. Inside he was informed that Congress was awaiting him in the Senate Chamber. As soon as the President was announced with great fanfare, the lawmakers and guests rose, and Washington, bowing to both sides of the audience, walked toward the Vice-President, who was standing on a dais with the Speaker of the House.

Adams formally welcomed the President and then began his own address. But the Vice-President, who had probably worried more about the occasion than anyone else, hesitated as if he had forgotten what he wanted to say. Then Adams finally started again: "Sir, the Senate and the House of Representatives are ready to attend you to take the oath required by the Constitution. It will be administered by the Chancellor of the State of New York." Pale and nervous himself, Washington simply replied, "I am ready to proceed," and he followed the Vice-President to the arched door that led into a small half-enclosed portico overlooking Wall and Broad streets. There the President watched the immense cheering crowd below. Next to Washington was an armchair, which he then sat in, and a small table draped in red, with a crimson velvet cushion that held a large leather-covered Bible borrowed from St. John's Freemason Lodge. The Chancellor, the Vice-President, and Governor Clinton moved closer to the President and behind him were the Secretary of War, Henry Knox, General Arthur St. Clair, and a host of distinguished guests.[4]

As soon as they moved into place, Washington rose and stepped toward the iron rail, where he was to receive the oath of office. The diminutive secretary of the Senate, Samuel Otis, squeezed between the President and Chancellor Livingston and raised up the crimson cushion with a Bible on it. Washington put his right hand on the Bible, opened to Psalm 121:1: "I raise my eyes toward the hills. Whence shall my help come." The Chancellor proceeded with the oath: "Do you solemnly swear that you will faithfully execute the office of President of the United States and will to the best of your ability preserve, protect and defend the Constitution of the United States?" The President responded, "I solemnly swear," and repeated the oath, adding, "So help me God." He then bent forward and kissed the Bible before him.

Livingston, himself probably a bit relieved, turned to the crowd and proclaimed, "It is done. Long live George Washington, President of the United States." Some members of the crowd cried out, "God bless our President." Soon a thirteen-gun salute was fired and a Spanish ship in the nearby harbor followed suit. Church bells rang and the President bowed again to the crowd, as the cheers resumed so strongly that one observer swore that they shook the very canopy over his head.

Washington moved slowly back into the Senate Chamber and took his seat on the dais while the rest of the members and guests resumed their places. Then he got to his feet to read his address, and the spectators rose with him. Washington bowed to them and they sat down. With some embarrassment and anxiety, he recited in a low voice the speech he had been working on for several months. The first part of it was a note of thanksgiving in Deist language, to the "Almighty Being" and the "Great Author of every public and private good." Then Washington, taking note of the opposition to the Constitution, recommended in cautious terms that Congress decide what amendments were necessary to relieve the "inquie-tude." He indicated that he would, as when he headed the army, take compensation only for actual expenses incurred and concluded his address on the somber note that he hoped that "the benign Parent of the Human Race" would continue to bless the American Union.[5]

Finished, he folded his paper, bowed, and sat down. Although nervous and not a particularly good speaker, Washington made a moving impression on those who saw and heard him. Fisher Ames called the performance, "an allegory in which virtue was personified, and addressing those whom she would make her votaries, her power over the heart was never greater." The whole audience, we are told, was moved to tears, and the French Minister, who was present, wrote home that "never had a sovereign reigned more completely in the hearts of his subjects than did Washington in those of his fellow-citizens. . . . He has the soul, look and figure of a hero united in him."[6]

From Federal Hall, Washington and members of Congress, with their guests, walked through the cheering crowd and passed by the New York militia as they went to St. Paul's Chapel, where the chaplain of the Congress began a service in the President's honor. In the dim chapel, Washington listened to some of the same hymns and prayers that he had heard as a boy in Virginia. Spared the usual sermon, the guests went on their way after the services were over, and the President left for a private dinner alone. At the end of the day, Washington was invited to a display of fireworks and to view some illuminated transparent paintings, which included a portrait of the new President surrounded by Fortitude, Justice (personifying the Senate), and Wisdom (personifying the House of Representatives). The pageantry of the American morality play finally came to an end sometime after dark, and Washington walked home to his residence, officially sworn in some fifty-seven days after he had been elected.[7]

11

THE PRESIDENTS
BEFORE WASHINGTON

As President of Congress, I repeat, I act faithfully, to the orders of Congress. I have no will of my own.

Henry Laurens, May 11, 1778

Although Washington was the first president elected under the new Constitution and charged with appointing executive officers, he was aware that the United States already had in place a small but long-standing bureaucracy and had officials called "president" before. From 1774 to 1789, fourteen individuals held that title and served as presiding officers of the Confederation congresses. Although their powers were minimal and their terms obviously short, there was still an element of continuity between that office and the new one Washington was to create.

From 1774 to 1781, seven men held the office of president for a period ranging from five days, for Henry Middleton, to nearly two and a half years, for John Hancock. The Congress was especially sensitive to the need for some geographical balance in filling the position; three men came from the South: Peyton Randolph, Henry Middleton, and Henry Laurens; and four came from New England and the Middle States: John Hancock, John Jay, Samuel Huntington, and Thomas McKuen.

The president of the Congress was regarded as the spokesman of that body and served as its social and diplomatic representative. Although the president received the same meager pay from his state as any other delegate, he often incurred substantial expenses in entertaining his colleagues and foreign ministers. The First Continental Congress named Peyton Randolph, the Speaker of the Virginia House of Burgesses, to serve as president, but after little more than a month's time, he resigned and was replaced by Henry Middleton of South Carolina, who served in that position for the remaining five days of the term. In the Second Continental Congress, Randolph was again elected, but after two weeks he left for Virginia in order to preside over a meeting of the House of Burgesses. His replacement was John Hancock, a high-living aristocrat from Boston, who was reputed to be one of the wealthiest men in America. Although he served in the position longer than anyone else, Hancock was frequently absent and not particularly impressive. He did, however, enjoy entertaining and was able to bear the expenses that were involved. Overwhelmed by the paperwork, he hired his own secretary to handle the correspondence. When, in October 1777, Hancock left the position, he reminded Congress, "I think I shall be forgiven if I say I have spared no pains, expense, or labors, to gratify your wishes, and to accomplish the views of Congress."[1]

Congress then turned to another rather wealthy merchant to preside over its deliberations, Henry Laurens of Charleston. Laurens, though, proved to be more of a critic of the Congress than the delegates were used to, and he charged that the assembly was marked by "venality, peculation and fraud." He insisted on participating in the debates and on one occasion quarreled with the congressional secretary, Charles Thomson, and threatened to boot him off the platform. A hostile Congress refused to pass the standard resolution of appreciation for his services until he apologized for some of his intemperate remarks.

His replacement was John Jay, who at the time of his selection was also Chief Justice of New York, a position in which he continued for most of the period he was president. Jay finally left to become minister to Spain and was replaced on September 28, 1779, by Samuel Huntington of Connecticut, who carried on in the position until July 6, 1781. In the last year before the ratification of the Articles of Confederation, the presidency passed from an ailing Huntington to Samuel Johnson, who promptly refused it, to Thomas McKuen, the Chief Justice of Pennsylvania and a delegate in Congress from the neighboring state of Delaware.

By the end of the year, Congress organized itself under the Articles of Confederation and chose as its first president John Hanson of Maryland. The Articles provided that Congress could appoint one of its own delegates to preside on condition that "no one person be allowed to serve in the office of president more than one year in any term of three years. . . . " The executive powers were generally absent from the Articles, or where they were mentioned, they were invested in the Congress. The first president is mainly remembered as the official who welcomed Washington after he arrived in Philadelphia with Cornwallis' surrender in hand. Then, on the morning of March 28, 1781, a cheering crowd watched as the General approached the tall and elderly Hanson to receive his congratulations. On behalf of the Congress, the president reaffirmed, "It is their fixed purpose to draw every advantage from [the victory] by exhorting the States in the strongest terms to the most vigorous and timely executions." Washington conveyed his thanks and asked Congress to urge the states to continue their efforts through the remainder of the war. Several days later, Washington took time out and wrote to Hanson, congratulating him on his "appointment to fill the most important seat in the United States."[2]

A year later Hanson stepped down and was succeeded by Elias Boudinot of New Jersey, who inauspiciously served his term and gladly relinquished it. The rotating chair then went to Thomas Mifflin of Pennsylvania, who was at one time part of the Convoy attempt to dismiss Washington during the Revolution. Ironically he now accepted, on behalf of a grateful Congress, General Washington's resignation from the army he had victoriously commanded.

The presidency continued to be a rather modest enterprise as was the entire national government. In 1784 there was some talk of making the president a "more powerful and serviceable official," but nothing came of that effort. Richard Henry Lee took over the position, complained about the press of duties, and was absent from the capital during most of the fall of 1785. He was succeeded by John Hancock, who had resigned from the governorship of Massachusetts but seemed lethargic and uninterested. Hancock insisted on staying with his wife at home, and during his absence, David Ramsey and later Nathaniel Gorham served as chairmen of the Congress, performing the duties of president as well.

When Hancock officially resigned, the Congress appointed Gorham for the last two months of his term. In that brief time, Gorham was involved in one of the most interesting schemes of the period. According to Rufus King, President Gorham, in 1786, invited Prince Henry, the brother of Frederick II of Prussia, to become king of the United States if the new Constitution provided for a monarch. The Founding Fathers, though, made no such decision, and Gorham's proposal is an interesting, if not bizarre, footnote in history.[3] After Gorham stepped down, the Congress elected General Arthur St. Clair, who later become governor of the Northeast Territory. By then the Philadelphia Convention had completed its work and the Congress now chose as its last president, Cyrus Griffin of Virginia. All together some fourteen men moved in and out of office, leaving little in the way of accomplishments.

These presidents performed various duties, including presiding over Congress, answering correspondence, and entertaining officials and dignitaries. In recognition of their services, Congress finally appropriated money for secretarial staff and provided a presidential household allowance in later years.

Despite the modest range of the office, Congress zealously defended the dignity of the position and gave it social rank over governors and other major officers. Some presidents found the office burdensome of inconsequential, but others, such as Thomas McKuen, who served for four months in 1781, found it an honor to be so named. When, in 1804, he was asked to be a candidate for vice-president, he declined, saying that the honor given him in 1781 "equaled any merit or pretensions of mine, and cannot now be increased by the office of Vice-President."

For others, though, such as Hancock and John Jay, their lackluster performances even in this office were remembered by their colleagues, and they were effectively eliminated as possible candidates for the new position created by the Constitution. As for Washington, few precedents were established that he could look to for guidance. He was acutely aware of the preoccupations with social etiquette and the extensive entertaining that surrounded the position, and after deep thought and some consultation, he issued his own guidelines to avoid being, as he put it, a maître d'hôtel.

Congress, in this period, had come to realize the importance of providing modest support and assistance to the president, a recognition that probably made Washington's own requests in 1789 a bit more familiar to the members of the first Congress, two-thirds of whom had served in at least one of the earlier congresses. Also, even with the limited range of their own responsibilities, the presidents had maintained contact with the executive departments that did most of the Confederation's business. These departments remained intact well into the first year of the Washington administration. By then, however, the department heads were not dealing with a presiding officer or a chief clerk, but with a powerful executive who had both considerable prestige and substantial influence, and who seemed intent on creating a respected branch of government.[4]

12

THE BUREAUCRACY
BEFORE WASHINGTON

I have reason, Sir, to apprehend that I have come into the Office of
Secretary for Foreign Affairs with Ideas of Duties and Rights somewhat
different from those which seem to be entertained by Congress.
John Jay, January 1785

On assuming office, Washington inherited four major executive departments: State, War, Treasury (including the Navy), and the Post Office. At
first, the President was rather reluctant to interfere with the Secretaries'
work, feeling that they were still answerable to Congress. But as time passed
and the legislative branch did not quickly create new agencies, the President
began reading dispatches and reports on file. He asked the department heads
to prepare for him a summary of their work, and Washington soon began
to assume a major role, especially in the direction of foreign affairs.

These four executive departments were the product of a long and sometimes common pattern of development that stretched back to the Revolutionary War. During that period, the Continental Congress established
numerous committees to manage different aspects of the war effort. The
most important of these ad hoc groups was the "Secret Committee," authorized on September 10, 1775, which was to import or have manufactured
gunpowder, arms, and ammunition. Later the Continental Congress established a "Cannon Committee" and a "Medical Committee." In early 1776,
after a direct appeal from General Washington, the Congress discussed
whether it should create a war office. Six months later, a Board of War
and Ordinance was established, chaired by John Adams with four other
members of Congress. It was staffed by a secretary and several clerks and
instructed to keep army records, take charge of supplies, help raise troops,
and forward money to the army. By October 1777 the Congress changed
the members of the Board by appointing five new members, none of whom
served in Congress. To Washington's dismay, three military men and two

civilians were chosen and General Gates was named president of the Board of War. With frequent turnover and little accountability, the Board grew increasingly unwieldy, and by February 1781 the Congress appointed a Secretary at War.

A similar change took place in the Treasury and Navy operations. The colonies originally had appointed a Treasurer, or Receiver General, who accepted, held, or paid out funds as ordered. By September 1775 the Congress moved toward the committee approach again, creating a group of thirteen delegates whose business it was to examine any claims against the United States. By February 1776 a new standing committee of five members was appointed by Congress to supervise minor officials, attend to bills of credit, and serve as a Ways and Means Committee of the legislative branch. In April, Congress altered that structure and established a Treasury Board headed by an Auditor General. Between 1776 and 1781 the Congress renamed, reconstituted, and reformulated the Treasury. Congress finally created a Superintendent of Finance in the same resolution that established a Secretary at War. In terms of the Navy, the same general policies were followed. The Congress at first created a Naval Committee, then a Marine Committee, then a Naval Board, and finally a Secretary of Marine.

In the important area of foreign affairs, the United Colonies in 1775 formed a "Committee of Secret Correspondents" with five members to write to "our friends in Great Britain, Ireland, and other parts of the world." The Committee soon evolved into a Foreign Office, but by 1780 even European governments were critical of the whole operation. Finally, on January 10, 1781, the Congress created a Secretary for Foreign Affairs.

The development of the Post Office was somewhat different from the other departments. The early postal service was started by a patent from the Governor of Virginia to Thomas Neale in 1693, and by the end of Queen Anne's reign, it was a branch of the general post office of England. In the colonies, mail moved extremely slowly and rather sporadically. Circuit riders were often elderly people who would knit winter garments as they leisurely moved from stop to stop. On July 26, 1775, the Congress established a Post Office department and appointed the versatile Benjamin Franklin, once a postmaster, to head it. Despite some major difficulties, especially in 1777, the department retained its original structure, with only some changes coming about in 1782.

In the War Department, after some delay, General Benjamin Lincoln, a strong supporter of Washington, was appointed Secretary through 1783. By then the war was over, and the importance of the office substantially declined to the extent that a chief clerk replaced Lincoln until General Henry Knox took over in 1785. In the Treasury, Robert Morris managed the precarious finances of the new nation until he finally despaired and resigned in 1784. The department was then placed under a new Board of Treasury, which also took control of naval affairs.

The most extensive changes after 1781 took place in the Foreign Office, where Robert R. Livingston started out advocating a major reorganization. Soon tired, though, of congressional interference and unable to live on his low salary, Livingston returned home to New York, where he continued to hold the office of Chancellor. After his retirement, the Secretary of Congress and then an undersecretary took over his duties until a year later, when John Jay was named to head the department. It took Jay nearly a year to return from his diplomatic position in Europe, but he proved to be a strong administrator who was willing to resist congressional pressures. With two assistants and two rooms in which to conduct business, John Jay carried on the foreign policy of the United States until the President named him the first Chief Justice of the Supreme Court.[1]

With these departments and their long and often complex developments in mind, Washington let it be known that he would not fill any subordinate positions until Congress completed its debates and he could name the senior executives first. Instead, he occupied himself with restating his position on the criteria he would eventually use for making appointments. All applications were confidential and should include a specific statement as to what position was being sought. If a person were in a state office that was being transferred to the federal government, he would continue in that post; if a division of duties occurred, the incumbent would be given preference for the better of the created positions. Although Washington's policies may not have furthered the development of a first-rate civil service, they did tend to create some order and stability. Also, in those cases where the President knew little about the applicants, he usually consulted the Senators from the individual's home state, although he said he was not bound to do so. Above all, Washington was particularly sensitive to the need to proceed carefully in dividing up the meager loaves and fishes.[2]

13

THE REMOVAL DEBATE

The decision that is at this time made, will become the permanent exposition of the constitution; and on a permanent exposition of the constitution will depend the genius and character of the whole Government.

James Madison, June 17, 1789

While Washington was leafing through the departments' dispatches and memoranda, days passed into weeks and still Congress had not created a new bureaucracy. Government was a much more leisurely affair in the eighteenth century, and many representatives entertained few presumptions about the national government entrusted to their charge. The pace was indeed slack, but there was also a major issue at stake that slowed matters somewhat—the right of the executive to appoint and especially to remove subordinates. The Constitution said little about removing administrative officers and mentioned dismissal only by means of the cumbersome impeachment process. Basically the central issue was would the president be able to hold members of his administration accountable to his wishes, or must he seek congressional approval for personnel changes. The Representatives knew all too well what the Constitution did and did not say, since some nineteen members of the First Congress had been at the Philadelphia Convention. The issue was less one of law than of logic, and Congress, with the President anxiously looking on, fully understood the implications of the first great legislative debate.

Starting off, Elias Boudinot slowly rose and in a deferential manner offered a motion to create new executive departments. Madison quickly added that the power to remove the heads of these departments should rest with the executive alone, although at first he had expressed a desire to have the legislature involved. That position was simple but not at all apparent to many of the Representatives in the House. As the debate went on, no less than four views emerged. Some Representatives argued that the only method of removal was impeachment and that no other one was permitted. A second group adhered to the view that the removal power grew out of the appointment process that the president and the Senate shared. Therefore, the executive could remove non-judicial officers only with the advice and consent of the upper house. A third view was that the Constitution delegated to Congress the authority to create new offices and make laws, and that the legislature could determine the tenure, duties, and compensation of such officers. Some Representatives who held this view, however, still believed that Congress should delegate its removal power to the president. And lastly, other members joined with Madison in holding that the Constitution gave the president the executive power, the initiative in appointments, and the responsibility to see that the laws were faithfully executed. The president alone, they concluded, retained the removal power.

As the debate progressed, most of the representatives were unwilling to press the position that the Senate should become, in a sense, an executive council with great powers to participate in the administration of government. The Senate was, in their eyes, too aristocratic in its leanings and too insulated from the currents of public opinion. They maintained then that the president, not the Senate, held the appointment power and that any attempt to give the upper house a voice in subsequent removals would force it, in Elias Boudinot's words, to be the judge in disputes between the chief executive and civil officers.[1]

To supporters of a strong presidency, the point was crucial—only the executive can be responsible for the actions done in his administration. As Fisher Ames warned:

The executive powers are delegated to the President, with a view to have a responsible officer to superintend, control, inspect, and check the officers necessarily employed in administering the laws. The only bond between him and those he employs, is the confidence he has in their integrity and talents; when the confidence ceases, the principal ought to have the power to remove those whom he can no longer trust with safety.[2]

Ames received strong support from James Madison, who went on to argue that the heads of the departments must be "responsible to the great executive power, and make the President responsible to the public for the conduct of the person he has nominated and appointed to aid him in the administration of his department." He further injected that a president who engaged in the "wanton removal of meritorious officers would be subject himself to impeachment for maladministration." Later, though, he confidently discounted the likelihood of such abuses by the executive and predicted: "We may fairly calculate that the instances will be very rare in which an unworthy man will receive that mark of the public confidence which is required to designate the President of the United States."[3]

In answer to all those who felt that Congress possessed the removal power because it authorized the original offices, Madison offered a sharp counter. The legislative branch creates an office, defines its powers, limits its duration, and fixes a rate of compensation, but "this done, the legislative power ceases."[4] Except in the case of the comptroller, who has both judicial and executive functions and answers to Congress, the president should retain the sole right to remove subordinates without interference. But Madison's opinion was not universally accepted in the House. Theodore Sedgwick, for example, argued the opposite view: "I do conceive, Mr. Speaker, that this officer will be the mere creature of the law; . . . now, this officer being the creature of the law, we may declare that he shall be removed for incapacity and if so declared, the removal will be according to law."[5]

Finally, the House decided to establish the Department of Foreign Affairs and approved Egbert Benson's clause, which noted: "The said principal officer shall be removed from office by the President of the United States. . . . " The House then approved similar language in creating the War and the Treasury departments, and went on to question Madison's view that the comptroller was partly a judicial officer and therefore could not be summarily removed by the president. The next day Madison simply withdrew his motion on the subject. In other bills before it, the House made no references to the tenure in office of naval officers, collectors, and surveyors involved in the collection of duties. In another action, the House, revising the government of the western territories, directed the governor to report to the president, rather than to Congress as before, and noted that all officers were to be appointed by the executive, subject to the advice and consent of the Senate. The president, though, was given the right to remove or reallocate commissions, except in the case of judges, who were given tenure.

In the Senate, some of the same issues were raised, and the role of the upper house in the removal process commanded more attention and support. Maclay refused to concur with the House bill and argued that the Senate was a "great check" in the process of republican government. He denounced the "court party" that he saw already forming and noted that the Vice-President himself had helped garner valuable support for the House bill. The Senate divided ten to ten over the issue, and an excited Adams cast the tie-breaking vote in favor of the original bill. The Senate moved on to approve the creation of departments of Foreign Affairs (renamed in September, State), War, and Treasury and each bill contained the following clause: "That where ever the secretary shall be removed from office by the president of the United States, or in any other case of vacancy in the office of the secretary, the assistant shall, during the vacancy, have the charge and custody of the records, books, and papers, appertaining to the said office."

The resolution of the question of removal power then seems clear at first glance, yet it has remained a source of bitter controversy, especially during the term of Andrew Johnson and even on into this century. In one case decided in 1926, Chief Justice William Taft, a former president, wrote that the First Congress recognized that the president's powers were unlimited in terms of removing executive appointees. Yet the record of the debates is more ambiguous as to what the Congress meant. The voting obviously shows that in the House, a majority favored allowing the executive sole power to remove such appointees at his pleasure. But less than a third of the representatives supported a theory of exclusive executive power in this area. Some representatives believed that the legislative branch still retained a say on the issue, but they favored delegating that authority to the executive alone. Congress would seek later to curtail that delegation, and Monroe, when president, signed a bill setting fixed terms for civil officers.[6]

Like so many matters of constitutional dispute, the end results seldom bring forth final victory for one particular philosophy or another. Historical crises, popular sentiment, the influence of personality, all tend to give circumstances a greater weight than mere expediency would allow. The coherence of dogma and philosophy becomes twisted and exposed to new realities, as judicious politicians and political judges reach accommodations. In the same way, the controversy over the removal powers was settled for a while, only to be reopened in future years. The First Congress, though, surely tilted the scales heavily toward the executive, where indeed they remain. As for Washington, he quietly avoided the controversy and anxiously awaited the establishment of the departments he now had to administer.

14

HIS HIGHNESS, THE PRESIDENT

From the time I had done breakfast and thence till dinner and afterwards till bedtime I could not get relieved from ceremony of one visit before I had to attend to another.

George Washington, 1789

While the First Congress was beginning its important deliberations on establishing executive departments, it was also involved in questions of etiquette and proper titles. The immediate cause of concern was what would be the most appropriate mode of addressing the president. In the Senate, Vice-President Adams saw this as a matter of great import and pleaded with that body to adopt a title worthy of the new office. Richard Henry Lee read off a list of titles of "all the princes and potentates of the earth" to show how widespread the term "highness" was. After a lengthy and sometimes one-sided debate, the title of "His Highness the President of the United States and Protector of the Rights of the Same" was chosen in preference to "His Elective Majesty," "His Excellency," and several other august expressions. In the House of Representatives, however, these preoccupations with titles were seen as aristocratic pretensions, and the only title that body would agree to was the simple designation in the Constitution: the President of the United States. As for the executive himself, Washington wisely avoided the whole controversy.[1]

The second major issue of protocol to come up was if and in what way the Senate should respond to Washington's inaugural address. The upper house doubted whether it should use the expression "gracious speech" in answering the executive. That term was a carryover from the British tradition when the Parliament acknowledged the king's address. Because the colonial and state legislatures had indeed responded to the executive's address, the Vice-President and eighteen senators decided to visit Washington at his residence on May 18.

There Adams, trembling with apprehension, put the address on the top of his hat and held on to it with both hands as he read the Senate's formal response. Washington then removed from his coat pocket a piece of paper containing his brief reply. But with the paper in his right hand and his own hat in his left, the President was unable to reach for his spectacles. Finally he put his hat on a nearby chimney piece, adjusted his spectacles, and responded without much emotion. The Vice-President and the Senate, having noted the "gracious speech," finally left, and Washington went on with his business. The whole procedure seemed a bit strained to all involved, and some of the more republican senators criticized Adams for his insistence on following such rituals. Senator Ralph Izard sarcastically remarked that since the heavy-set Vice-President was so enamored with titles, he should be given an appropriate one too—"His Rotundity."[2]

Even with his great sense of decorum, Washington was finding the social functions of the position burdensome. Since his arrival, the President had spent nearly every day receiving visitors and many nights returning calls and going to civic events. Overwhelmed by these demands, he brooded that there was no time left for public business. As he was aware, the presiding officers of the Confederation Congress had entertained lavishly and their tables were open often to the public. Washington, on one occasion, bluntly remarked that the presiding officer was a "maître d'hôtel," and he wrote to Adams, Hamilton, Jay, and Madison for advice on how to avoid that fate.[3] Could he reduce these public gatherings or levees to one a week? How should he treat personal friends or political leaders when it came to invitations? Should he travel throughout the country to see what were the customs in these areas? If so, who would pay for these ventures, and how?

Hamilton answered that he favored one levee a week, and it should be open to those properly introduced. The President should stay at these affairs for a half hour or so, and he should not accept invitations to parties or return visits. Hamilton advocated about two to four entertainments a year. Adams, on the other hand, argued for two levees a week and no public entertainments. After giving the matter great thought, Washington decided on a dinner every Thursday at four o'clock for government officials only, with their families occasionally invited through a system of rotating names. On Tuesday afternoons there would be a levee for men only, and tea parties would be held for men and women on Friday evenings. Both events would be open to the public.[4]

Such entertainment proved costly, and in the first nine months in office, Washington spent almost $2,000 on liquor alone—an astronomical figure in the era of 1789. On assuming office, he had asked Congress not to give him a salary, but only to reimburse him for official expenses. Washington had done rather well under that arrangement during the Revolutionary War, and it allowed him to maintain the Southern pose of noblesse oblige. Congress, however, refused his request and insisted on paying him a salary of $25,000 and no expenses.[5]

As Washington continued to go through with his ceremonial duties, some vocal republicans found him to be a bit pompous and pretentious in these appearances, seeing a man who had aristocratic ambitions. But more likely his stiffness was an old soldier's awkwardness in prolonged social situations. Privately, Washington noted his dislike of these occasions and wrote that he would rather be "at Mt. Vernon with a friend or two about me than to be attended at the seat of government by the officers of state and representatives of every power in Europe."[6]

When his wife, Martha, arrived, Washington finally seemed to relax somewhat, the parties became more entertaining, and at informal tea parties, the President began to pass by the men and spend more time with the ladies. At formal dinners, the President and Mrs. Washington sat opposite each other at the middle of the large dinner table, with the ladies seated on both sides of Martha and the gentlemen flanking the President. Senator Maclay noted in his diary that on one occasion when he was a dinner guest, the menu consisted of soup, fish, roasted and boiled meats, gammon, fowls, apple pie, pudding, iced creams, jellies, melons, apples, peaches, and nuts. There were endless toasts and the President told a not particularly humorous story, the Senator sourly related.[7]

Washington understood the importance of making a fine impression and exhibiting the proper style becoming a leader of state. Although he was not an aristocrat or personally inclined toward what his foes saw as monarchial habits, he was still no social democrat. He had worked hard and sacrificed much to separate himself from the mass of men, and he enjoyed the advantages that the good life can bring. Since his youth, he had acquired a special fondness for fine equipage, and as president, he ignored his own rule against accepting gifts and took possession of a grand carriage with the four seasons painted on its doors and six cream-colored horses.

Despite the press of important business, Washington spent a considerable amount of his time being concerned about his household, and he paid for a staff of fifteen servants and six attendants for the stables. Still he found his first official residence too modest and insisted on moving to another mansion on Broadway, which at one time had been the French Ministry. The new lodgings cost him £1,000 a year, and he began to have it recarpeted and decorated for his purposes. New plateaux were purchased, lighting was improved, two cows were acquired, and the Council of New York was persuaded to add street lamps in front of the residence. While Congress was busy in late 1789 and early 1790 with important public business, the President often seemed more preoccupied with the trappings of office and the comforts of home.[8]

15

THE DEBT ASSUMPTION DEAL

Every breach of the public engagements, whether from choice or necessity is in different degrees hurtful to public credit.
                                        Alexander Hamilton, January 9, 1790

The most pressing issue facing the new republic was of course neither etiquette nor appointments, but the state of the economy. Much of the justification for passing the Constitution and creating a new form of government was based on the widely held view, especially in the commercial classes, that the Confederation was too weak to promote economic development and guarantee financial stability. For those groups, it was fortuitous that the most brilliant and energetic cabinet member in the administration was Alexander Hamilton.

Hamilton took office as Secretary of the Treasury on September 11, 1789, and ten days later he received the House of Representatives' request that he send to them a plan for the "adequate support of the public credit." That simple inquiry was the immediate cause of Hamilton's far-reaching design to expand the federal government's power and tie it to the interests of merchants and bankers. Blessed with a remarkable mastery of detail and a gift for tactical leadership, Hamilton unfolded a monumental economic policy. In his own mind, he was the prime minister of the new administration and mainstay of the Federalist faction.

The most difficult problem he faced first was the matter of paying off the debt acquired during the Revolution. As with most of their colonial initiatives, Americans avoided a systematic economic policy and created an ad hoc set of arrangements that varied widely. The Revolutionary War had been financed through a crazy-quilt array of measures, and the states and national government had been unable to settle the problem of who owed what to whom. The states were originally supposed to finance the war by contributing funds at an equitable ratio to the Continental Congress and allowing it to administer the disbursements. But in addition to those modest amounts raised, the Congress and the states both spent many more millions of dollars, and the exact war debt was difficult to calculate.

The largest part of the debt was intergovernmental credits and obligations. The total amount the state government spent for the war was somewhere over $100 million, and under the Articles of Confederation and various ordinances passed by Congress, those expenditures were to be audited and then the costs reapportioned. Those states that had given more than their share would be reimbursed from the general treasury, and those who had paid less than their share would have to pay into it. The main dispute soon became the methods of auditing and verifying such expenses. While some Americans, like the meticulous New Englanders, tended to ask for and keep receipts for their expenditures, others, such as many Southerners, often did not. Also, some states, Massachusetts and Virginia, for example, insisted on charging all their military expenditures to the federal government, including those expenditures that were more for state ventures than for national ones. On top of those problems, the United States owed about $8 million to the government of France and $2 million to the bankers of Holland. In addition to those obligations, the old Congress had made direct expenditures by issuing unsecured paper money (called "Continentals"), selling bonds or loan office certificates, and authorizing its military officers to pay and supply troops by signing promissory notes. The paper money had depreciated to virtually nothing, and the loan office certificates and fixed expenditures totaled together nearly $27 million. Even the interest on this amount had not been paid since 1783. Lastly, there were state debts that were contracted independently of these other transactions. Some states had paid off the debts, while others had not.

Despite the intensified activity of speculators after 1787, between 25 and 40 percent of the securities were still in the hands of the original holders, including some states that retained large blocks of such currencies. The largest single concentrations of the Continental securities were held by the state treasuries of New York, Pennsylvania, and Maryland; these deposits constituted together about one-third of the total national debt, and Dutch investors held another one-fifth. Complicating the picture was the fact that many of the American speculators bought vast tracts of land from Congress or the states and paid for them with government securities at *par value*. While this group had an interest in keeping the price of these securities low, still other speculators bought up public securities, gambling that the price would rise and they would make a fortune overnight. Overall, the public debt situation seemed politically intractable because of conflicting state interests. Massachusetts, Connecticut, and South Carolina had large public debts because of the war, and they would gain if the federal government assumed those obligations. Virginia, Maryland, North Carolina, and Georgia, on the other hand, repaid most of their debts and were anxious for a rebate.

In trying to reach some solution to the debt assumption question, Hamilton was influenced by a variety of authorities. He was aware of the English experience in trying to deal with the public debt. Charles Montague, Lord Halifax, as a member of Parliament and Chancellor of the Exchequer, had advocated a Bank of England, excise taxes on malt and liquor, the institution of the public debt, and the first tontine in England. The tontine was a complex life annuity plan, and both William Pitt the Younger in England and Hamilton, following his example, were to divide up the tontine into six classes. Pitt's scheme was detailed in an article in the December 2, 1789, issue of *The New York Gazette of the United States*. The English Prime Minister had also successfully introduced the sinking fund as a method for financing the public debt, and one of his predecessors, Robert Walpole, had long since used the excise tax as a way to raise revenue and curtail smuggling. Meanwhile in France, Jacques Necker had presented to the Estates General a financial plan to deal with his nation's problems, and Hamilton was probably influenced by that as well.

The new Secretary had, in the past, worked closely with both Robert Morris and Gouverneur Morris, who tried to deal with the nation's financial problems. During the latter part of the Confederation period, Hamilton kept up a steady correspondence on those issues with major financiers and public officials, such as William Bingham of Philadelphia, and some of their views would later be found in his drafts. Also, as a man of ideas as well as practical pursuits, Hamilton was familiar with David Hume's work on public credit and the views of Hobbes and Montesquieu on the importance of honoring contracts. These philosophers were all well-known figures, men whose works still constitute a major part of Western political thought. Yet probably the most influential source was the *Universal Dictionary* of Malachy Postlethwayt, which the Secretary had used before and which he paraphrased in parts of his "Report on Public Credit." Hamilton agreed with the author's emphasis on the need to honor debts, promote the easy transfer of securities, and encourage the rapid circulation of funds.[1]

Hamilton, then, approached his task with a great deal of background and some important European, especially English, precedents. On January 14, 1790, he submitted his "Report Relative to a Provision for the Support of Public Credit" and followed it up with two more reports eleven months later. The first series of recommendations quickly dismissed the notion of outright repudiation of the debt or of discriminating on the basis of whether the holder was the initial loaner or not. Hamilton estimated the debt as foreign, $11,710,000, including principal and unpaid interest; national, $27,383,000 plus $13,030,000 in accrued interest and allowance of $2,000,000 for old accounts not yet liquidated; and state debts set at a level of $25,000,000. All of these debts were to be funded, but the interest rate would be reduced from the existing 6 percent to a little over 4 percent.

Hamilton called for a new loan to the U.S. government using the old securities. Creditors had a choice of repayment options. They could receive two-thirds of the value of their securities in the new government bonds that would yield 6 percent interest and take the remainder in Western lands at 20¢ an acre. Thus they could take the full value of their subscriptions in 4 percent interest-bearing bonds and be compensated for the reduced interest by receiving seventy-nine acres of Western land for every $100 subscribed. Or, if they did not want any land, they could take 66.66 percent of each $100 of old securities at 6 percent and the remaining 33.33 percent would entitle the holder to $26.88 in new stock at no interest for the first ten years and at 6 percent thereafter. Any subscriber who pledged half in old security and half in gold or silver would receive stock bearing 5 percent interest on it. Creditors who refused all of these options could keep their securities and receive 4 percent interest on them; however, the interest would be payable only if there were a treasury surplus after servicing the subscribed debt. Installments on the principal of the foreign debt would be met by new loans abroad. Interest on the debt plus $600,000 for ordinary operations of the government would total $2,839,163.09. This sum would be raised from existing duties on wines, spirits, teas, and coffee. Finally, Hamilton proposed a sinking fund to be used to reduce gradually the national debt. The sinking fund commissioners would apply the money through a national bank—an idea that Hamilton indicated that he would develop in a later report.

At first glance, Hamilton's proposal was a brilliant mosaic of economics, politics, and statesmanship. It was meant to restore American credit both domestically and abroad, and it put the new nation firmly behind its full faith and credit promise. Hamilton's proposal also protected the land speculators who paid in installments, by not increasing to par the value of securities that they were using to pay for those lands. Thus they were still allowed, although at a reduced rate, to pay for Western land with the full value of inflated currencies. Later Hamilton provided for two measures: the continuation of the tariff and the creation of the national bank that would further solidify the allegiance of the wealthy to the new government. The Secretary believed that the future of the new republic was dependent on the forbearance of the rich, and his national financial structure provided for investment, access, and opportunities for them.

When Hamilton presented his January Plan on debt assumption and funding, the Congress was a bit taken back. The House had indeed instructed the Secretary to come forth with a report on the public credit, but the size and intricacies of Hamilton's proposal were unexpected. Fenno, the arch Federalist editor and admirer of Hamilton, scornfully looked at Congress' reaction and then penned:

The Secretary makes reports
When'er the House commands him;
But for their lives, some members say
They cannot understand him.
In such a puzzling case as this
What can a mortal do?
'Tis hard for ONE to find REPORTS
And understanding too.

By the end of January, speculators were moving into the hinterlands, hoping to buy up securities before news of Hamilton's plan reached its inhabitants. When the House warily began deliberations, the debate went through three phases: first, a discussion of whether there should be discrimination between original holders and assigners, an argument that lasted for eleven days, until February 22; then, until March 9, the topic was whether the war debts of the states should be assumed by the federal government; lastly, the plans for modifying the debt were discussed and then recommitted on March 30, finally being reconsidered along with the former question of assumption.

The main spokesman for Hamilton's Plan was Elias Boudinot of New Jersey, a well-respected figure of the Revolutionary period who served as president of the Continental Congress and as a delegate to the Constitutional Convention. Few people knew that he had been a foster father to Hamilton when the Secretary was a schoolboy. Boudinot outlined the origins of the debt and reminded the House of the importance of honoring the payment of debts. He warned that "A bankrupt, faithless, Republic would be a novelty in the political world, and appear, among reputable nations, like a common prostitute among chaste and reputable nations."[2]

The House quickly approved the provisions to pay the foreign debt and interest. The question of discrimination, though, was discussed at length, with Madison arguing for such a differentiation between original holders and speculators. Before Madison's proposal came to a vote, Hamilton and his followers circulated the story that it was impossible from the records to tell the difference between the original and the present security holders. This was not true, but only the Secretary knew that, and on February 22 Madison's discrimination plan was defeated thirty-six to thirteen. The second and third propositions drawn from Hamilton's proposal dealt with laying aside permanent funds to pay the interest and discharge the principal of the debt and provide that arrears on interest should be paid on the same terms as the principal.[3]

The major provision that attracted the opposition was the method of calculating the debts of the states. Hamilton had originally counted on Madison's support, and now he was faced with the Virginian's strong opposition. Whether Madison and his associates were simply trying to get a better deal for their states or whether they were philosophically opposed to the plan remains unclear. In either case, while Congressmen from the states of New Hampshire, Pennsylvania, North Carolina, and Georgia argued that their states had already paid off their debts and they wanted no refunding of the obligations, the delegations from Virginia and Massachusetts demanded that the assumption package include the costs incurred by private armies as well. Virginia's Representatives prepared a series of amendments to improve their state's position, thus raising the costs of the proposal. Hamilton, fearing defeat, approached the Massachusetts delegation and floated a deal under which the federal government would assume nearly all of Massachusetts' war debt. Federalist leader Theodore Sedgwick from that state saw Hamilton's plan as a way of avoiding future Shays' Rebellions, which he argued were based on state taxes levied to pay the war debt. But other representatives, such as John Jackson of Georgia, conceived the whole plan to be a product of Hamilton's ambition—a calculated attempt to centralize the debt in his hands in order to show his skill at managing it. After various tangential discussions, the House, sitting as a Committee of the Whole, passed the resolutions embodying the Report on March 13. Although the tally was unrecorded, it is probable that the majority margin was only four or five votes. The House then went on to discuss antislavery petitions, and some of the sectional bitterness began to spill over when debate resumed on the debt package. With North Carolina's representatives seated, the assumption resolution was taken up again and this time defeated thirty-one to twenty-nine. The Committee of the Whole was then discharged from considering the assumption question, although the remainder of the Report passed. Hamilton had lost the battle for the major reform in his package. The bill went to the Senate for deliberation.

There that body was already discussing the establishment of a new capital city. On July 1 the Senate voted to move the government from New York to Philadelphia by December 1790, and then, after ten years, a permanent residence was to be established near the Potomac River area. What at first seemed a clear decision became confused in a medley of political pressures, private interests, and sectional controversy. Some members of the Senate and the House began to link the capital site and the debt bill by adding the assumption provision. The House in turn rejected it thirty-two to twenty-nine. The delegations from Pennsylvania and Virginia both had the same idea: trade their votes on the debt issue for support from Hamilton's allies to bring the permanent capital to their area. To head off the Pennsylvanians' proposal, pressure was brought on Madison to approach Hamilton and come up with a compromise on the assumption question. Madison had already led the opposition, so his withdrawal would be tactfully difficult. One historian, though, has suggested that Madison was less reluctant than has been generally assumed. Madison had been planning to acquire lands in the falls area of the Potomac region and would reap a great profit if the

capital city ended up there. Thus, it is argued, his real strategy was to block
Hamilton's financial package until he and his allies could force a bargain
that guaranteed a Potomac site. Whether this is true is rather questionable,
but for Hamilton, the problem remained: he needed some way to compromise both issues.[4]

Then, as the tale goes, fortune took a hand. One day a deeply depressed
Hamilton was passing in front of Washington's residence after the House
defeat. There he met Jefferson, who had recently arrived in New York to
assume the position of Secretary of State. Hamilton besieged Jefferson to
find some way to help him and the financial plan. Jefferson agreed that
something had to be done to settle the debt issue and complimented Hamilton for having come up with the only comprehensive approach. Concerned
about the views of foreign bankers and governments, and probably anxious
to show that he was loyal to the new administration, Jefferson invited
Hamilton and Madison for dinner the next night. Some thirty years later,
Jefferson described the events:

Hamilton was in despair. As I was going to the President's one day, I met him in
the street. He walked me backwards and forwards before the President's door for
half an hour. He painted pathetically the temper into which the legislature had been
wrought; the disgust of those who were called the creditor states; the danger of the
secession of their members, and the separation of the States. He observed that the
members of the administration ought to act in concert; that though this question
was not of my department, yet a common duty should make it a common concern;
that the President was the centre on which all administrative questions ultimately
rested, and that all of us should rally around him, and support, with joint efforts,
measures approved by him, and that the question having been lost by a small
majority only, it was probable that an appeal from me to the judgment and discretion
of some of my friends, might effect a change in the vote, and the machine of
government, now suspended, might be again set into motion. I told him that I was
really a stranger to the whole subject; that not having yet informed myself of the
system of finances adopted, I knew not how far this was a necessary sequence; that
undoubtedly, if its rejection endangered a dissolution of our Union at this incipient
stage, I should deem that the most unfortunate of all consequences, to avert which
all partial and temporary evils should be yielded. I proposed to him, however, to
dine with me the next day, and I would invite another friend or two, bring them
into conference together, and I thought it impossible that reasonable men, consulting
together coolly, could fail, by some mutual sacrifices of opinion, to form a compromise which was to save the Union. The discussion took place. I could take no
part in it but an exhortatory one, because I was a stranger to the circumstances
which should govern it. But it was finally agreed, that whatever importance had
been attached to the rejection of this proposition, the preservation of the Union and
of concord among the States was more important, and that therefore it would be
better that the vote of rejection should be rescinded, to effect which, some members
should change their votes. But it was observed that this bill would be peculiarly
bitter to the southern States, and that some concomitant measure should be adopted,

to sweeten it a little to them. There had before been propositions to fix the seat of government either at Philadelphia, or at Georgetown on the Potomac; and it was thought that by giving it to Philadelphia for ten years, and to Georgetown permanently afterwards, this might, as an anodyne, calm in some degree the ferment which might be excited by the other measure alone. So two of the Potomac members (White and Lee, but White with a revulsion of stomach almost convulsive) agreed to change their votes, and Hamilton undertook to carry the other point. In doing this, the influence he had established over the eastern members, with the agency of Robert Morris with those of the middle states, effected his side of the engagement; and so the Assumption was passed, and twenty millions of stock divided among favored States and thrown in a pabulum to the stock-jobbing herd. This added to the number of votaries to the Treasury, and made its chief the master of every vote in the legislature, which might give to the government the direction suited to his political views.[5]

Jefferson was to denounce Hamilton for setting the stage for corruption and a party of courtiers paid by the largesse of the government. He and Madison had been outwitted, he claimed, overwhelmed by their dedication to the new Union. Yet his recollections ring hollow. Both he and Madison were astute judges of men, and everyone, even the Pennsylvanians who felt cheated by the outcome, knew what was at stake and what benefits could occur. After the dinner, Virginia's allowable debt assumption jumped to nearly $19 million, which came within $100,000 of wiping out the total debt, and even that amount was never collected by the federal government.

On August 4, 1790, Hamilton's proposal, with some modifications, was passed and signed into law by the President. As for Washington himself, during some of this period, he was severely ill with pneumonia and nearly died. Clearly he had let Hamilton carry the burden by himself during this controversy. Overall, Washington's view of the presidency was somewhat different from the views of present-day leaders. He generally refused to tell Congress what legislation it should pass, and he regarded his Treasury Secretary as partially answerable to the Congress. His diffidence was due in part to the law that made the reporting lines of the Treasury Secretary more ambiguous than those of the Secretaries of State and War. Congress retained some direct access to the treasury, and Hamilton adroitly used his ambivalent status to increase his personal influence. In addition, Washington knew little about finance, and Hamilton seemed to be in touch with the influential financiers who had a direct interest in the whole matter. As his correspondence indicates, Washington surely supported privately the Hamilton proposal. But this was less of a strong personal commitment than a realization that his Treasury Secretary was trying to deal with a major national dilemma and was doing so in a capable way. Washington was also aware of the financial problems that had so afflicted the early Confederation and the bitter charges leveled against the Superintendent of Finance, Robert

Morris, who tried to deal with these financial problems and, at the same time, keep the General's army in the field.

Yet the President stayed clear of controversy, and Hamilton, like the prime minister he envisioned himself to be, maneuvered, traded, and cajoled the bill through Congress. There is no evidence that Washington played any part in the backstage dealings or the fateful dinner at Jefferson's home. Some mild criticism did appear in *The New York Daily Advertiser*, which published an open letter addressed to the President, arguing that the proposed move from New York to Philadelphia was unconstitutional. When Jefferson reassured him it was not, Washington signed the bill. In *The New York Journal*, a writer named "Z" charged the President, in careful terms, with ingratitude, but generally, Washington benefited from his own discretion and from Hamilton's propensity for the limelight.[6]

16

THE ESTABLISHMENT
OF THE BANK

It may be laid down as an incontrovertible position, that all the powers contained in a constitution of Government, which concern the general administration of the affairs of a country, its finances, its trade, its defense ought to be construed liberally, in advancement of the general good.

Alexander Hamilton,
February 1791

By the fall of 1790 it was apparent that Hamilton was the foremost member of the cabinet and the single most important political operative in the new government. The major issues of the first few years were economic, and the Treasury Secretary was more than capable of realizing their importance. Having succeeded with the debt assumption proposal, Hamilton moved on to the next proposal, which was an outgrowth of his first report—the creation of a national bank. In December 1790 the Secretary presented the outline of his plan: a bank with one-fifth of the $10 million capitalization subscribed to in cash by the national government. The government in turn would borrow $2 million from the bank, and the remaining stock would be sold to private investors, with three-quarters of their subscriptions payable in new 6 percent government bonds, the rest in specie. The Secretary of the Treasury could remove government deposits, inspect the books, and require periodic statements from the bank. The government would accept the national bank notes at par for all taxes and other obligations, and the bank would be the main depository and fiscal agent for the U.S. government.

Hamilton originally proposed his national bank on December 13, and after a month of debate, behind closed doors, the Senate passed a bill incorporating the bank and sent it on to the House. There the earlier opposition on the debt bill was transformed into even stronger criticism, for now Hamilton was proposing to establish an institution that many Representatives felt would benefit only the merchant class and be of no use to farmers.

In its March 17, 1790, issue, the *Philadelphia Gazette*, with its crude verse refrain, had criticized the secretary for his tax program:

> Tax on Tax young Belcour cries,
> More impost and a new excise,
> A public debt's a public blessing
> Which 'tis of course a crime to lessen.
> Each day a fresh report he broaches,
> That spies and Jews may ride in coaches,
> Soldiers and farmers don't despair,
> Untax'd as yet, are Earth and Air.[1]

Now opposition was becoming more intense and organized. By the beginning of 1791 Jefferson voiced his own dissatisfaction with the administration's direction of the nation, and by February he was writing to political friends in New York, Virginia, and Kentucky, asking, "Are the people in your quarter as well content with the proceedings of our government as their representatives say they are?" However, the real leader of the nascent faction in the Congress was not Jefferson, but Madison, Hamilton's onetime ally and a Washington confidant.[2]

During the debate, Madison argued in vain that the bank was unconstitutional, but the House passed it by a vote of thirty-nine to twenty. Within the councils of the administration, Jefferson and Attorney General Edmund Randolph wrote opinions, at Washington's request, that argue along similar lines. Their main point was that the Tenth Amendment, which had not yet been ratified, prohibited the federal government from exercising any power not expressly delegated to it.

Jefferson's opinion was replete with erudite legal terminology that the layman Washington must have found confusing. Although he favored the concept of a national bank, Washington was especially disturbed by the questions being raised about its constitutionality. He held several conversations with Madison and discussed the problem at length. Madison reminded Washington that at the Constitutional Convention, the framers had discussed giving Congress the power to incorporate institutions and that the proposal was laid aside. Washington countered that the Continental Congress had, in 1781, incorporated the Bank of North America, but Madison argued that that act was a product of necessity and no such problem existed now.

Washington, who believed that one of the primary purposes of giving the president the veto power was to guard against unconstitutional acts, found himself in a difficult position. Madison, who generally favored a stronger national government than the President, now was arguing in terms of limiting its powers, and Jefferson and Randolph agreed. The President then penned, on February 16, 1791, a formal note to Hamilton, informing him of Randolph's and Jefferson's views and requesting, in an icy tone; "That I may be fully possessed of the argument *for* and *against* the measure before I express any opinion of my own, I give you an opportunity of examining and answering the objections contained in the enclosed papers. I require the return of them, when your own statements are handed me (which I wish may be as soon as is convenient); and further that no copies of them be taken."[3]

Hamilton, at first startled and then angry, took up the challenge. Meanwhile Washington asked Madison to summarize the major points that should be contained in a veto message. Within forty-eight hours, Hamilton wrote his "Defense of the Constitutionality of an Act to Establish a Bank" and forwarded it to the President on February 23. In one of the most brilliant state papers ever written, Hamilton demolished the major objections and argued in the process for a broad interpretation of the Constitution. He undertook a linguistic analysis of Jefferson's use of the word "necessary" that left the Secretary of State's position in wreckage. In a quandary, Washington carefully read the arguments presented to him. Jefferson had advised against signing the bill but then added that if the President was undecided in his own mind, he should support the legislature's will after all. Washington finally decided to sign the bill, creating the Bank of the United States. Thus the second major part of the Hamiltonian system fell into place, but not without a struggle.[4]

Why Washington finally signed the bill is not clear. Perhaps he was swayed by the precedents of 1781, when the Continental Congress created a bank, or he may have been overwhelmed by the apparent logic of Hamilton's brilliant brief. Interestingly, at the same time, Washington was also involved in setting the Potomac site for the capital. The President had rejected the advice of his three-man commission and decided to move the capital to a location that happened to be some three miles outside the authorized southeastern location and closer to his own estate. He apparently realized that the effect of these transactions would be to increase the value of his own property. Somewhat uncomfortable because of his decision, Washington decided that he wanted the Congress to approve retroactively his action by amending the federal district act. One biographer of Hamilton had argued that Washington's request got caught up in the debate over the bank. In the Senate, the bank supporters, with Hamilton's knowledge, held up approving Washington's desired site changes until the President approved the bank bill. On February 25 the President overcame his constitutional objections, and that day the Senate took up the capital site bill. Thus once again the new seat of government had been part of a shrewd trade that helped put in place the Hamiltonian economic system.[5]

After Congress recessed on March 3, 1791, the President made plans to take a tour of the Southern states, similar to the one he had taken of the New England states the summer before. He instructed his secretaries of State, Treasury, and War to consult with the Vice-President, should any occasion arise that needed attention and he would "approve and ratify" what they decided on, or, if necessary, he would return as fast as he could, if summoned.

On April 17 Washington set out for the Carolinas and Georgia. He traveled along the East Coast and passed through Richmond, Wilmington (North Carolina), and Charleston to Savannah, and then up the interior to Columbia and Charlotte toward Prince Edward, Fredericksburg, and Mount Vernon. The President was surprised at the barrenness of the land and the poverty of the people in some of those areas. Over the difficult roads, Washington's carriage covered nearly 1,900 miles. At some stops, the inhabitants were startled to find their president at the local inn without any notice. But in more cosmopolitan cities, such as Charleston, the President was accorded full social honors. There Washington, dressed in a velvet suit, yellow gloves, steel sword, and a profusely powdered wig, danced with the Southern ladies. At Charleston, the President was surrounded by 256 elegantly dressed ladies in an afternoon dancing assembly, and in the evening, he noted fondly in his diary, "at least four hundred ladies, the number and appearance of which exceeded anything of the kind I have ever seen." The tour lasted for two months, and Washington failed to find any immediate criticism of either the bank or the liquor tax.

On July 6, 1791, Washington returned to Philadelphia and learned of the public reaction to the sale of the stock in the new bank. Hamilton, to counter the charge that he favored the rich, had priced the scrip at $25 a share. When the sale began, crowds rushed to purchase the shares. The stock was immediately oversubscribed by 4,000 shares, and the price of the stock shot up from $25 to $325. The credit of the new government was unquestionable, and Washington concluded that the "astonishing rapidity with which the newly instituted bank was filled gives an unexampled proof (here) of the resources of our countrymen and their confidence in public measures." Coincidentally it was at this point that Washington began to sign his letters to Hamilton with the same ending he used with Madison and Jefferson, "affectionate regard."[6]

Overall, the Bank of the United States proved to be a worthwhile endeavor for the nation. With its bank notes, it provided a circulating currency, and the new credit helped to stimulate capitalist enterprise. When, in the 1790s, the number of state banks rapidly increased, the Bank of the United States exercised some control through its power to require other banks to redeem their notes and checks with hard money. The Bank loaned the government money, transferred government funds, and aided in foreign exchange. The Republicans bitterly noted that some thirty members of

Congress were stockholders and directors in the Bank of the United States, and the Republicans fostered the establishment of state banks to counter the economic and political power of the new U.S. Bank. They complained that while the Bank served well the interests of the government and of the merchants, when the question came up of loaning money to Southern planters, using tobacco warehouse receipts as security, Hamilton objected. In succeeding years Congress refused to provide enough money to pay off the government's debt to the Bank, and the government eventually sold its large blocks of stock so that by 1809, foreigners owned 18,000 of the 25,000 shares. The Bank of the United States, despite the criticisms of a narrow-based Republican faction, survived the Federalist period and became an established part of the national structure until the Jackson administration. Then, once again, the forces of partisan appeal, wild speculation, and strong state interests found a more belligerent popular champion than either Jefferson or Madison could ever become.[7]

17

WASHINGTON AS ADMINISTRATOR

General Washington is, I believe, almost the only man of an exalted character who does not lose some part of his respectability... by an intimate acquaintance.

Tobias Lear

Although there was no executive office surrounding the first president, Washington did have, as was his custom, some personal assistants who performed all sorts of tasks. Like most individuals used to responsibility and leadership, Washington tended to bring to a new undefined office the same work habits he had followed so successfully before his election. As an owner of a large plantation, he was disposed to delegate responsibility to overseers, while at the same time retaining a control over detail. Being the major American military figure in the Revolution, Washington, as commander-in-chief, had gained even more valuable experience in working with a contentious Congress, watching the varied experiences of the war governors, and presiding over the main continental operation the fledgling nation supported. He retained a knowledgeable storehouse of names and information that served him well now in making appointments for the new government. In his day-to-day dealings, he continued to be respectful of Congress but was also concerned about the need to establish and assert his own prerogatives. He appointed aides to help him sort out the paper work and named able cabinet heads to preside over the departments. These heads turned out to be so strong that even Washington had a trying time keeping his house in order. When both Jefferson and, later, Hamilton resigned, Washington outwardly retained his cabinet form of government, but in reality, Washington, like other strong presidents, such as Lincoln and Franklin Roosevelt, moved away from close consultation with subordinates after the first term in office. There is no training ground for being president, and presidents, as they stay longer in office, come to believe that they know more about what they should do in the office they have held. It is a view that is in one sense quite correct and in another quite dangerous. Incomplete truths are sometimes worse than outright falsehoods, for the former are so covered with reason and logic that enlightenment takes all the more time. In the case of Washington, it can be said, though, that of all the strong presidents, he was less prone to make serious errors while in office. As Thomas Bailey has noted, Washington may very well have been the greatest president because he never made a major mistake.[1]

As for his personal staff, Washington fell back on the lessons he had learned during the war. Early in the Revolution, he was faced with the need both to plan strategy and look after details, and he complained that "at present my time is so taken up at my desk, that I am obliged to neglect many other essential parts of my duties." To relieve himself of the press of such work, he hired aides-de-camp, men who could "write a good letter, write quick, [and] are methodical and diligent." The aides slept together in one room, usually opposite the General's own bedroom, and they were on call twenty-four hours a day. One aide, Tench Tilgham of Maryland, wrote his father: "You need be under no apprehensions of my [losing my health] on the score of excess living. Vice is banished from the General's family. We never sup but go early to bed and are early up."

Over the years some thirty-two young men served as aides to the General, with the most capable and important being Alexander Hamilton. One of Hamilton's earliest friends, Robert Troup, commented that "the pen for the Army was held by Hamilton; and for dignity of manner, pith of matters and elegance of style, General Washington's letters are unrivaled in military annals." Hamilton's duties extended beyond simply answering correspondence. With Washington's approval, he assumed responsibilities generally entrusted to a person holding a rank far superior to that of colonel. On occasion he was even sent by Washington to command other generals to dispatch their troops in order to accomplish particular objectives.

The relationship between Washington and Hamilton was a strangely complex one. Hamilton's name was originally recommended by General Nathanael Greene, although others were also aware of Hamilton's vigorous leadership during the battles of Princeton and Trenton. Washington not only used Hamilton's skills and brilliant organizational ability, but also came to form a strong personal attachment toward the young man. A passionate but highly controlled person, Washington seldom reached out to form close friendships. Although married to a widow with children, he had no offspring of his own, perhaps as a consequence of the smallpox he had contracted years before. While Washington became more dependent on Hamilton and somewhat protective, the ambitious colonel began to chafe under Washington's strictures, precipitated a quarrel, and resigned over the alleged slight. Finally the two men parted. Although Washington said little about the incident, Hamilton, less discreet, insisted on telling friends, "The truth is our dispositions are the opposites of each other." Yet, even with their uncomfortable parting of the ways, both men remained in contact with each other after the war and during the 1780s.[2]

Washington, in retirement, continued to hire aides to help him run his affairs. He solicited from close friends the names of prospective young gentlemen who could compose a good letter, handle his account, organize his papers, and devote some time to the initial schooling of the two Custis children. In 1785 Washington's loyal confidant, Benjamin Lincoln, recommended a twenty-four-year-old Harvard graduate from New Hampshire, Tobias Lear. Lear was a sober and industrious lad who was good-natured and willing to work for the $200 a year the General had set aside as a salary. At first, Lear was offended by Washington's aloofness and reserve, and considered resigning from the position. But he soon noted that Washington "began to relax and gradually drew me toward him by every tender and endearing tie." Lear became part of the family, ate with the group, and, in the evening, played cards with the President.[3]

Lear tried manfully to make sense out of Washington's personal accounts and discovered that during the war, the General had lost at least £10,000, mainly because debtors had paid him in depreciated Continental currency instead of in specie. In addition, some of the debts owed by his wife's relatives and other individuals were simply uncollectable, and other individuals refused to pay unless sued—a recourse Washington thought was useless. Lear also handled the President's move from Mount Vernon to New York City and later to Philadelphia.

In addition to these domestic responsibilities, Lear began to assume other administrative and political duties. In 1793 Lear was asked by the President to investigate discreetly the problems arising from land claims in the Rock Creek area of the proposed capital. Later Lear represented the President when the Potomac Company met to discuss the site, and when the architect, Pierre L'Enfant, was giving the commissioners some difficulty, Lear wrote him, urging cooperation. L'Enfant proved to be uncompromising, personally rebuffing Lear's intercession, and consequently Washington had Jefferson dismiss him.

The President also had Lear keep a record on whether Congress had accepted his occasional recommendations so that Washington could decide if he should press for passage of those items overlooked in the rush of business. Lear also kept in contact with members of Congress and with the Cabinet secretaries. In one instance, Henry Knox informed him that he would not respond to a particular question raised by the President until he had consulted with his fellow secretaries, Jefferson and Hamilton. On another occasion, Washington, who was considering a second term, asked him to "find out from conversation without appearing to make the inquiry" whether there was support building in the capital for any other candidate. When Lear found that the mention of any other name aroused "apprehension," the President checked with Jefferson to see if the same held true in the South, which it did.

As the years passed, Lear joined with Jefferson in believing that Washington's public appeal was being hurt by Hamilton's economic policies. Even Washington seemed to understand that most of his political, as well as social, contacts were with members of the Federalist faction. He urged Lear to keep in contact with Republicans and added that "mixing with people in different walks, high and low, of different descriptions and political sentiments, must have afforded you an extensive range for observation and comparisons; more so, by far, than could fall to the lot of a stationary character who is always revolving in a particular circle." Lear did indeed continue his relationships with Republican partisans and so fell under their spell that when some of them attacked Washington, Lear tried to convince a skeptical Washington that it was really the Federalists who were behind these criticisms in order to help discredit their opponents in the President's eyes!

During his service as aide, both Lear and his wife lived on the third floor of the executive mansion, and the Washingtons shared in the joy of the birth of their children and the deep sorrow when Lear's wife died. Soon after her death in 1793, Lear left Washington's employ and went into business for himself. Later, with the help of the President and Jefferson, Lear became a diplomat and was involved as consul general in trying to negotiate a treaty with Tripoli. When the proposed treaty was bitterly criticized, Lear returned home and finally took a job as an accountant in the War Department. In 1816 he committed suicide, leaving no explanation for his deed.

Washington never really found anyone after 1793 who could replace Lear as both secretary and confidant. He hired Bartholomew Dandridge to handle some of his financial affairs, including renting Mount Vernon and selling some of his western lands. It was Dandridge who, after the President was bitterly denounced in the *New York Daily Advertiser*, wrote the editors that since Washington was a busy man, he had little time to read newspapers and the subscription should be cancelled. By early 1795 Dandridge expressed a desire to leave his job, but Washington proposed that he take an extended vacation instead. By the summer of 1796 Dandridge abruptly disappeared, returning in July.

Beside Lear and Dandridge, Washington hired other staff people. He retained a strong affection for Colonel David Humphreys, the son of a Continental minister, who earned a Master of Arts degree from Yale at the age of eighteen. Humphreys had served in the Revolution and after the war worked with Washington on his autobiography. He had a flair for coining a good phrase and helped Washington compose his seventy-three-page inaugural address draft. The President-elect, though, had some reservations and asked James Madison to look it over. Humphreys also went with Washington on his trip from Mount Vernon to New York City and remained associated with the President in the early years of his administration. Washington also hired, in September 1789, Major William Jackson, a friend of Benjamin Lincoln and the secretary at the Philadelphia Convention. It was Jackson who supervised the medical care given to Washington in 1790 when he almost died of pneumonia.

Throughout his first term, the President, then, had some personal staff and several nephews and sons of friends to assist him with the burdens of both official correspondence and domestic matters. In addition, Washington had a strong cabinet and a wide circle of friends and acquaintances. His years of national service had given him a vast network of people who were all too willing to share with him private gossip and public information and offer advice on affairs of state.[4]

By today's standards there was no real presidential office. Yet the pace and range of responsibilities are nowhere near comparable. From his diary for February 1 through February 14, 1790, we can get a fairly good representative view of Washington's activities.

February 1790

Monday 1	Agreed on new house.
Tuesday 2	Exercized in the carriage with Mrs. W., on return met Blair, Associate Judge, Attorney General of the U.S. and Colonel Bland; Levee today.
Wednesday 3	Visited new home and directed stables to be built.
Thursday 4	Received an Act from Congress; dinner with important members of Administration and Judges.
Friday 5	Received a list of names for North Carolina revenue offices; submitted to Senators for their "inspection and alteration."
Saturday 6	Walked to new lodgings to conclude agreement on stables; nominated Iredell for Supreme Court.
Sunday 7	Chapel.
Monday 8	Nominated revenue officers, Iredell and Major Samuel Shaw (as consul for Canton, China); signed bill sent on Thursday.
Tuesday 9	Levee; exercized on horseback in the forenoon.
Wednesday 10	Sat from 9–11 for portrait; dispatched commissions and necessary Acts to Revenue officers.
Thursday 11	Exercized on horseback in forenoon; dinner with some Congressmen.
Friday 12	Sat from 9–11 for portrait. Mrs. Washington had company.

| Saturday 13 | Walked to new house and gave directions for furniture arrangement. |
| Sunday 14 | Wrote letters to Virginia.[5] |

In a government of this size and an administration of modest aspirations, the president was able to be an executive with control over detail. The world of large bureaucracies, a diffuse welfare state, and massive military budgets make all that supervision and care impossible. A president so consumed in detail today would lose sight of the broad general policy questions and forfeit the possibilities inherent in the office. But for Washington—and indeed for most of the presidents through Herbert Hoover—the presidency was an important, but still very small office. There is some truth to the facetious remark that before the New Deal, the role of the federal government was to deliver the mails and watch the shorelines for invaders.

One can get a good sense of the early presidency from Jefferson's description, written in 1801, of Washington's administrative style:

Having been a member of the first administration under General Washington, I can state with exactness what our course then was. Letters of business came addressed sometimes to the President, but most frequently to the heads of the departments. If addressed to himself, he referred them to the proper department to be acted on: if to one of the secretaries, the letter, if it required no answer, was communicated to the President, simply for his information. If an answer was requisite, the secretary of the department communicated the letter and his proposed answer to the President. Generally, they were simply sent back with an informal note, suggesting an alteration or a query. If a doubt of any importance arose, he reserved it for conference. By this means, he was always in accurate possession of all facts and proceedings in every part of the Union, and to whatsoever department they related; he formed a central point for the differing branches; preserved a unity of object and action among them; exercised that participation in the suggestion of affairs which his office made incumbent upon him; and met himself the due responsibility for whatever was done. During Mr. Adams' administration, his long and habitual absences from the seat of government rendered this kind of communication impracticable, removed him from any share in the transaction of affairs, and parcelled out the government, in fact, among four independent heads, drawing sometimes in opposite directions. That the former is preferable to the latter course, cannot be doubted. It gave, indeed, to the heads of the departments the trouble of making up once a day, a packet of all their communications for the perusal of the President; it commonly also retarded one day their dispatches by mail. But in pressing cases, this injury was prevented by presenting that cause singly for immediate attention; and it produced us in return the benefit of his sanction for every act we did. Whether any change of circumstances may render a change in this procedure necessary, a little experience will show us. But I cannot withhold recommending to heads of departments, that we should adopt this course for the present, leaving any necessary modifications of it to time and trial.[6]

Not only was Washington well organized in his administrative practices, but he was also quite sensitive to the types of appointments he made. During his two terms, Washington nominated more than 350 officials in addition to department heads and Supreme Court justices. The government bureaucracy grew rapidly, and by 1792, 780 persons were employed by the federal government, 660 in the Treasury Department alone. By the time Jefferson took over as President, the number was 2,120, with 1,615 in the Treasury Department.

Although some of Washington's appointees were men of modest achievements, the general standards that he used were higher compared with other western nations, including Britain and France. Unlike Lincoln, who was plagued by applicants for public office, the first president saw no such aspirants personally and gave no commitments until he had completed his selection process. Washington generally tried to find out how well regarded a person was in his local community, and he gave preference to former holders of state offices, especially in the customs service, who had had similar positions before and conducted themselves well. He also gave preference to veterans but refused to extend that claim to their dependents.

Washington was quick to exclude people known to be lazy and those prone toward alcoholism. He also was unwilling at first to appoint his own relations, and on one occasion in 1789 turned down his nephew, noting that "my political conduct in nominations even if I was uninfluenced by principle, must be exceedingly circumspect and proof against just criticism, for the eyes of augur upon me, and no slips will pass unnoticed that can be improved into a supposed partiality for friends or relatives." But just several months later, he changed his mind and began appointing relatives of his wife to various federal posts.[7]

Washington is often pictured as a president who was above partisan considerations. Even John Adams went so far as to criticize his predecessor, noting, "Washington appointed a multitude of democrats and jacobins of the deepest hues . . . I have been more cautious in this regard." In fact, Washington was extremely sensitive to the need to appoint friends of the Constitution, that is, Federalists, and he systematically passed over Anti-Federalists and later Republicans. In the process, the President routinely consulted Federalist leaders about appointments and respected their views.[8]

The President also relied heavily on Hamilton's opinions concerning appointments, and since three-quarters of these positions were in his department, the Federalist party, as it later grew up, was well provided for. But the President was not a passive partisan. Washington, on one occasion, signed a commission for a Wilbur Perry to be inspector of internal revenue in Maryland and then discovered he was a Republican. The President informed Hamilton that Perry was to be dropped, and that the Secretary was to move on to a less qualified Federalist applicant, William Richardson.

The Washington administration did more than reward friends of the

Constitution; it used its patronage powers as a way to create a base for the Federalist party. One of the most prized positions was the postmastership, which helped to support the editors of party newspapers. Although the salary was small, the local postmaster could mail their newspapers free, and some of them were retained to print up the session laws of Congress. Jefferson complained, quite correctly, to Madison that the post office had become "a source of boundless patronage to the executive."[9]

In addition, the Federalist party was assisted greatly by the collectors and customs officials who were closely involved with the mercantile and financial interests of their respective states. Their influence was added to that of internal revenue service officers who were able to travel around and often were involved in actual campaigning for Federalist candidates. Although the Internal Revenue Service in our own time has not been free of discretionary administration of the laws and of political influence, there is no real comparison to these early years of partisanship. Americans have, in this century, gone through periods of non-partisanship or anti-partisanship, and the civil service has, as a result, come to be somewhat insulated from politics. That development has made governments often unresponsive, arrogant, and excessively bureaucratic as well as more honest and independent.

The same changes can be seen in the American judiciary. In the Federalist and Jeffersonian periods, the courts not only bent to public sentiments, but also were fierce actors in the partisan struggles. Judges delivered opinions that embodied the nationalist philosophy of the Federalist party and were intensely involved in that party's activities. Of the twenty-eight men who sat on the U.S. bench as district judges in the 1790s, fourteen had been delegates to the Philadelphia Constitutional Convention or state ratifying conventions, and another seven had been politically active in favor of the Constitution outside the conventions. Once appointed, these men continued not only to uphold the Constitution, as they were sworn to do, but also participated in party meetings, spoke openly about the partisan issues of the time, and, most unfortunately, used the courtrooms in which to press their opinions. Some of these judges abandoned any claim to impartiality, and in impanelling juries, in giving them charges, and in writing legal opinions, they clearly proselytized. Federalist judges often were the most vigorous supporters of the administration's foreign policy and unreservedly implemented the hated sedition laws.[10]

When Jefferson and the Republicans took over, they began to purge the Federal judiciary, and the President bluntly advocated reciprocity in dealing with Federalist opponents. He had been especially incensed that the federal attorneys and marshals were used to stifle dissent and impanel juries that persecuted notable Republicans. He singled out seven of the seventeen incumbents and promised to remove them promptly from office when he came to power.[11]

The Federalists, and soon after the Republicans, used the judiciary for partisan purposes in ways that clearly emulated the English example. Only after the judiciary became more established and the legal profession more conscious of its own worth did the sanctity of the law and the importance of impartiality become generally accepted. By then, politicians also learned that the American populace could be fickle in their choices. Those politicians who had been ruthless when in power might find themselves one day on the outside, facing the hostilities of a newly constituted judiciary. A rough-and-tumble consensus emerged on what were to be the rules of the game, rules designed not to protect the people, but to protect the political leadership. One could fool, lie, and bamboozle the electorate, cheat and name-call, engage in demagoguery or race baiting, but political persecution—at least of mainstream parties—was gradually abandoned in the nineteenth century. The traditions of the Founding Fathers were changed, probably for the better.

Yet with all the competition for patronage positions, Washington found it increasingly difficult to fill the top spots with competent men, especially after 1795. Many distinguished people refused to leave their home states, and the federal government's meager compensation and its limited role in people's lives made the positions not particularly coveted. Some of the Supreme Court appointments also presented difficulties. Jurists disliked riding circuit, and in the early years of the Republic, most of the case work was at this level and even Supreme Court justices were involved in lower court hearings. In 1791 an exasperated Washington wrote to Charles C. Pinckney and Edmund Rutledge, noting to both of them that a seat on the Supreme Court was vacant and asking them to decide which one would accept it. Both declined.[12]

The President had other problems filling cabinet posts and diplomatic positions in the later years, and some of his appointments ran into opposition in the Senate. In 1794 Washington, replacing Gouverneur Morris as minister to France, decided to appease the Republicans by nominating one of their own, if they could agree on a name. The Republican leaders suggested Aaron Burr, and Madison and Monroe presented the President with that name. Washington had put himself in an embarrassing position, and he had no choice but to say bluntly that he would not nominate a person whose integrity he found questionable. The Republicans held firm at first when an angry Washington countered that he would accept Madison or Monroe, but not Burr. Finally Monroe went off to the position, later to Washington's regret.[13]

Washington did consult with Congress on other major appointments, and there is one case in which, after he received a list of nominations for the position of revenue officer from a North Carolina representative, the President asked the state's Senators to look at the list for "inspection and alteration." On five occasions the Senate rejected the President's nominees, two of these in major appointments. The first such instance was the nomination of Benjamin Fishbourne to be naval officer in the port of Savannah. Washington was infuriated at the rejection and reminded the Senate that Fishbourne had been repeatedly elected or appointed to offices in his state and obviously had the respect of his neighbors and fellow citizens. Later the Senate rejected the President's nomination of John Randolph of Virginia to be a Supreme Court justice. Some Senators felt he was an erratic personality, although others questioned his party loyalty.

After the early debates on the removal power, Washington did replace some seventeen officials, including three ministers—Monroe, William Carmichael, and Thomas Pinckney (the last at his own request)—two consuls, eight collectors, and four surveyors of the internal revenue. In addition, he essentially forced Edmund Randolph to resign as Secretary of State. Washington then did exercise considerable authority in appointing and removing officials and in choosing men who were both friends of the Constitution and adherents to the new party. But he was also faced with the reality that service in the federal government in the temporary capital cities was not a sought-after reward for men of position and stature. The same experience held true for Congress. Of the ninety-four men who served in the Senate from 1789 to 1801, thirty-three resigned before their terms were up. Only two served through that full period, and some fifteen returned to become governors, twelve others were made judges, and twenty-four went back to serve in the state legislatures. Clearly the Federal government was not viewed as the center of the new Union, and its closest adherents tended to remain political provincials at heart.[14]

18

THE TRIBES AND THE LONG KNIVES

It is melancholy reflection that our modes of population have been made more destructive to the Indian nations than the conduct of the conquerors of Mexico and Peru. The evidence of this is the utter extermination of nearly all the Indians in the most populous parts of the Union. A future historian may mark the causes of this destruction of the human race in sable colors.

Henry Knox

Although most accounts of the first term of the Washington administration concentrate on the economic program, the major issue that occupied the President's attention was the situation on the frontier. Although Washington was willing to leave the funding of the war debt to Hamilton, he retained considerable control over the day-to-day operations of military affairs, Indian policy, and frontier diplomacy.

In working out his policies in these areas, Washington's closest advisor was his old friend and confidant during the Revolutionary War, Henry Knox. Born in 1750, Knox was the seventh of ten sons whose father was a shipmaster. Knox originally worked as a bookseller and owned The Corner Bookstore in Boston. Somewhat interested in military matters, he joined a local militia and was present at the Boston massacre. Knox is supposed to have protested Captain Thomas Preston's decision to fire on the patriot mob—an incident that sparked intense resentment throughout the colonies. By 1772 Knox joined the respected Boston Grenadier Corps and was named second in command. In those years before the war, Knox studied, in a more serious way, engineering and the principles of military strategy. He loved to parade in his uniform, and he cut such an imposing and impressive figure that he courted and won the hand of Lucy Flucker, the daughter of the royal secretary of the province. When British–American hostilities began, Knox decided to leave the Royal Army and joined the patriots. He was soon named a colonel and head of the infantry, and acquired a reputation for resourcefulness and audacity when he led a train of artillery through the harsh snows from Fort Ticonderoga to Boston. Before the war was over, Knox distinguished himself in the battles of New York City, Trenton, Princeton, Brandywine, Germantown, and Monmouth. He was one of the best-known American soldiers of the period, and after the Revolution, he conceived and organized the Society of Cincinnati, a group of former military officers under Washington's nominal aegis.

In the new administration, Knox and his wife were important figures in the President's official social circle. The Secretary and his wife entertained elegantly and spent much more than his small salary allowed for such events. Both of them were heavyset, weighing nearly 300 pounds each, and they were labeled, "the largest couple in New York." Knox was an amiable, yet forceful person who could be generous and hospitable, and his wife exhibited those same virtues. Despite her occasional social awkwardness and sometimes tasteless remarks, she became one of the main hostesses in the capital and a good friend of Mrs. Washington. With expensive tastes, Knox, like many of his contemporaries, was a major speculator, and over the years he was frequently involved in legal suits. He died at the age of fifty-six when a chicken bone became lodged in his intestine and could not be removed.[1]

Knox had served under the Articles of Confederation as the Secretary at War, and when the First Congress established the new departments, Washington retained him and changed his title to Secretary of War. Intent on reorganizing the army, Knox soon found himself involved in two unrelated disputes between the Senate and the President. The first controversy arose from the Senate's rejection of Washington's nomination of Benjamin Fishbourne of Georgia to fill a post in Savannah. Despite the fact that Fishbourne had been a fine officer in the war, and afterward compiled a good record, the Senate, by secret ballot, rejected the nomination. As noted previously, an angry Washington sent Knox to the Senate with a letter suggesting that the body notify him when a nomination appeared "questionable" so that he could give his reasons. Washington then enumerated Fishbourne's qualifications but finally proceeded to nominate another man. Because the Georgia delegation originally objected to the Fishbourne nomination and the full Senate upheld its colleagues, some historians have cited the example as the first use of "senatorial courtesy." However, it is unclear from the record that the Senate had developed any such notion at this early date.

In any case, Knox had acted as an intermediary in a difficult situation that had little to do with his major duties. Then, a few days later, he accompanied Washington to the Senate to obtain its advice and consent for a proposed treaty with the Creek Indians. Washington sat in the Vice-President's chair with the Secretary beside him. Adams read the text of the treaty to the Senate, but as the noise from the busy street outside grew louder, his voice was hard to hear. When the Vice-President asked the Senate to give its advice and consent to the treaty, Robert Morris, a staunch Washington supporter, requested that a section be reread. When that was done, Senator Maclay insisted that some additional papers be read, and Knox gave the senators more information on the situation with other Indian tribes. Knox then was asked when General Benjamin Lincoln, the newly appointed commissioner to the Indian tribes, would be in New York, and he responded, "Not 'til Saturday next." This brief exchange marked the first and probably the only time a member of the cabinet has been interrogated in front of the full Senate.

As the debate dragged on, a member of the Georgia delegation asked that the whole matter be postponed until the next Monday. An annoyed Washington is supposed to have blurted out, "This defeats every purpose of my coming here." Regaining his composure, the President left in what one observer characterized as "sullen dignity." On Monday the President reappeared in a more placid mood and listened for several hours to the debate, but as he left the Senate, he was overheard to complain that he would be "damned if he ever went there again." The treaty finally passed with some minor changes, but Washington never again appeared for the Senate's debates. Interestingly enough, the formal role of the Senate also changed from advice and consent to one in which it would simply approve or disapprove final treaties.[2]

Knox's main relations with the Congress, though, involved trying to get support for the establishment of a national militia. The new Congress, however, retained the traditional American distrust of standing armies, especially when commanded by federal authorities. Knox sought, with Washington's approval, to enroll all male citizens between the ages of eighteen and sixty into legions, subdivided into three classes: the Advanced Corps, the Main Corps, and the Reserves. Each subdivision was to consist of 2,853 commissioned officers. Congress, however, on March 5 approved a much more modest and scaled down plan.

Knox also turned his efforts to recruiting, and issued instructions that new soldiers were to be enlisted for three years, paid a bounty of $8, be at least five feet five inches tall, possess good character, be in good health, preferably be single, and be between the ages of eighteen and forty-five. No blacks or mulattoes were enlisted, and no one could join the army while he was in a state of intoxication.

Knox's support for a strong national army came out of his own commitment to the military as well as to the wide-ranging problems the new government faced on the frontier. The presence of Indian tribes in the hinterlands presented serious difficulties for the Washington administration in both its foreign and domestic policies. Some tribes, even after the Treaty of Paris ended the Revolutionary War, joined with the British in the western areas and, to a lesser extent, the Spanish in the South in refusing to acknowledge the new borders of the United States. As the American settlers and land speculators pushed deeper inland, the Indians became impediments to their ambitions.

Nearly all white politicians and leaders agreed that the tribes had to move, but some adopted a more benevolent attitude toward "the noble savage." They emphasized the values of white civilization and the benefits of commerce, usually linking the two together. Other leaders, especially those on the frontier, urged a policy of forcible removal and subjugation that, on occasion, bordered on and often became genocide. Washington and Knox followed the first approach, although their policy of paternalism was combined with a steady willingness to subdue the tribes in troubled spots.[3]

Washington was especially sensitive to the fact that the Indian situation was compounded by the informal and formal alliances some of the tribes had with foreign powers. During the Confederation period, the Wyandot, Delaware, and Shawnee Indians, with British support, raided white settlements. Washington, before his presidency, was in constant contact with Knox and others about Indian attacks, and he urged that mustered-out Continental army officers and enlisted men be encouraged to settle on the frontier.

At this time, in 1783, General Philip Schuyler of New York also wrote to the Congress, advising that the Americans had to be more flexible in dealing with the Indians. The Indians would, of course, have to lose some of their lands because of their support of the British, although they would retreat in many cases because of the scarcity of game as civilization advanced. Thus, if the Americans were patient, they would not have to pay compensation for these lands. Washington agreed with Schuyler's general policy and proposed that a discernible, but not necessarily permanent, boundary be established between the settlers and the Indians to avoid conflicts. At all costs, war should be avoided, for "there is nothing to be obtained by an Indian War but the soil they live on and this can be had by purchase at less expense," Washington counseled.

The Indians, however, did not accept the logic of American expansion, nor did they want to give up their ties to the land and to the way of life that for them often had religious significance. Tribal leaders did not see how they were obliged to surrender large tracts of land because of their alliance with the British during the war. The lands were historically theirs, and the British were simply protectors of the tribes' right to them. In a practical sense, the Indians were also in firm control of most of these land areas and were determined to resist any attempts to push them back.

From 1784 to 1786, Congress tried to use negotiations, persuasion, and verbal threats in dealing with the Indians. At Fort Stanwix in New York, the commissioners extracted from the Six Nations major concessions of land west of Pennsylvania. Flushed with success, the Americans tried a similar approach at Fort Intosh with the Wyandots, Delawares, Ottawas, and Chippewas in order to gain lands in the eastern and southern Ohio regions, and again they were successful. In January 1786 the American government dictated terms to the Indians in the Old Northwest, including, for a time, the difficult Shawnees. By the end of the year, though, Indian resistance was growing, and at a general council of the tribes, the Indians demanded that the American government renegotiate their treaties.

The problems in the South were even more complex. State leaders in North Carolina and Georgia pursued their own Indian policies and resented any congressional intrusion; other settlers were forming a semi-independent state of "Franklin," which was meant to break off from North Carolina, and these individuals conducted their own aggressive actions against the Cherokees. Despite the attempts of Congress in 1785 and 1786 to deal peacefully with the southern tribes, the Indians were on the verge of all-out war. By the end of 1786 the Indian policy of the national government was in ruins in the North and collapsing in the South. Unwilling to abandon the advantages of acquisition and speculation, and yet unable to establish a firm peace, the Americans were increasingly concerned with military security in these areas. As for the tribes, their position was becoming more belligerent and threatening. The tribes were not led by semi-human savages or by gracious noble redmen. The chiefs were, as a group, determined warriors, skilled in frontier warfare and as capable of brutality as their white neighbors.

Knox, trying to set policy during the Confederation period, found the troops "utterly incompetent" to protect the vast Old Northwest frontier. The Secretary argued vigorously that the government should purchase those Indian lands already ceded in the 1784–1786 treaties. In early 1789 General St. Clair committed the government at Fort Harmar to giving about $9,000 worth of commodities to the Indians in the Northwest in order to get them to reaffirm their previous treaties. But again, many of the Indians were affronted by the terms, and hostilities continued. In the South the situation had grown worse as speculators and settlers confronted aggressive and confident Indian leaders. By 1789 the Ohio area was the site of pillage and murder, and Knox tried to intervene by offering peace negotiations.

When Washington assumed office, Knox laid before the new President his options: a war involving 2,500 soldiers and costing $200,000, or a concerted effort to offer bribes and presents that would cost $16,000. For a small and frugal national government, these costs were significant. Indeed, from 1790 to 1796, almost five-sixths of the general expenses of the government went to pay for the wars in the West.[4]

The new administration soon received petitions and letters from the Ohio Valley communities requesting assistance. Washington forwarded to Congress a letter from St. Clair asking for authorization to call out the frontier militia. Congress was then in the midst of a debate on a bill to reorganize the current military establishment, and some representatives prophetically objected that this simple authorization would grant to the President the power to start, in effect, a war against the various Indian tribes. But Washington's personal prestige, his experience in Indian affairs, and the press of other business led to congressional approval. Later, when the Indian campaign in Ohio ran into difficulties, Washington cited this language as authorizing the campaign. Then the Congress realized, as did so many other congresses after it, that it had given the president permission to wage war without ever being aware of it at the time.

Neither Knox nor the President wanted war, and neither recognized that their policy would lead to major campaigns against the Indians. Yet, even with Washington's often-stated policy of peace, he followed an inconsistent pattern that made war probably inevitable. Although the administration talked of treaty and conciliation, it used the army to punish the various Indian tribes into negotiations, forcing them to reach agreements along the lines the government wanted. The Indians undoubtedly regarded this use of limited force as total war, and they responded by retribution.

Within a year, the agitation in Kentucky increased markedly, and some settlers began to press for detaching that region from the United States and linking it up as an independent nation under Spanish protection. Land speculation also increased and the Indians became more inflamed. The new administration found its prestige on the line, and the President and Knox decided to take a firm stand. On January 12, 1790, Washington asked Congress for another regiment of regular infantry. The Senate cut back the request, but the administration moved ahead along the obvious path by approving the assignment of eight militia scouts for each frontier county.

Washington found himself in a difficult position as hostilities between the Indians and the settlers increased. He saw strong sentiment in parts of the West for a separation from the weak new Republic, as the United States, without a large standing army, seemed unable to protect its own citizens and deal with British and Spanish intrusions. In Congress the costs and the very establishment of a standing army frightened some Federalists from New England who were less concerned about the frontier than their Republican counterparts who had political support in that area. The President sent out agents to treat for peace, while at the same time he was seriously considering military action against the more aggressive tribes. As so often happens in politics, the impetus for war easily overtook the general impulses for peace.

In the Southwest, General Anthony Wayne wanted to move aggressively against the Cherokees and their allies, the Creeks and Choctaws. But Knox, once again, turned away from full-scale confrontation and persuaded the President to invite one of the major Creek chiefs, Alexander McGillivray, to the capital. Rather astute and well educated, McGillivray understood the fluidity of the frontier situation. Although in the pay of Spain, McGillivray recognized the need to deal with the new American government. Washington, at first, sent a special emissary, Marinus Willett, to the Creek nation, and he argued that the new President wanted none of its lands and only desired to see that all proper claims were settled. In sentiments that were to be repeated countless times by other government agents, Willett said that the Creeks could send a delegation to New York City, where a treaty would be made "as strong as the hills and lasting as the rivers." While McGillivray doubted that Washington was moved only by feelings of "justice and humanity" as Willett claimed, nonetheless the chief believed that he could obtain some advantages for the Creeks. So, together with his entourage, the chief made his way through the wilderness, into North Carolina, and then on to Richmond, Fredericksburg, and Philadelphia. When McGillivray and the twenty-nine other Creek chiefs arrived in New York on July 20, 1790, they were greeted by the newly organized Society of St. Tammany, whose members were dressed in full regalia and who escorted the Indians to Federal Hall and on to meet the President.

After some discussion and amid great festivities, the government and the tribal chiefs concluded a major peace treaty on August 7. The treaty provided for the normal expressions of peace and friendship and placed the Creeks under the protection of the United States. A joint commission of "three old citizens of Georgia and three old Creek Chiefs" was to establish the boundaries. The Creeks were left to punish any white intruder who settled on their land and American citizens were forbidden to hunt there; Creeks committing capital crimes were to be delivered over to the U.S. government. The Indians were to be given cattle, tools, and the services of interpreters. Most important, the Creeks agreed to give up most of the disputed lands in Georgia. After the ceremony, the President gave each Indian a string of beads and a package of tobacco. In return, the Creek leaders sang a "song of peace," and Washington personally appointed McGillivray a brigadier general in the army and a U.S. Indian agent. The Senate promptly approved the trip, and it appeared that some of the President's and Knox's efforts were beginning to bear fruit, at least in the Southwest.[5]

In the Northwest, however, the administration's earlier tough stance led to one disaster after another. After the Miami and Wabash Indians continued their attacks on the boats in the Ohio and Wabash rivers and began burning villages and killing settlers, Washington agreed to begin a military campaign in that area, to be headed up by the governor of the Northwest Territory, Arthur St. Clair. By late May 1790 Knox reviewed the reports of the Indian pillage and urged that the troops "strike a terror in the minds of the Indians." The President apparently agreed, and on June 7 Knox ordered St. Clair and General Josiah Harmar to organize the expedition.

The American force under General Josiah Harmar, a man known for his appreciation of the non-medicinal uses of liquor, included a 1,500-man force that assembled at Fort Washington (now Cincinnati). Both Knox and the President advised St. Clair that he and the commander should attempt to identify friendly Indians first, and try to get the Wabash tribes to agree to a peace treaty. But St. Clair and Harmar argued for a military solution and planned a two-pronged attack to destroy quickly the Wabash and Miami villages. After some misgivings, Washington and Knox approved the strategy, trusting the judgment of the men in the field. Military strategy took precedence over the political objectives it was supposed to serve. The Indian tribes, however, proved to be more effective than imagined, and despite Harmar's later claims of victory, the American army was overpowered and badly defeated.[6]

When news of the defeat reached Philadelphia, Congress was shocked. Serious questions were raised about the ability of the War Department to provide direction and matériel for the army, and the entire administration strategy was being criticized in Congress. Washington, a longtime survivor of defeats and miscalculations, quickly laid the full written record of his reservations and warning before Congress, and he allowed Harmar to take the brunt of the criticism.

The President and Knox were fully aware that the Indian tribes in that area would now become more confident because of their victory. The administration moved to send a 3,000-man army to the Ohio territory, and had the army supplemented by volunteers enlisted by the government for the duration of the campaign. In the wake of Harmar's defeat, Congress grew skeptical about the costs of escalating the war and creating a substantial volunteer army. To sway the Congress, Knox released a long and pathetic letter from Rufus Putnam, the leader of the Ohio Company, which in frightening terms outlined the massacre that had taken place at Big Bottom and begged for help. Partially as a result of that letter, Congress supported the Administration's request and gave the President the authority to create another regiment, call up 2,000 volunteers, establish new posts, and appoint officers without Senate approval.

The War Department moved quickly to assume more centralized control over the army and its operations. Knox continued to urge negotiations, but the language of one of his "requests" is rather instructive: "Reflect that this is the last offer that can be made; that, if you do not embrace it now, your doom must be sealed forever." A continuation of war was clearly the likely outcome, and a concerned Knox sent Timothy Pickering to urge the Six Nations to remain neutral in case of war in the Northwest. Meanwhile in the Southwestern Territories, Governor William Blount attempted to guarantee Cherokee neutrality.

On the frontier, St. Clair, plagued by supply problems and personal illness, moved his troops toward Miami Village. On November 4, when he was halfway there, his army of 1,400 men was nearly annihilated. In addition, more than fifty women camp followers were killed, and according to one officer there, "some of them [were] cut in two, their bubbies cut off, and burning." Washington learned of St. Clair's humiliating defeat while he was giving a dinner party in early December 1791. Going into the hallway, an angry President read the dispatch from the Ohio area detailing St. Clair's defeat at the hands of the Miamis and their allies, under Chief Little Turtle. Some 550 regulars had been killed, 200 wounded, 41 militia dead, 34 wounded. Washington rejoined his guests and conversed pleasantly throughout the evening until ten o'clock, when his guests left. Then he went into his study and furiously denounced the expedition to Lear:

It's all over!—St. Clair defeated!—routed: the officers nearly all killed, the men by wholesale; the rout complete; too shocking to think of, and a surprise into the bargain! Yes, here on this very spot, I took leave of him: I wished him success and honor. "You have your instructions from the Secretary of War," said I. "I had a strict eye to them, and will add but one word, Beware of a Surprise! You know how the Indians fight us. I repeat it, Beware of a Surprise." He went off with that, my last warning, thrown into his ears. And yet! To suffer that an army to be cut to pieces, hacked, butchered, tomahawked, by a surprise—the very thing I guarded him against—O God! O God! He's worse than a murderer! How can he answer it to his country'! The blood of the slain is upon him—the curse of widows and orphans—the curse of heaven.[7]

Washington found himself once again in a bad political situation, and this time the House of Representatives ordered an investigation and appointed a committee to look into the cause of the defeat. The committee called on the President and asked for relevant War Department documents. Their inquiry was the first legislative request for executive documents, and Washington was clearly aware of the precedent he was establishing. Although some historians in the 1960s have argued that the claims of executive privilege originated in the Eisenhower term, the record is clear that from the time of the Washington administration, presidents have maintained a right to withhold information and have done so at various times.

Washington summoned one of his first cabinet meetings and, as Jefferson related it, at the time "neither acknowledged nor denied nor even doubted the propriety of what the House was doing, for he had not thought upon it, nor was acquainted with subjects of this kind: he could readily conceive that there might be papers of so select a nature, as they might not be given up."[8]

The cabinet members took time to think over the matter, and two days later they urged that in the future, all requests for information go to the President rather than to individual ministers, with the executives using, in each case, his own discretion on what to release. The cabinet members seemed to agree that such papers should be given where "the public good would permit and [the executive] ought to refuse those, the disclosure of which would bring injury to the public." Interestingly enough, they consulted the proceedings of the House of Commons in the case of Robert Walpole.★

Jefferson recorded that he thought Hamilton feared that any inquiry would reveal how much the Treasury Secretary and his allies "had been dabbling in stocks, banks, etc." Hamilton supported the request, however, concluding that "there was not a paper which might not be properly produced." Washington turned over the papers as the House requested and sent his Secretaries of War and Treasury to testify in person before Congress. The committee finally cleared St. Clair but he resigned, a major general.

Washington took on more responsibilities both in terms of frontier diplomacy and in the activities of his army in those regions. In 1792 he bluntly demanded to know from Knox "who is Mr. Rosencrantz, and under what authority has he attended councils of the Indians at Buffalo Creek? . . . No person should presume to speak to the Indians on business of a public nature except those who derive their authority and receive their instructions from the War Office for that purpose."

The details and span of Washington's authority can be seen in the correspondence between the various secretaries of War and General Wayne. When the federal government found out that some settlers intended to strike Indian villages at Sandusky, Ohio, Knox wrote in June 1792, "You will in the name of the President of the United States, positively forbid any such incursion, until the effects of the pacific overtures be known." Through his secretary of war, Washington ordered at one time or another reevaluations of court martial proceedings, instructed Wayne where to lay camp and how to discipline and train troops, designated what the destination of the troops should be, approved and disapproved promotions to higher rank, stopped a collateral expedition to the rapids of the Miami River, and laid out the terms of a proposed peace treaty. When Wayne decided to brand the forehead of a deserter with the word "Coward," Knox warned the impulsive General against "uncommon punishments." Frustrated by the various controls placed on him, Wayne wrote to Knox words that have since been repeated by many military commanders chafing under political restraints: "Would to God that my hands were untied."[9]

As Washington exercised more authority in the Indian problem, he seemed to express disagreement with his own general policy over the years. On at least one occasion he advised that "no idea of purchasing land from

---

★The precedents that Jefferson cited from the 1741 parliamentary debates were somewhat more complex than the proposed St. Clair inquiry. Three major motions were offered in the House of Commons: the first was to refer to a select committee several papers that had been laid before the House on the Conduct of the War. That motion was defeated, as was the second motion to conduct an inquiry into the conduct of public affairs over the previous twenty years. A third major motion to investigate the conduct of Robert, Earl of Oxford, did pass.

them [Indians] ought to be admitted—for no treaty or other communication with the Indians have *ever* been satisfactory to them when this has been the subject." Still, recognizing the weakness of his army and the broad expanse of the frontier, Washington could not give up on diplomacy altogether. After St. Clair's disastrous rout, Washington decided to deal directly with the Senecas, who had close ties with the more aggressive Western tribes. The President invited the Seneca chief, Cornplanter, to attend a council in Philadelphia. On December 1, 1790, Cornplanter promoted the Indian case in eloquent terms, arguing that the Americans had broken the treaty signed at Fort Stanwix and had taken land that was the Indians' and not the property of the British.

Father: The voice of the Seneca nation speaks to you, the great councilor in whose heart the wise men of all the Thirteen Fires have placed their wisdom. It may be very small in your ears, and we therefore entreat you to hearken with attention: for we are about to speak of things which are to us very great. When your army entered the country of the Six Nations, we called you the town destroyer; and to this day, when the name is heard, our women look behind them and turn pale, and our children cling close to the necks of their mothers. . . .

Everyone said that your hearts were yet swelled with resentment against us for what had happened during the war, but that one day you would reconsider it with more kindness. We asked each other, what have we done to deserve such chastisement? . . . What the Seneca nation promise, they faithfully perform; and when you refused obedience to that king, he commanded us to assist his beloved men in making you sober. In obeying him we did no more than you yourselves had led us to promise. The men who claimed this promise told us that you were children, and had no guns; that when they had shaken you, you would submit. We hearkened to them, and were deceived; but your people, in teaching us to confide in that king, had helped to deceive, and now we appeal to your heart—Is the blame all ours? . . .

All the lands we have been speaking of belonged to the Six Nations; no part of it ever belonged to the King of England, and he could not give it to you. The land we live on, our fathers received from God, and they transmitted it to us, for our children, and we cannot part with it. . . .

Father: Innocent men of our nation are killed one after another and of our best families; but none of your people who have committed the murders have been punished. We recollect that you did not promise to punish those who killed our people, and we now ask, was it intended that your people should kill the Senecas, and not only remain unpunished by you, but be protected by you against the revenge of the next of kin.

Father, these to us are very great things. We know that you are very strong, and we have heard that you are wise, and we wait to hear your answer to what we have said, that we may know that you are just.

In his written response, Washington answered that some of the difficulties that the Six Nations had were under the old Confederation and that now the federal government had the power to make a treaty with the Indian tribes:

Here then, is the security for the remainder of your lands. No State, nor person, can purchase your lands, unless at some public treaty, held under the authority of the United States. The General Government will never consent to your being defrauded, but it will protect you in all your just rights. Hear well, and let it be heard by every person in your nation, that the President of the United States declares, that the General Government considers itself bound to protect you in all the lands secured to you by the treaty of Fort Stanwix. . . .

Washington condemned the attacks of the Ohio Valley Indian tribes and warned the Six Nations not to join them:

Remember my words, Senecas! Continue to be strong in your friendship for the United States, as the only rational ground of your future happiness, and you may rely upon their kindness and protection. . . . If any man bring you evil reports of the intentions of the United States, mark that man as your enemy; for he will mean to deceive you, and lead you into trouble. The United States will be true and faithful to their engagements.[10]

The Indian leaders returned to the main Seneca village near Buffalo and assembled the neighboring tribes. After some discussion, the New York chiefs pondered whether to send a delegation to the Ohio tribes to try to induce them to meet with General St. Clair at a council at Fort Washington, but they were unable to agree.

After the meeting of Cornplanter and Washington, the President tried personal diplomacy again and had invitations extended to the leading chiefs of the Six Nations to visit the capital in late 1791 and early 1792. Some fifty chiefs accepted the invitation, but the leading chief, Captain Joseph Brant, was hesitant and did not come. The other chiefs, however, arrived on March 14 and, escorted by the fife and drum corps of the militia, made their way into Philadelphia. Washington clearly stated his purposes for the meeting when he indicated that he wanted peace and desired no lands but those obtained by treaty. He implored both the New York tribes and those in the West to understand his true objectives. After about six weeks of negotiations, Washington presented the great Indian orator Red Jacket with a huge silver medal—some seven by five inches—that depicted Washington presenting a peace pipe to an Indian chief while a white woman in the background was plowing with a yoke of oxen. On the back of the medal was the familiar American eagle and the motto "E Pluribus Unum." Red Jacket, usually suspicious of white men, was delighted with the gift and was frequently seen with it.

Some time later, Brant decided that he, too, should visit the President in Philadelphia, and Washington and Knox entertained him lavishly and offered him bribes, which he honorably turned down, being already in the employ of Britain. However, Brant did offer to intercede with the Ohio tribes and relayed Washington's request for peace. Indeed, various Indian chiefs from the New York and Canadian tribes sought to address the Northwest tribes, and at one major tribal conference, Red Jacket pressed eloquently for peace. But the Shawnee, the most bellicose tribe, responded that the "United States have laid these troubles, and they can remove these troubles. And, if they take all their forts and move back to the ancient line [the Ohio River], then we will believe that they mean to have peace, and that Washington is a great man—then we may meet the United States at Sandusky in the spring."

Although Washington and Knox pursued peace negotiations, they were faced with the problem of increasing hostilities on the frontier. After the defeats of Harmar and St. Clair, the administration felt that it necessary to establish a strong military presence in the Northwest, and after some reservations, Washington and Knox appointed Anthony Wayne to head the army in that area.

Wayne's army, named by Knox the Legion of the United States, had 2,800 men plus 1,500 Kentucky mounted militia and was well supplied. Despite an initial bout with influenza, Wayne was ready for action and he moved toward Greene, Ohio. By August he had forced the Indians to retreat to the areas near Fort Deposit in northwestern Ohio. The Shawnees and their allies, the Wyandots, however, decided to continue the war, and it was only Wayne's victory at Fallen Timbers on August 20, 1794, and the Treaty of Greenville a year later that ended the major conflicts with the Indians in the Old Northwest. Finally, in November 1796, just before his retirement from the presidency, Washington invited the leaders of the Ohio tribes to the capital and once again made them a familiar promise: a lasting peace and a life of great abundance.

Faced with serious problems over the years in the Old Northwest, the government tried to keep the Southwest tribes placated, but some Indians were being stirred up against the American settlers. In 1793 Jefferson noted that Spain was trying to instigate a quarrel with the United States, and the French minister Edmond Genet also tried to ally the Indians with the French by promising them full and peaceful possession of their former lands. Finally, Genet's demise and the treaty of October 27, 1795, with Spain ensured free navigation on the Mississippi and an end to hostilities on the frontier.[11]

Overall, then, the Indian policy of Washington and Knox was at times confusing and contradictory. Basically, they believed that tribes would move peacefully to open up the frontiers to settlers if only the Indians were treated properly. Washington and Knox both favored some compensation for these lands, including those given up in the various treaties of the late Confederation period. Despite his suspicions about Indians, the President generally insisted that the government pay for disputed lands. To Western-oriented politicians, such as Jefferson and Blount, Washington's concern seemed unwarranted, for these lands were once British and after the war became part of the United States. But in his dealings with the Indians,

Washington resisted tremendous political pressures from the Western frontier leaders and fairly consistently spoke out against speculators and lawless settlers. He pursued negotiations intensively but was willing to show citizens in the West that the federal government was able to protect them and their interests. Thus the President found himself pulled by different forces. First, there were strong political pressures to protect the frontier from Indians and from the British and Spanish. Second, there was an element of the West that was quite willing to secede and form a separate unit if the new government proved weak. Third, the President and his Secretary were committed to a policy that would generally treat the Indians in a civilized way. Knox, in fact, advocated intermarriage as the solution to the hostilities. Washington probably thought in less personal terms, yet together they opposed the demands for wholesale removal and unbridled exploitation. What is remarkable about the Washington–Knox policy is that it worked reasonably well after so many military and diplomatic fiascos.

For the Indians, though, the consequences were the same—constant pressure to give up the land that was the very source of their pastoral or agrarian ways of life. The conflict between those ways of life and their acquisitive and speculative landholding neighbors was inevitable. Washington and Knox sought to contain that conflict, to deal with it, usually in a moderate way, and their success can be appreciated only if one is familiar with the brutal Indian policies of future administrations. Then the ugly forces of exploitation and racial hatred were given full sway, as the government itself at times pursued a policy amounting to nothing less than tribal genocide. Although their policy was not free of nastiness, presumptuousness, and arrogance, still, taken in total, Washington and Knox were not part of the new world to come. Surely, though, as they cast a cold eye over the frontier, they would see the seeds of it being sown.[12]

19

FATHERING THE PARTIES

These lawyers, and men of learning, and moneyed men expect to be
the managers of this Constitution, and get all the power and all the money
into their hands.

Amos Singletary,
Massachusetts Ratifying Convention, 1788

In our era of still identifiable parties and partisan voting, it is difficult to realize that for a long period in American and European history, the growth of
factions and parties was resisted by most respectable elements of society.
Surely personal cliques and groups often sprung up around a popular leader
or family, but cohesive and long-lasting alliances were rare in early
America.[1]

Historian Jackson Turner Main had found, however, that on the state
levels in colonial times, one could see legislative blocs arising that had
common attitudes that tended to persist over time. One group, which he
called "Cosmopolitans," came from relatively urban, more affluent areas
with an economy based on overseas trade, extensive internal commerce,
limited manufacturing, stable crops, and a concentration of fluid capital.
The second group, "the Locals," lived primarily in inland areas that lacked
easy access to markets, were more recently settled, and were agricultural
communities that had fairly egalitarian social structures.[2]

On a national level, the main political divisions were not based on such orientations, but on the geographical and social differences between New England
and the Southern colonies, with the Middle States and their delegations often
being uncohesive. These divisions were important and intense at times, but they
did not immediately lead to a party system in the new nation.

Several factors retarded the growth of parties. First, influential Whig
thinkers in both England and America had long opposed the development
of factions, as they called them, fearing that they destroyed the unity and

resolve of a nation. Indeed, one of the most articulate proponents of this line of thought was James Madison, who later was, ironically, the prime mover behind the Democratic–Republican party. A second factor was that in some states, such as Virginia, a strong tradition of deference was still entrenched, and the majority of voters tended to support the will and desires of the upper class. In still other states, the electoral system was so structured that opposition parties were virtually eliminated. In Connecticut, for example, the secret ballot was abolished and nominations were controlled in order to prevent major challenges. From 1788 to 1818, all members chosen for the Senate, the House of Representatives, and the upper house in the state legislature were from the Federalist party. Although Connecticut was clearly an exaggerated case, other states, in lesser degrees, used the electoral laws as a way to smother party development.[3] Oddly enough, though, it was Washington who both impeded at first and accelerated later the party system. In the new nation, communications were poor before 1790 and the government lacked any great visibility. The election of Washington in 1789 was so clearly a foregone conclusion that little partisan activity took place and factions did not grow up around the most important office in the land. Except for some sentimental support for the aged Franklin and some mention of John Hancock, who was thought to be a bit erratic or too ambitious, Washington's name monopolized the pre-election conversations. After some mild stage managing by pro-Constitution figures in major cities, the General won unanimous approval.[4]

In one sense, then, Washington's selection muted the need for a party system, and yet, because of his policies and leadership, his administration unwittingly furthered the growth of a partisan spirit and institutions. Supporting a strong nationalistic economic policy and asserting executive prerogatives in the areas of foreign policy and frontier security, Washington made the executive branch a rather visible and somewhat controversial establishment. The basic issues that were to divide Americans were the Hamiltonian economic policies, the foreign policy of neutrality, and, to a lesser extent, the Indian question and the growth of a strong military. In following these directions, Washington not only split his own administration, but also helped to create a national agenda that allowed local candidates to differentiate themselves back home and in the capital. The first President was to learn quickly what most modern executives have found out: that to make decisions is to make enemies, and in politics, enemies coalesce and multiply. Increasingly in the First, the Second, and then the Third Congress, members began to become polarized, and long-lasting factions acquired leaders and ideologies.[5]

In the First Congress, the congressional parties had a clear sectional base, with New Englanders and Southerners voting almost en bloc on the major issue of locating a permanent seat of government. In the Second Congress, the issue of reapportionment of the House led to the same sort of regional coalitions. But on other issues, such as debt assumption, frontier policy, and Indian affairs, there does not seem to be partisan voting patterns. On the debt issue, for example, voting cohesiveness was not regional or partisan, but based understandably on the specific monetary interests of the different states. Two strong Federalist leaders, Rufus King of New York and Oliver Ellsworth of Connecticut, voted differently, according to their states' relative indebtedness.

But as the conflicts became more intense and the public became more aware, opposition to the administration was organized and began to hold from one issue to another. In the Third Senate in December 1793, the two factions were locked in a bitter controversy over the establishment of a national bank. In the House, during the next session, the two factions demonstrated considerable cohesiveness in voting on issues involving the Whiskey Rebellion, Democratic–Republican societies, frontier security, and Indian affairs. Thus by the end of the Third Congress, parties were being created and voting was following such allegiances.

The birth of parties is generally attributed to the intense debate over the Jay Treaty, but actually the two voting blocs were emerging somewhat even before then. The administration, by its economic policies, strongly favored certain interests at the expense of others, and its foreign policy seemed pro-British, or at least certainly anti-French, in its orientation. Both parties were likely to generate opposition, and able leaders like Madison, Giles, Beckley, and even Jefferson became the central figures of the opposition party.

Although Washington had a great deal of support in Congress, still there were limitations on how far he could transfer his personal authority to controversial policies. The debt assumption proposal probably passed only because of the deal on the capital site. There was strong opposition to the excise tax among the rural communities, and although Republicans in Congress and outside did not formally support the Whiskey Rebellion in 1794, they were strong enough to oppose successfully in the House, support of the President's condemnation of the Democratic–Republican societies. In foreign affairs, the Neutrality Proclamation was not rejected by leaders in Congress, but their position was one of caution rather than of vigorous support for the chief executive. Later, by submitting the Jay Treaty, the first President became involved in an explosive controversy that rocked segments of the nation and sent tremors through Congress. Thus, although many people respected, and even revered, the name of Washington, they were not passive when it came to opposing at first the policies of his ministers and then the policies of the President himself.

In another way, the growth of partisanship was also facilitated by the increase in communications and the general rise in what one might call political consciousness. In the decade from 1790 to 1800, the number of newspapers in America doubled to 200, and by 1810 there were more journals of public opinion per capita in the United States than anywhere else in the world. There was also a dramatic upsurge in the number of post offices from 28 in 1776 to 75 by 1790 and 453 in 1795.[6]

Politics became more of a popular concern and news, even delayed news, was widely disseminated. Some people not only read about politics, but they began to join partisan clubs as well. The most important of these groups were Democratic–Republican societies, and the first appeared in 1793, organized by the Germans in Philadelphia. These societies were dedicated to political education, common action, and a diligent oversight of government actions. Between 1793 and 1798, more than forty-two societies were formed, and such prominent figures as David Rittenhouse, George Logan, and Alexander J. Dallas were members.

While some Federalist leaders were quick to charge that the societies were Jacobin clubs sponsored by the impetuous French minister to America, Genet, and that they were financed by French gold, the origins of the political club movement are more complex. In England there had been a "Revolutionary Society" dedicated to the celebration of the Revolution of 1688, and later in the colonies there were the "Sons of Liberty," "The Regulators" in North Carolina, and various "Whig" clubs that were all precursors of the Democratic–Republican movement. Some of the impetus for these new American clubs came from major republican figures who had initially opposed the adoption of the Constitution and who pushed for a bill of rights.

The most important factor contributing to the creation of the societies, though, was the increasing controversy over Federalist policies. The democratic clubs were made of a diverse group of people: local merchants who did little business with Britain, manufacturers in competition with British industries, mechanics, seamen, and other elements of what one Federalist called "the swinish multitude." A good number of physicians and some intellectuals mixed with land speculators and Western frontier democrats in filling the ranks of the clubs. The great pamphleteer Thomas Paine gave his royalties to these societies, and his friend Jefferson called the clubs a rekindling of the spirit of 1776.[7]

Political unrest increased in the United States and in France, and then in England, Ireland, and other parts of western Europe. The rise in population, the dislocations owing to the economic and technological changes, and the increase in communication, all helped to create a new concept of citizenship and greater demands for political reform. In the United States, the ferment was localized, and national political issues only later became focal points of controversy. At first, the loose collection of states and territories had no national parties, no national partisan principles, no national political organizers. When issues materialized and divisions occurred, a nascent party system was created and the leaders emerged out of the President's own cabinet. The early unity of the new nation was quickly shattered by the contentious spirit and by the crass calculus of personal interests.[8]

20

A FALLING OUT OF SONS

Are the people in your quarter as well contented with the proceedings of our government as their representatives say they are?
                    Thomas Jefferson to Robert Livingston,
                                        February 4, 1791

While Washington sought to create a strong cabinet to administer the new government, he ended up choosing men who not only acted often independently, but who also became focal points of partisan controversy. The major adversaries were his Secretary of Treasury, Alexander Hamilton, and his Secretary of State, Thomas Jefferson, both of whom mixed personal animosity, raw ambition, political acumen, erudite philosophy, and backstage intrigue in volatile ways. What is remarkable, though, is not that Hamilton and Jefferson opposed each other on great public issues, but that Washington was able to harness both for so long in the same cabinet. For him it was important to keep them together, but that decision was one the President would pay dearly for before the end of his term in office.

Hamilton at thirty-seven was a dashing figure with incredible intellectual gifts and a fiercely burning ambition. With a fair complexion, rosy cheeks, dark—almost violet—eyes, and reddish hair that was tastefully styled and powdered, he was the picture of the handsome courtier. As one historian has noted, Hamilton was "graceful and debonair, elegant and courtly, seductive and ingratiating, playful or impassioned, he could have fitted into the picture at the Versailles of Louis XV." Born in the West Indies, he was the illegitimate son of a drifting trader. He attended King's College (later Columbia) and served at the age of twenty-two as Washington's aide-de-camp. Washington, in some ways a reserved and lonely man, began to develop a close attachment to Hamilton, perhaps out of a paternal need that he could not fulfill, having no children of his own. But Hamilton rebuffed Washington, concluding that the General was "neither remarkable for delicacy nor good temper," and adding that he wished "to stand rather on a footing of military confidence than of private attachment."[1]

Hamilton tried to move on to a more glamorous command, but Washington was reluctant to let the talented Hamilton leave his service. Finally Hamilton provoked an argument, refused to accept Washington's apology, and left the General's household. After the war, Washington returned to Mount Vernon and finally agreed to preside over the Philadelphia Constitutional Convention. There he watched as Hamilton proposed to an incredulous convention that they create a British form of government with an executive elected for life. That speech would haunt Hamilton for the rest of his life, and to latter-day Republicans, it explained much of his economic policies and his anti-democratic sentiments.

After the war, Washington's most influential circle of friends included old army officers like Benjamin Lincoln and Henry Knox and fellow Virginians like the brilliant Mr. Madison, but not Hamilton; he was once again an outsider. Indeed, although Washington heeded the advice of Robert Morris and James Madison and chose Hamilton to be secretary of the treasury, the relationship was, in the beginning, rather formal for two people who had once been so close.[2]

As for Jefferson, Washington was obviously familiar with him but more by reputation than by personal acquaintance. They were both from the gentlemen planter class, but their personal relationship was limited. They had served in the House of Burgesses together, but when Jefferson went to the Continental Congress, Washington had left to become Commander-in-Chief. As Governor of Virginia during the war, Jefferson corresponded regularly with Washington, who was then in the North. When the war was over, Washington and Jefferson continued to write to each other frequently, until Jefferson left to become Minister to France, replacing Benjamin Franklin.

In appearance, Jefferson was quite different from his rival Hamilton. Although he, too, had red hair (as did Washington as well), the forty-six-year-old Virginian was as tall as Washington (6'2"), loose-jointed, gangly, and sometimes disheveled. To some extent, he presented the image of an easygoing, wealthy planter who had just finished working on the account books back home. But under that exterior, Jefferson was a man with an insatiable curiosity about life and a dreamy love of leisure and quiet. The author of the most memorable statement of American ideology, he still felt at middle age somewhat of a failure and, like Washington, was haunted by bouts of loneliness. A widower at thirty-nine, Jefferson swore never to remarry and he was to spend the rest of his life a passionate man devoted to passionate causes, trying to express himself in temperate ways. Fearful of controversy, sensitive to personal attacks, he was to become the most controversial public figure of his generation.[3]

In August 1789 Jefferson was still enjoying the culture and romance of

France and nearby Italy, and planning to return home. Then Washington, through Madison, approached Jefferson to be Secretary of State. Jefferson had serious reservations about continuing public life, but he finally took the position on March 21, 1790, after having received the offer in December of the previous year. Jefferson, whose father died when he was only fourteen, had a profound, almost filial respect for Washington, regarding him as one of the greatest, if not the greatest, men of his age. Both Hamilton and Jefferson sought to please the President, and there is in the correspondence of both secretaries elements of personal jealousy and sibling-like rivalry that interweave with the major political and philosophical controversies of the period.

As far as is known, Jefferson and Hamilton had not personally met each other before March 1790. When Jefferson arrived, Hamilton was clearly the major figure in the cabinet and his ideas on debt assumption and funding were being debated regularly in the capital. Jefferson seemed to be raising no objections to plans that he admitted he only vaguely comprehended. During this major controversy, Washington was taken ill with pneumonia, nearly died, and thus provided his secretaries with little guidance on the matter.

Many historians believe that it was during this summer that Jefferson, Hamilton, and Madison made their so-called deal, linking debt assumption to the location of the capital. Jefferson, as has been noted, said later that he had been "duped" by Hamilton, and that "of all the errors of my political life, this has occasioned me the most regret." Yet, at that time, Jefferson saw the particular deal as a necessary compromise to solve a difficult economic problem and prevent growing political turmoil in the New England states. His eventual disillusionment was partly due to his later clashes with Hamilton and to the fact that he probably did not fully comprehend the full dimensions and objectives of the Hamilton plan. After the bank controversy, Jefferson and Hamilton began to part company, and their personal differences became entangled in the major political controversies of the 1790s.[4]

The rivalry between the two Secretaries was apparent in a variety of situations. Jefferson, with some justification, resented Hamilton's communications with the British minister in the United States and regarded such actions as an interference in his department. Yet, in 1791, Jefferson attempted to get Tench Coxe appointed Comptroller of the Treasury, an obvious intrusion in Hamilton's domain. Furthermore, during that period, when Congress debated the presidential succession bill, Jefferson's supporters pressed for the Secretary of State to be next in line after the Vice-President, while Hamilton had his followers oppose this designation and substituted the president pro tem of the Senate and the Speaker of the House ahead of the cabinet officers.

Hamilton had one great advantage in the first year or so of the administration. The major issues were economic and his department controlled nearly all the patronage appointments in the new government. Whereas the State Department employed 4 clerks and the War Department had 3, the Treasury supervised 1,000 custom house officers and revenue agents, 30 clerks, a treasurer, a comptroller, and several other officials.

Like a great patriarch presiding over a quarrelsome extended family, Washington, by his own account, recognized that there were some differences of opinion and temperament, but he did not at first comprehend the full dimensions of the animosity. Shrewdly, he tried to manage the conflict by flattery, fatherly admonitions, joint meetings, personalized attention, and even, on occasion, a picnic. The President attempted to channel the energies of Hamilton and Jefferson into a common set of policies, and for a time, he seemed to be successful.

However, in early December of 1790, Jefferson was beginning to have some misgivings about the Hamiltonian program. He wrote to several friends to see if the people in their areas were pleased with the new economic policies. Despite his own discontent, though, it was really Madison who assumed the leadership of the Republican cause, not Jefferson. From his position in the House, Madison began to oppose Hamilton for what seemed at first to be sectional differences. But by the time of the bank controversy, he was clearly in the forefront of the opposition. His objections about the Bank of the United States, linked with Jefferson's and Randolph's opinions, nearly caused Washington to veto Hamilton's major initiative.

Then, in early 1791, Jefferson found himself in one of those controversies that he fell into from time to time because of an indiscreet remark or released letter. Madison had sent his fellow Virginian a copy of Paine's *Rights of Man* and asked Jefferson, on reading it, to forward it to Jonathan B. Smith, whose brother was to reprint the work. Jefferson, in a friendly gesture, decided to send along a personal note, rather than a simple letter of transmittal. He indicated that he was pleased to find that the pamphlet was to be printed in Philadelphia and approved that "something was at length to be publicly said about the political heresies which had of late sprung up among us, not doubting that our citizens would rally around the standard of Common Sense." When the pamphlet finally appeared, Jefferson's cursory note was printed as the foreword. His opponents accused him of fomenting trouble in the administration, and Hamilton let it be known that he was critical of such sentiments. An embarrassed Jefferson decided to say nothing, hoping that the controversy would pass. However, the incident led some to see Jefferson as the major defender of republicanism and as a central antagonist in opposing Hamilton's programs. In the midst of the controversy, Jefferson and Madison made their famous trip up the Hudson River to Lake George and Lake Champlain to examine the foliage. According to Hamilton's friends, Jefferson and Madison were cementing an alliance between Virginia and New York to undercut Hamilton's allies.

There is really no evidence that the Virginians did more than take notes on the botanical wonders of the area, but to the Federalists, the trip was not scientific in the least.

When Madison and Jefferson returned, the controversy over the latter's foreword was still causing comment. A writer called "Publicola" attacked Paine and defended John Adams' recent conservative political work *Discourses*, which Jefferson's note had, by implication, slighted. Most political leaders quickly assumed that the writer was the Vice-President himself, but it turned out to be his twenty-four-year-old son, John Quincy Adams. Soon the younger Adams' attack was followed by a host of Republican responses, and a pamphlet war ensued.[5]

As the controversies continued, Jefferson and Madison came to believe that the Republicans needed a paper that could counter Federalist propaganda, especially John Fenno's influential *Gazette of the United States*. Madison, who pursued the matter with more vigor than Jefferson, suggested that they help set up in business his old Princeton classmate and poet of the Revolution, Philip Freneau, who was then working for the *New York Daily Advertiser*.

To provide him with some small income, Freneau's name was suggested to Jefferson for an opening as a translating clerk in the State Department. Jefferson quickly agreed and offered him the position at the meager annual salary of $250, but Freneau declined, citing his desire to establish a paper in Monmouth County, New Jersey, instead. Madison, however, persevered and continued to discuss the project with Freneau until he consented to take the job in the State Department and arranged to publish a new gazette in Philadelphia. Convinced of the need to support a party organ, Madison started rounding up subscriptions and Jefferson made a financial advance to Freneau to help the paper along. Although outnumbered in Congress and outflanked in the cabinet, the Republican message would now be presented to the nation at large, a message that sought to attack the "monarchial" impulse whenever it reared its ugly head.

For the first couple of months, Freneau's publication was generally moderate in tone, but by March 1792 the *National Gazette* launched a series of broadsides criticizing Hamilton's funding system and his bank proposal, and taking aim at the stockholders and alleged speculators who occupied seats in Congress. Fenno counterattacked, and by midsummer a fierce partisan newspaper war was underway.[6]

As for Washington, he watched these developments with some dismay. The split between his two ambitious and sensitive Secretaries seemed at first to be grounded more in personal differences than in philosophies. As time passed, though, the controversies multiplied and increasing acrimony resulted, leading to the growth of factionalism, the rise of Democratic–Republican clubs, a national division over the French Revolution, and a full-scale and bitter debate about the directions of American foreign policy.

The Hamilton–Jefferson feud was a prism through which these controversies were refracted, and even Washington, with all of his care and goodwill, was unable to master the currents. He was to know controversy as he had never known it before.

21

THE FIRES OF
FACTIONALISM, 1792

My earnest wish and my fondest hope . . . is that instead of wounding suspicious and irritable charges, there may be liberal allowances, mutual forebearances and temporizing yieldings on *all sides*.

Washington to Jefferson,
August 26, 1792

As the estrangement between Hamilton and Jefferson became more severe, the administration was also faced with several diplomatic controversies that were to heighten that dispute. In August 1791 the French government sent over a new minister to the United States, Jean Baptiste Ternant, who was a friend of Lafayette and who had served as an officer in the American Revolution. Despite his Francophile reputation, Jefferson, as Secretary of State, was careful to maintain a rather proper and formal relationship with Ternant. It was Hamilton, continuing to fashion himself as a prime minister, who cornered Ternant and talked of a need for a new commercial treaty. The French minister understandably believed that he was being sounded out on a proposed American policy, and he became confused when Washington seemed to be as reserved as his Secretary of State.

The situation was further complicated when some time later the British decided to send to the United States a twenty-eight-year-old Minister Plenipotentiary, George Hammond, to reestablish full diplomatic relations. Hammond had been carefully instructed to cultivate influential people in his new post, especially Hamilton. The young minister found Hamilton to be a man characterized by a "just and liberal way of thinking," and he was sure that the Secretary belonged to the "party of the English interest."[1]

Both Secretaries had dealings with Hammond. Jefferson, however, was primarily interested in getting the British out of the Northwest frontier posts, and he closely questioned the minister on that point of contention between the two nations. It soon became clear that the British minister could discuss such matters but could not conclude any agreements. Hammond relayed the British position that several articles of the Treaty of Paris had not been fully lived up to on the American side either, especially those provisions dealing with the recovery of old debts and the confiscation of Loyalist lands. Jefferson's view was that the British wanted to grant no concessions and avoid American discriminatory tariff measures. As for Hamilton, he continued his own diplomatic overtures to Hammond, hoping to forge closer ties between the two nations and, in the process, undercut the administration's Secretary of State.

With foreign ministers arriving at Philadelphia and problems arising on the frontier, Washington moved to name his own ministers to three major posts. He asked the Senate to approve the selection of Thomas Pinckney for London, Gouverneur Morris for Paris, and William Short for The Hague. The Senate immediately raised the general question of whether it was really desirable to appoint ministers plenipotentiary at all to reside permanently at foreign courts. Jefferson wrote for the President a strong declaration of executive prerogatives in which he asserted that, constitutionally, the president was the sole competent judge on questions of grade and designation of ministers. Congress could periodically review the entire diplomatic establishment and could withhold its consent to particular nominees, but the executive retained specific prerogatives in this area.

Washington decided to let the challenge pass by quietly, and the issue was simply referred to a Senate committee. The three nominees passed the Senate, although Morris was approved by a vote of sixteen to eleven and Short's nomination was forwarded only after the vice-president broke a tie. In the latter case, the Senate was uncertain if the United States needed a minister to The Hague at all. But as for Morris, the opposition was sparked by strong personal dislike. Washington, in a cordial but frank letter, told Morris:

It was urged that your habits of expression indicated a hauteur disgusting to those who happen to differ from you in sentiment, and among a people who study civility and politeness more than any other nation, it must be displeasing; that in France you were considered as a favorer of aristocracy and unfriendly to its Revolution (I suppose they meant constitution). That under this impression, you could not be an acceptable public character. . . . That the promptitude with which your lively and brilliant imagination is displayed allows too little time for deliberation and correction and is the primary cause of those sallies which too often offend, and of that ridicule of characters which begets enmity not easy to be forgotten, but which might easily be avoided if it was under the control of more caution and prudence. In a word, that it is indispensibly necessary that more circumspection should be observed by our representatives abroad than they conceive you are inclined to adopt.

In this statement you have the pros and cons. By reciting them, I give you a proof of my friendship if I give none of my policy or judgment. I do it on the presumption that a mind conscious of its own rectitude fears not what is said of it, but will bid defiance to and despise shafts that are not barbed with accusations against honor or integrity. And because I have the fullest confidence (supposing the allegations to be founded in whole or in part) that you would find no difficulty . . . to effect a change and thereby silence, in the most unequivocal and satisfactory manner, your political opponents.

Of my good opinion and of my friendship and regard, you may be assured.[2]

Despite his reservations, Washington supported Morris' appointment because of their close friendship and because Morris shared his skepticism about recent occurrences in France. After some initial sympathy, the President was becoming apprehensive about the course the French Revolution was taking. One good example of his feelings was exhibited when the King addressed a letter to the United States announcing his acceptance of the new French constitution. The President passed it on to the Congress for their information. The House overwhelmingly passed a resolution of support and asked the President, in his reply to the King, to express their approval of "this great and important event." Washington, feeling that the House was attempting to invade his prerogatives, was unwilling to send any statement of approval. Commenting on the situation, Jefferson moved to reassure Washington that the House's expression of support of the French constitution, if it were an invasion of executive prerogative, was a rather faint one. But privately the Secretary told others that the larger issue was that Morris, "a high-flying monarch-man . . . had kept the President's mind constantly poisoned with his forebodings."[3]

Jefferson not only was suspicious of Morris' attitudes, but also believed, with good reason, that Hamilton was involved in pursuing a pro-British foreign policy. The Secretary of the Treasury had been involved in conversations with Hammond that ran counter to Jefferson's tough bargaining position, and Hamilton falsely told the British minister that Washington had not read Jefferson's position papers, and thus did not support the Secretary of State's policies.

Jefferson's anger mounted and he indicated to Washington early in 1792 that he intended to resign his post at the end of the President's term. When Washington and Jefferson discussed Hamilton's plan to put the Post Office under the Treasury rather than the State Department, Jefferson bluntly expressed his pent-up outrage. He told the President that the Treasury "possessed already such an influence as to swallow up the whole executive powers, and that even the future presidents (not supported by the weight of character . . . [Washington] possessed) would not be able to make head against this department." The President tried to soothe Jefferson by expressing his sense that the Secretary of State's role was more important than that of the Secretary of the Treasury, and for good measure, he assigned the newly established Mint to his jurisdiction.

Although the President was generally aware of some personal tensions between his cabinet members, he did not at first grasp the full ramifications. When he expressed general dismay to Jefferson, the secretary responded that the issue was the Hamiltonian economic system, which encouraged speculation, corrupted some members of Congress, and fostered an aristocratic view of the Constitution. As Washington realized, Jefferson was not alone in his criticism. In Congress, Hamilton was subject to a barrage of accusations posed by William Giles, a follower of Madison and, by implication, of Jefferson. These discontented Republicans, in Hamilton's view, wanted nothing less than to drive him in disgrace from office and into retirement. He was, to a large extent, correct in his assessment; the Republican faction was becoming more cohesive, and with its newspaper allies, led by Freneau's *National Gazette*, it was ready to challenge the policies of the first administration.

Hamilton was never one to suffer quietly, and on July 25, using the designation "T.L." in Fenno's *Gazette*, he attacked Freneau for collecting a salary in the State Department while at the same time criticizing the administration and disturbing the public peace. When Freneau questioned the public printing contracts given to Fenno's press, Hamilton responded anonymously that Freneau was "the faithful and devoted servant of the head of a party from whose hands he receives the boon." The allusion to Jefferson and his allies was clear and the literary style made the author fairly obvious.[4]

Washington tried to quiet the growing partisan war in his own house. When Jefferson wrote to him and listed some twenty-one objections to Hamilton's policies, the President forwarded the general accusations to his Secretary of the Treasury and asked for a response. Hamilton knew immediately who was the author of Washington's inquiries, and he became even more bitter toward Jefferson and his allies. By August 18 his reply was ready; he admitted that some speculation occurred but went on to show the overall benefit of his policies. Hamilton denounced those who had cast aspersions on his integrity and that of Congress. He denied that he had advocated a royal government at the Constitutional Convention, as his opponents charged, and concluded: "Those, then, who resist a confirmation of public order are the true artificers of monarchy."

Within a week, Washington, staying at Mount Vernon, wrote both of his Secretaries the same sort of letter, pleading to each for greater personal toleration and for an end to "tearing our vitals out." Hamilton wrote back a conciliatory letter, expressing his own dismay at the President's unhappiness and concluding that if harmony were not restored, the contesting parties would have to be replaced sooner or later. Hamilton noted that he was the hurt party in the controversy, and that he had exercised great restraint, especially in the incident concerning the Paine pamphlet. He had indeed retaliated after Jefferson attempted to undercut his position with Congress and after the Secretary of State's instigated attacks in the newspapers, but he pledged cooperation and peace in the future.[5]

Jefferson's response was less conciliatory. He argued that Hamilton's economic system was calculated to undermine and destroy the Republic by placing "his [Treasury] department over the members of the Legislature." He denounced Hamilton's interference in foreign policy and asked the President "which of us has, notwithstanding, stepped farthest into the control of the department of the other?" He blamed Hamilton for Fenno's attacks and added that he intended to retire soon as Secretary of State. Bitterly he concluded: "I will not suffer my retirement to be clouded by the slanders of a man whose history, from the moment at which history can stoop to notice him, is a tissue of machinations against the liberty of the country which had not only received and given him bread, but heaped honors on his head."[6]

The tensions within the cabinet continued to spill out into the public. Even Washington was coming under attack for his supposed preoccupation with pomp and the trappings of power. The rival newspapers continued to criticize one another intensely for nearly two months, and from September 8 to October 31, 1792, the Federalist and Republican editors unleashed a barrage of salvos. The congressional elections heightened the sense of partisanship, and factions became more cohesive, especially outside the South.

The Second Congress, in December 1792, was still in office and its successor would not meet until nearly a year later. So the Republicans began to launch a major effort to force Hamilton's resignation before the session ended. The House of Representatives adopted a resolution requesting the President to give the Congress an accounting of all foreign loans, including details on interest and balances. In January 1793 Giles pressed the case further by demanding copies of the authority under which loans had been negotiated, an account of payments made to France, Spain, and Holland, a statement on the balances between the federal government and the Bank of the United States and its seventeen branches, a full account of the sinking fund, and a report on all unapplied revenue and money derived from loans. The House approved these far-reaching requests, and Hamilton was forced to turn his attention to writing detailed reports justifying his stewardship.

Giles' objective was clear: on February 27 he introduced a set of resolutions censuring the Secretary, accusing him of making unauthorized financial arrangements, exceeding his authority in making loans, failing to give Congress financial information, negotiating an unnecessary loan and of "indecorum" in his behavior toward the House's official inquiry. The Republicans intended to remove and disgrace their most powerful foe.

Giles' attack was not an isolated move by a frenzied partisan. In Jefferson's personal papers, in his own distinctive handwriting, is a draft of Giles' resolution, which indicates that the Secretary of State was either the author or at least a major leader in the censure attempt. Once again, though, Hamilton was to outflank his accusers. His brilliant defense led the full House of Representatives to back away from the Giles resolutions. Although the Congress was becoming increasingly partisan, the traditions of independence and fair scrutiny were still powerful in the legislative branch. Some Representatives shied away from an obvious political attack on Hamilton; others felt that any censure would reflect on the President, and still others were intent on simply going home. At no time could the Republicans get more than fifteen votes for the censure motion.[7]

The Republicans, in the midst of their attack on Hamilton's public record, came into possession of some information about his private indiscretions as well. In late 1792 several Republicans in the House were informed about the Secretary's affair with a Mrs. Maria Reynolds. Mrs. Reynolds had, at first, approached Hamilton to help her husband, and apparently the Secretary's cooperation soon became mixed with tenderness, which turned into passion. Her husband was supposedly outraged when he found out and demanded blackmail payment from Hamilton to keep the matter quiet. Whether Hamilton was deliberately led into a compromising situation by the Reynolds couple is unclear. But he continued to pay financially for his indiscretions until James Reynolds and a cohort were arrested for fraud in another matter. Reynolds then sought to use Hamilton's influence to get out of prison, and when the Secretary refused to cooperate, Reynolds met with some Republican leaders and detailed new allegations of Treasury corruption. The Republican leaders—Frederick Mühlenberg of Pennsylvania, and James Monroe and Abraham Venable of Virginia—confronted Hamilton, charging him with using Reynolds in a speculative scheme. To their surprise, Hamilton unearthed the full story of his affair and the blackmail payments and convinced them that the speculation charge was false. The congressmen swore, as gentlemen, that the story would remain confidential, which it did until someone, probably Monroe, later publicized it during another controversy.[8]

As the partisan atmosphere increased in 1792, the President suffered some criticism in the newspapers, but generally his public support remained high. Most Americans assumed that Washington would stay in office for a considerable length of time, perhaps for life, but at least beyond his first term. Washington, however, indicated to his cabinet and Madison that he did not intend to stand for reelection. Madison quickly argued that the new government was weak and still required his leadership. But the President candidly responded that he "had from the beginning found himself deficient in many of the essential qualifications, owing to his inexperience in the forms of public business, his unfitness to judge legal questions and questions arising out of the Constitution." At age sixty, the President felt that he was in a state of physical decline, suffering from various maladies, and generally weary of the "fatigues and disagreeableness of his situation."[9]

Madison, though, was unwilling to accept Washington's reservations. He argued to the President that his judgment had been competent and his very presence seemed to unify the new nation. No one else could perform that latter function. Adams and Jay were too disposed to monarchy; Jefferson was determined to retire, and even if he did not, he was distrusted in the North. Once again, Madison appealed to the President's sense of duty and patriotism.[10]

Jefferson joined Madison and urged Washington to continue, lest the forces of division prevail. He saw the President as a powerful bulwark against the mounting monarchial sentiment, for the Secretary felt that while he had differences with the President and his tolerant attitude toward Hamilton, nonetheless Washington remained a true devotee of liberty. Jefferson and Madison received support this time from Hamilton himself, as the Treasury Secretary warned Washington that a premature resignation would be "critically hazardous to your own reputation."[11]

By the summer the political winds of revolution shook the ancient orders in Europe, and at home, discontent was mounting in the mountain areas over the excise tax on whiskey. Even the moderate Attorney General, Edmund Randolph, warned of civil war. A disconcerted Washington asked his personal aide, Lear, "to find out from conversation, without appearing to make the inquiry," what preferences people had for the presidency. Lear reported back universal support for Washington's reelection and Jefferson confirmed that judgment. Washington then agreed to let his name be put forward, but he was extremely guarded in his actions. While he was rather reserved in the election of 1788, this time he was almost reticent. He said little about the election, and when a congressional candidate in Maryland reported that he had the President's support, Washington wrote him a strongly worded letter, indicating that he regarded it as improper to interfere in any election. Washington then waited, seemingly removed from the process and yet admitting that he would be chagrined if he did not after all receive a fairly substantial portion of the electoral vote. On February 13, 1793, the official tally came in—Washington was unanimously reelected. He had retained the support of his countrymen once again. While the partisan newspapers raged at each other and his own cabinet split asunder, the President continued to be a unifying symbol around which controversy swirled.[12]

The real election intrigue was over the second spot, the vice-presidency—a position for the heir apparent if the diffident Washington decided finally to resign before his second term was over. The election of 1793 brought forth a new political figure, Aaron Burr of New York, one of the most enigmatic and interesting personalities of the period. Burr (1756–1836) was the son of the president of the College of New Jersey (later Princeton) and his wife was the daughter of the great Puritan divine Jonathan Edwards. He served in the army during the Revolution and was in the official household of Washington until they developed a mutual dislike of each other. Burr then went on to study law in New Jersey, and he soon formed an alliance in New York with the Clinton and Livingston factions to help defeat Philip Schuyler, Hamilton's father-in-law. Burr served as a senator from 1791 to 1797 and developed ties with the St. Tammany Society, an early political machine made up of small businessmen and mechanics.

In the election of 1796, Burr's name was prominently mentioned for vice-president, and Hamilton quietly wrote to influential friends, attacking his fellow New Yorker's character and judgment. In Virginia, Jefferson's Republican allies had real misgivings as well. Monroe argued that Burr, who was a year older than he was, should be told that people opposed his nomination for vice-president "solely on his youth and late arrival on the national scene." But that assessment was untrue. As Jefferson was to remark years later, Burr was a "crooked gun, or other perverted machine, whose aim on shot you could never be sure of."

Other Republicans, however, were more favorably disposed toward Burr. To some, such as Dr. Rush, Burr was the type of young leader the nation needed. As he wrote to Burr, "your friends everywhere look to you to take an active part in removing the monarchial rubbish of our government. It is time to speak out, or we are undone."[13] The Republican leadership met in caucus at Philadelphia on October 16 to decide whether to support Burr or the more reliable and durable George Clinton. Finally the New York and Pennsylvania representatives apparently decided on Clinton, and although Jefferson stayed away from the caucus, his close friends, Monroe and Beckley, pushed Clinton as well.

In the general election, Adams retained enough support to win over Clinton by an electoral vote of seventy-seven to fifty. Nonetheless, the Republicans had mounted a strong campaign against the incumbent vice-president and Clinton carried not only New York but also did well in the South, especially Virginia, North Carolina, and Georgia. The impulses toward factionalism were growing all the more intense, and national parties were beginning to coalesce around major economic interests and ambitious public personalities.

22

TOWARD NEUTRALITY

There you Gallic Brethren see
Struggling, bleeding to be free.
Oh! Unite your prayers that they
May soon announce their natal day.

Ann Eliza Bleecker,
July 4, 1793

While the Hamilton economic measures strained the unity of the cabinet and created consternation in Congress, the origins of the first party division grew less out of domestic affairs than out of foreign policy. The major disputes in Washington's term revolved around worsening Franco-American relations, and in that area, the President himself had provided the controversial directions.

In the first year of his administration, Washington looked out over a hostile world. The British, despite the provisions of the Treaty of 1789, retained military posts on the Northwest frontier and had decided generally to ignore American protests. The British encouraged Indian hostilities in that area and the Spanish in the Southwest seemed equally unfriendly to the new and fragile American union. The Spanish retained possession over Louisiana and Florida and controlled the Mississippi River and the major port of New Orleans, and they, too, encouraged their agents and the indigenous Indian tribes to reject American peace overtures. Other agitators were sent out to stir up the frontiersmen and encourage them to secede and join the Spanish empire. One of the most skillful of these figures was James Wilkinson, an officer in the American army as well as a paid agent of the Spanish government. Born in Maryland, Wilkinson had studied medicine, served with Washington as a lieutenant colonel, and later joined the Conway Cabal against the General. After the war, he migrated to Kentucky and led the movement to split that territory from Virginia. He convinced the Spanish that he was working to promote dissension and ended up with an annual pension from them of $2,000. To most of his neighbors, though, he posed as a loyal American, anxious to promote their interests and secure markets for them in New Orleans.

Wilkinson continued his intrigue in the West and eventually came into conflict with General Anthony Wayne on how to handle the Indian tribes in what is now the Detroit area. By 1801 he became so involved with Aaron Burr that when the Republicans took over control of the government, Jefferson appointed him as his representative to the various Indian tribes. The Spanish, however, continued to pay him for his services, and he invested the money in sugar speculation. By 1805 he was appointed governor of the Louisiana Territory and became even more involved with Burr, and finally ended up as the chief witness against the New Yorker at his treason trial. Through all of these ventures, Wilkinson continued his ties with the Spanish and was the recipient of their attention and bribes for a considerable period of time. Although he was one of the more accomplished Spanish agents, Wilkinson's ability to play off both governments was due in part to the ambiguous and often uncertain state of frontier diplomacy. Far from the capital, living in a rough land of speculators, drunks, and paid mercenaries, the Wilkinsons of the world not only survived, but also prospered. Such circumstances made it difficult for Washington to either set down a fixed policy or be able to make it work reasonably well from one month to another.

The President, however, did try to exert control when the situation deteriorated to the point of threatening the federal government's authority. For example, when the Georgia legislature granted large tracts of what it considered to be its western land to three companies, the President decided to step in. A conflict with Spain seemed in the wind, and one company, led by a Wilkinson protégé, Dr. James O'Fallon, was prepared to negotiate with the Governor of New Orleans and recognize Spanish authority in the region. Washington denounced the proposed action and issued a proclamation that warned the Western settlers of O'Fallon's true intent. On March 19, 1791, the President specifically attacked O'Fallon as a person who was disturbing the public peace and violating American treaties and statutory law. O'Fallon's support quickly vanished as some of the settlers, especially in the Kentucky area, pressed for separate statehood and not secession. The Georgia legislature repealed its charter and the whole proposal fell through.

From the earliest months of his administration, the President carefully evaluated the frontier problem and America's policy toward both the Spanish and the British. When both those nations were near war in 1789 because of trade disputes in the Nootka Sound, the President called his department heads together to discuss what the government's policy should be if the British attacked Louisiana from Canada by marching across U.S. territory. Hamilton supported favoring the British as a way of establishing stronger ties with them later. Jefferson pressed for an alliance with Spain and, if possible, France, to balance the British presence in the New World. Although the controversy passed, the initial division of opinion remained and became a central problem for the President in the days to come.[1]

Jefferson, as Secretary of State, sought to negotiate with the Spanish minister, Don Diego de Gardoqui, in order to settle some of the more pressing frontier problems. But before those discussions progressed, Citizen Genet, the French Minister to the United States, arrived with his own flamboyant plans. Although young, Genet was not a novice in the world of diplomacy. He was the son of the head of the Bureau of Interpreters in the Ministry of Foreign Affairs at Versailles. At the age of six, he could read French and English and recite Greek; at about fourteen, he translated *The History of Eric XIV* from Swedish and received a gold medal from the King of Sweden. He worked for a while with his father and then served as secretary to the French embassy in Berlin and later in Vienna. By 1787 he was assigned to the court of Catherine II in Russia, but when she heard of his support for the French Revolution, she expelled him in 1792. The Girondians, then in power, warmly welcomed him home and soon named him as the new minister to the United States. With France and Spain at war, Genet tried, at first, to organize three expeditions against the Spanish in North America and he gained the support of the Revolutionary hero George Rogers Clark, who wanted to attack New Orleans, the heart of the Spanish territory. Genet, delighted, wrote back to his government, "I provision the Antilles, I excite the Canadians to free themselves from the yoke of England, I arm the Kentuckians."[2] Although Jefferson had desired some disruption along the Mississippi in order to persuade Gardoqui that negotiations had to move along, he was somewhat concerned about Genet's ambitious plans. Washington, though, had no such ambiguous sentiments: he intervened directly and warned the Governor of Kentucky about any such activities. Before Genet could further his policies, he was removed by the new French regime and ordered home.

Genet's objectives were clearly to replace the declining Spanish power with French revolutionary fervor and form ties with the American frontiersmen while he helped to seize Louisiana, the Floridas, and finally Canada. He had the support of a variety of figures in his adventure—not just George Rogers Clark, but also Thomas Paine, Joel Barlow, a poet, and Gilbert Imlay, a Revolutionary War soldier who lived with feminist Mary Wollstonecraft, the mother of Shelley's wife, who also created the fictional monster Frankenstein. But Genet lacked one important character in his cast, Washington, and the President was determined to protect the American frontier and avoid getting involved in the French and British war.[3]

Despite his early enthusiasm for the French Revolution, Washington had serious reservations about the course of events. He was deeply moved when Lafayette sent him the main key of the Bastille prison, that "fortress of

despotism," as the Frenchman proclaimed. Linking up the two great revolutions he had been part of, Lafayette gave the key as "a tribute which I
owe as a son to my adoptive father, as an aide-de-camp to my general, as
a missionary of liberty to its patriarch." Surely the oppressed French had
come to bear witness to the American experiment and sought to emulate
its success. But as the revolution became more radical and its leaders engaged
in terror, Washington backed away. The French, he felt, were being overwhelmed by the consequences "resulting from too great eagerness in swal-
lowing something so delightful as liberty."[4]

The Federalists in general were less circumspect: to them the French
republic became the epitome of anarchy, atheism, and vice. France was
what America stood in danger of becoming—a wild beast set free from the
constraints of God and society. The Republicans, on the other hand, tended
to overlook the excesses of the Revolution. In a moment of enthusiasm,
Jefferson noted that although the Reign of Terror was unfortunate, it was
probably necessary, for if the "liberty of the whole earth was depending
on the issue of the contest . . . rather than it should have failed, I would have
seen half the earth devastated."[5]

Soon, though, Lafayette ended up in jail and Americans of all persuasions
were dismayed by the twistings of French politics. Events were to prove
Washington, and not Jefferson, more correct. The French Revolution was
different from the American Revolution; indeed, it was different from any
upheaval the world had previously seen. The French, in their cycles of
bloodshed, terror, anarchy, and finally military despotism, were to alter
society in ways neither Washington nor Jefferson could understand, let alone
approve. Although Jefferson urged a revolution every twenty years or so
to water the tree of liberty, his statement was more of a rhetorical gesture
than a prescriptive one. The class structure of the New World romantics
and dreamers was a mild one compared with the feudal society still encrusted
in Europe. America had escaped millennia of history, generations of abuse,
and the rigidities of class, king and church. To the colonists, revolution
was a one-time thing, whereas to the French, it became a way of life. The
Founding Fathers in America assumed their proper places of respect in the
new order, while across the ocean the revolution consumed its fathers and
haunted their sons.

But to many Americans in late 1792 and 1793, the French Revolution
was an extension of their own great cause. They welcomed the egalitarian
principles of the French and looked at their own society to see if they had
lapsed from republican virtue. On December 12, 1792, the *National Gazette*
carried an article, called "Forerunners of Monarchy and Aristocracy in the
United States," by a writer using the *nom de plume* of the revolutionary
Mirabeau. This widely quoted piece attacked the use of titles in America
such as "excellency," "honorable," or even "esquire," and it criticized a
variety of alleged abuses, ranging from levees, birthday celebrations for

public servants, ceremonies, parades, high salaries, public debt, and "swearing, drunkenness, debauchery or a want of justice in the payment of debts." Clearly some of those abuses were seen as being part of the Federalist administration.

Other Republican newspapers joined in these convenient denunciations. Men were encouraged to address one another, as in France, by the title "citizen," and marriage announcements even used this prefix for both parties. Federalists mocked the whole move as nonsense, and one wondered if a woman were to be called "citess" or "civess," and if a slave was to be sold with the cry, "Twenty pounds for Citizen Alexander—who bids more?"

But the Republicans were not discouraged. For them, as for so many fervent partisans, language was not a convention, but a true barometer of commitment. Phi Beta Kappa and other academic societies at Harvard College were denounced as being inimical to the "principles of liberty and equality." Streets were renamed to purge any allusion to royal terms and endless odes were written to the fall of the Bastille, July 14, Lafayette, Paine, equality, liberty, and the death of Louis XVI. Freneau published a series of such odes, satirizing leading Federalists, including Adams, Hamilton, and Knox. Fourth of July orators and college rhetoricians celebrated the unity of the two revolutions and the new age dawning in Europe. As Joel Barlow wrote:

> Freedom at last, with reason in her train
> Extends o'er earth her everlasting reign.
> See Gallia's sons, so late the tyrant's sport,
> Machines in war and sycophants at court,
> Start into men, expand their well-taught mind,
> Lords of themselves and leaders of mankind.

The French influence seemed dominant in the American mind. At Harvard College, one student, William Ellery Channing, who entered in 1794, wrote later that the "college was never in worse stage than when I entered it. Society was passing through a most critical stage. The French Revolution had diseased the imagination and unsettled the understanding of men everywhere. The old foundations of social order, loyalty, tradition, habit, reverence for antiquity, were everywhere shaken, if not subverted. The authority of the past was gone." A classmate of Channing noted how the patrons and governors of Harvard distributed to each student a copy of Watson's *Apology for the Bible* to counteract the influence of Paine's *Age of Reason*, but to no avail, for the "college could not escape the contagion of their principles."

By the beginning of 1793 an intense pro-French feeling swept across the states, bringing forth an incredible display of republican solidarity. In Philadelphia, Savannah, Baltimore, Charleston, Providence, Norfolk, and dozens of smaller cities, celebrations led the populace to new heights of excitement. The most memorable feast was held in Boston on January 24, 1793. There the Civic Festival, as it was called, began with a cannon salute and at eleven o'clock a great procession started. In the procession was a roasted ox covered with ribbons and displaying gilded horns adorned with both French and American flags. In front was the gold inscription "Peace Offering to Liberty and Equality." The procession moved through the town and passed Liberty Square, where a sixty-foot-high liberty pole had been erected. A great banquet at Faneuil Hall was later held, presided over by "Citizen" Samuel Adams. The hall was elaborately decorated with a figure of Liberty crushing under her feet the symbols of despotism—a crown, scepter, mitre, and chains. The hall was dressed with American and French flags and various mottoes and inscriptions celebrating Liberty, Equality, Justice, and Peace. The evening ended with the usual display of fireworks and bonfires.

Other prominent politicians, such as John Hancock, spoke of the Revolution in his Thanksgiving proclamation in 1793, and the Governor of Vermont praised the French experiment in his Fast and Thanksgiving proclamations as well. Even the fledgling American theater was affected. In New York, when an actor dressed up to play an English officer, he was hissed by the audience, which included some Sons of Tammany Hall. He quickly indicated to the audience that he was representing a coward and a bully so the uniform was appropriate. Elsewhere, pro-French audiences frequently demanded that Marseillaise be played in the theaters before each play, and the owners booked such plays as "Tyranny Suppressed," "The Demolition of the Bastille," "Liberty Restored," and "Helvetic Liberty."

On the other side, the opponents of the new France concentrated on the rancorous nature of the Revolution and its endless bloodshed. One issue of popular dismay was the execution of Louis XVI, the sovereign who had supported the American cause. Whereas Washington and Patrick Henry disapproved of the execution, Republican leaders like Jefferson and Madison accepted it. One article simply summarized the event, "Louis Capet has lost his Caput." And at a Philadelphia meeting, the head of a pig, representing the King, was passed around and mangled.

When the yellow fever struck Philadelphia in 1793, some ardent Federalists were convinced that it was God's punishment for those who supported the atrocities in France. The Federalists attacked the atheism of the French radicals, their preoccupation with equality, and their fixation with trivialities, such as abolishing titles and addresses. Noah Webster, after expressing some sympathy for the Revolution, asked, "What shall we say to the legislature of a great nation waging a serious war with mere names, pictures, dress and statues? Is this also necessary to the support of liberty? There is something in this part of the legislative proceedings that unites the littleness of boys with the barbarity of Goths."[6]

With such intense feelings at home and the threat of European war, Washington found that France's foreign policy placed the new nation in considerable peril. Because the United States had an alliance with France dating back to 1778, did this mean that America had to go to war against Britain? Washington's response is an interesting chapter in presidential leadership, for while his Secretaries debated what was to be done, the President, in his own mind, had decided to pursue a policy of neutrality.

On March 27 the news of France's February 1 declaration of war on Britain and Holland reached the United States. By April 7 the rumor was confirmed, and Jefferson wrote to the President, who was staying at Mount Vernon. The day after he received Jefferson's message, Washington left his estate and arrived in Philadelphia on April 17. Quickly he submitted a series of thirteen questions "with a view to forming a general plan of conduct for the executive." Both Randolph and Jefferson were sure that the questions were originally drawn up by Hamilton, for, as the Secretary of State noted, "it was palpable from the style, their ingenious tissue and suite that they were not the President's, that they were raised upon a prepared chain of argument, in short that the language was Hamilton's and the doubts his alone."[7] The inquiries dealt with a variety of issues: the future of the Franco-American treaty, the need for a neutrality statement, the manner of receiving the new French minister Genet, America's conduct toward the European war, and whether Congress should be called into session.

Jefferson at first downplayed the importance of the crisis. When the President first arrived on April 17, the Secretary of State greeted him with a stack of routine correspondence and said nothing about neutrality. Although Jefferson fervently desired to stay out of the war, he opposed issuing any proclamation announcing neutrality. He argued that "it would be better to hold back the declaration of neutrality as a thing worth something to the powers of war, that they would bid for it and we might reasonably ask a price, the *broadest privilege* of neutral nations."[8] In addition, Jefferson maintained that the President did not have the right to declare that there should be no war, any more than he could unilaterally declare war, for those issues were in the prerogative of Congress. Hamilton not only pressed for a proclamation, but also argued for a temporary and provisional suspension of the treaty with France. To Jefferson's consternation, the Treasury Secretary maintained that treaties could be unilaterally declared void in such instances.

At their next meeting, both Hamilton and Jefferson presented briefs to the President on the nature and legal underpinnings of treaties. There is no question that Jefferson's strong and well-documented argument was superior to Hamilton's presentation. One of Hamilton's main arguments was that the treaty had been made with the King of France, Louis XVI, and his heirs, and that since Louis had been driven from the throne, America's obligations were now somewhat different. Although Hamilton conceded that treaties had historically been made with nations and not specific regimes, he argued that it was unjust to turn an alliance to the clear disadvantage of the king and his heirs who had originally made the treaty. The only way out of this dilemma was to suspend the treaty. Also, the alliance was a defensive pact and Hamilton argued that it was clear that France was the aggressor in the European war, and thus America was not bound to come to its aid. Most importantly, he asked what would happen if the United States supported France and France lost the war.

As for his response, Jefferson, in one of his best state papers, dealt rather effectively with much of Hamilton's theoretical arguments. He maintained that the treaty was still valid and binding. The President could not annul treaties, nor could he suspend them unilaterally. Whether Washington was much influenced by the lawyer-like arguments of his subordinates is unclear; what he wanted was neutrality. So he asked, probably with Jefferson's consent, that Randolph prepare a draft that would stress America's impartiality. Washington's choice of Randolph was an obvious attempt to restore some level of cohesion after the strained debate between his two principal Secretaries. The Attorney General produced a document that stated America's neutrality without using the word—an obvious concession to Jefferson's sensitivities. The proclamation, signed by Washington and approved by the full cabinet, acknowledged the hostilities and declared that "the duty and interests of the United States require, that they should, with sincerity and good faith, adopt and pursue a conduct friendly and impartial toward the belligerent powers. . . . "[9]

Although the word "neutrality" was not used, it soon found its way into the President's public papers. When disagreement appeared in the cabinet about the use of the word in a presidential speech in November, Washington interrupted the discussion by stating, as Jefferson recalled, that "he had never had an idea that he could bind Congress . . . or that anything contained in his proclamation could look beyond the first day of their meeting. His main view was to keep our people in peace. He apologized for the use of the term neutrality in his answers." Still his intention was obvious to all.

A major difference of opinion then developed over enforcement procedures. Hamilton argued that all violations should be reported to customs officials who would in turn notify the Secretary of the Treasury. Jefferson vigorously objected, writing Randolph on May 8, 1793, that "the collectors of the customs are to be made an established corps of spies or informers against their fellow citizens, whose actions they are to watch in secret, inform against in secret to the Secretary of the Treasury, who is to communicate with a convenient weapon to keep down a rival, draw a cloud over an inconvenient censor, or satisfy mere malice and private enmity." As an alternative, Jefferson proposed that the government rely on the grand juries, "the constitutional inquisitors and informers of the country." Washington, again heading off confrontation, directed the Attorney General to instruct the district attorneys to require from the collectors of the several ports information on all infractions of neutrality. Thus both Hamilton and Jefferson were sidestepped in one deft stroke.[10]

Unlike some of his actions during his first term, Washington exhibited a commanding presence in the neutrality decision. Faced with a delicate situation, Washington tried his best to formulate a consensus among his advisors (called, by this time, his cabinet) and yet clearly and strongly assert American foreign policy aims. He realized, as did even Jefferson, that the weak but expanding United States was unable to honor its treaty commitments. However, he chose not to suspend the treaty abruptly, as Hamilton argued, but simply to lay it aside. And unlike Jefferson, he was both neutral and impartial, with a firmness that remained unwavering.

The proclamation, however, did not close the debate. The Republicans were critical of Washington's request that Americans remain "impartial" and called to mind the sacrifices France had made to the American cause. They argued that he was acting unconstitutionally by issuing his declaration, and some attacked his "evil counsellors," especially Hamilton.

In response, Hamilton, who had a penchant for anonymous journalism, decided to write a series of articles setting the record straight and encouraging support for the controversial policy. Under the pen name "Pacificus," he defended Washington's Neutrality Proclamation against Republican attacks. Most of the articles repeated his views that the Franco-American treaty should be abrogated, and that the United States had no obligation to come to the aid of the new regime. However, in his first essay, published on June 29, 1793, Hamilton dealt mostly with the question of whether the executive had stepped beyond the bounds of his constitutional duty. Hamilton argued that the legislative department is not the "organ of intercourse" between the United States and foreign nations, because the president has all executive powers except those that are expressly qualified in the Constitution. Hamilton then maintained that although the legislature has the right to make war, it is the duty of the executive to preserve the peace until war is declared. However, the legislature is "free to perform its own duties according to its own sense of them, although the executive in the exercise of its constitutional powers may establish an antecedent state of things which ought to weigh in the legislative decisions. From the decision of the executive there results in reference to it a concurrent authority in the distributed cases. Hence, in the case stated, though treaties can only be made by the President and the Senate, their activity may be continued or suspended by the President alone."[11]

At Jefferson's insistence that he must "take up his pen," Madison proceeded to answer Hamilton's contentions. Madison, however, mainly directed his attention to Hamilton's reflections about executive power rather than to the actual Neutrality Proclamation. In his first letter, using the pen name of "Helvidius," Madison took to task Hamilton's theory that the powers of making war and treaties are, by their nature, executive except where the Constitution specifically says otherwise. Madison argued that the natural province of the executive is to execute the laws and that of the legislature is to make them. A treaty has the effect of law and is "to be carried into *execution*, like all *other laws*, by the *executive magistrate.*" Madison argued further that the commander-in-chief clause of the Constitution does not grant this power to make treaties. Indeed, it shows the incompatibility of the two powers, for those "who are to *conduct a war* cannot in the nature of things, be proper or safe judges, whether *a war ought* to be *commenced, continued* or *concluded.*" No other clauses of the Constitution contain such appropriate justifications, and thus the only source of this doctrine lies in the royal prerogative of the king. Madison cited Federalist Paper 75 (written, he knew, anonymously by Hamilton), which maintained that the legislature must participate in the operation of treaties as well as law.

"Pacificus" had argued that although the Congress judges the situation and can declare war, still the executive has the right to judge the situation as well. Madison countered that this view represented an intrusion into the legislature's domain and is contrary to principles of well-organized governments. "Pacificus" had also maintained that because the President was responsible for receiving ambassadors and ministers, he could decide if he chose to recognize particular regimes. Madison, again quoting a Federalist Paper, this time 69, penned also by Hamilton, argued that this power was a "matter of dignity rather than authority." "Pacificus," Madison maintained, sought to create from this etiquette a new set of executive prerogatives.

Madison was particularly critical of the assertion that the executive can "lay the legislature under an obligation to declaring war," and argued that the legislature must be able to make its own judgments on the matter. He warned that the executive is particularly incapable of dealing with the decision, for "war is in fact the true nurse of executive aggrandizement." Then, citing again Hamilton's Federalist Paper 75, Madison warned that "if a free people be a wise people also, they will not forget that the danger of surprise never be so great, as when the advocates for the prerogatives of war can sheathe it in a symbol of peace." Just as an executive cannot declare war under the Constitution, so, too, he cannot "judge and conclude that war ought to be made." Thus the Neutrality Proclamation was improper. A proclamation is always understood to relate to "the law actually in operation," and if it is "exclusively executive in nature, it is addressed to the citizens and subjects, but not to foreign governments as the Neutrality Address was." In effect, Madison noted that the arguments of "Pacificus" had used the word "government" to really mean "the will of the executive."[12]

These erudite discussions were to continue in a variety of places, and the issue of presidential prerogatives, especially on matters of war and peace, remains a difficult question. But for Washington, the policy was set and he pursued his course, in the process alienating both British and French governments over the years of his second term. As he did so, the President soon found the government involved in a series of legal cases and diplomatic confrontations that clearly tested whether Washington's policy would come undone and whether he had enough political support to stand firm.

Under Article 17 of the Treaty, the French could capture enemy ships and bring them into American ports. After Genet arrived, he began to confer privateering commissions, and insisted on the right of French counsels to act as admiralty prize courts for the condemnation and sale of every prize brought into American ports by French privateers. When the French dragged some ships, including the British merchant vessel *Grange*, into Delaware Bay, the Secretary of State was delighted. It was another example, he wrote to Monroe, that the spirit of 1776 was still alive. But the British Minister Hammond protested that the *Grange* was not on high seas, but in American waters. Washington and Jefferson quickly ordered the French to return it, and the Americans decided not to allow French privateers to be outfitted and commissioned in American ports.

Then the administration found itself faced with another dispute—the question of whether the ship *Little Sarah*, taken on the high seas off the Virginia Cape and held by the French, should be returned to British control. Jefferson and Randolph insisted that the American government had just issued the proclamation and had no time to enforce its injunction. The most the British should hope for was some sort of apology against the outfittings of privateers, but surely they could not expect the Americans to force the French to release the ship. Hamilton and Knox, however, argued the opposite position: the ship must be returned.

Washington was at Mount Vernon and Jefferson asked Genet to agree that the ship would not set sail until the President reviewed the dispute. The Minister at first concurred, but then he abruptly countered his order before the President could arrive. Once in the capital, Washington again turned to his Attorney General and concluded that although the ship, renamed *The Little Democrat*, could not be restored to the British, the privateer that brought her to port and several other French corsairs outfitted illegally in Charleston were to be denied sanctuary in the United States.

The administration thus continued to pursue its difficult neutrality policy, but even the courts proved uncooperative. The government had prohibited Americans from enlisting on French privateers in American ports, and when two citizens, Gideon Henfield and John Singleton, violated that restriction, they were arrested and jailed. Genet correctly argued that there was no law prohibiting their enlistments, but Randolph responded that treaties were the law of the land, and that Henfield's action violated treaties that the United States had with three nations then at war with France. Thus he had disturbed the peace and was indictable under common law.

In the trial before the Circuit Court in Philadelphia in July, the judges declared that if the charges against Henfield were true, he had committed a crime under existing law. The jury was simply to determine if he committed the offense as alleged. The jury, probably unwilling to give the proclamation the true force of law, found the defendant innocent, and Genet and some Republican leaders celebrated the verdict as a true triumph of liberty.

Faced with mounting legal problems, the administration, on July 18, decided to appeal directly to the Supreme Court for an advisory opinion on what was proper in implementing its general policy. The Court, however, citing the separation of powers, refused to provide any guidance, thus setting an important early precedent about its role. But finally a major case arose and went to the high court. A French privateer had captured the *Betsy*, which was owned by neutral Swedes and Americans. The vessel was sent to Baltimore for adjudication as a prize by the French consul, and the owners appealed to the U.S. district court for relief. The district court in Maryland, however, decided that American courts had no jurisdiction over French prizes. The government then appealed to the Supreme Court, which unanimously ruled that the district court did indeed possess the power to determine the legality of prizes brought into American ports. It further held that no foreign power could set up courts in the United States unless stipulated by treaty, and that admiralty jurisdiction exercised by the consuls of France was not warranted.

Meanwhile Genet not only concentrated on the privateers issue, but also pressed Washington for a renegotiation of the treaties of 1790. To further entice the Americans, the French, in February, had decided to open up the West Indies to U.S. trade, and the Revolutionary government allowed the construction and sale of American vessels in its nation. The French regime was obviously seeking to draw the Americans closer at the very time the President was attempting to create some distance. In the United States, Genet pressed for the liquidation of the American debt ahead of schedule so that he could use the $2.5 million to outfit and arm the French army. As the controversy grew, Republican newspapers openly attacked Washington's integrity and his commitment to republican ideals. Even Madison wrote to Jefferson that the Neutrality Proclamation was an error that left the President open to charges of "Anglomany."

As Genet pressed his claims, Hammond was demanding full restitution for British losses, and the Spanish, then in alliance with Britain, were inflaming the Indians in the Southwest. Meanwhile, on August 11, Jefferson tendered his resignation but consented to stay on until the end of the year, and Hamilton and Tobias Lear also expressed a desire to leave government service, although the Secretary of the Treasury continued in office through 1794. Washington was becoming increasingly dependent on his own resources and judgment.

As the crisis continued, Genet's conduct was becoming even more objectionable to the administration. In July the President had received reports that the Minister was threatening to "appeal from the President to the people." Even Jefferson became a target of Genet's harangues, and the Secretary was telling Madison that Genet's appointment as Minister was a calamity for the cause of liberty. He was, Jefferson complained, "hotheaded, all imagination, no judgment, passionate, disrespectful, and even indecent towards the President. . . . He renders my position immensely delicate."[13]

While all these events were going on, the President decided to send his Attorney General to the South to see what the public sentiment was. When Randolph returned, he reported back that there was substantial public support for the proclamation and that the President's judgment was widely respected. As so often has happened, a President had alienated segments of the capital and the media but still retained the broad-based goodwill of the citizenry.

By the end of July, Washington called his cabinet together to write some specific rules governing neutrality. Seeing an opportunity, Hamilton pressed for a release of the full record of Genet's conduct to the public, but Jefferson opposed such a step, arguing that it would make the President into a partisan figure and one who seemed to compete with Genet for the public's attention. Knox, instead of dealing with the issue at hand, showed Washington the latest attack on him in the *National Gazette*. Suddenly the President's anger exploded as he denounced the "rascal Freneau" and cried out that he would rather be dead than be president. He went on and dared anyone to single out one selfish act promulgated by him while in office, and then he finally sputtered and dismissed his cabinet.

On August 2 the American government decided to ask for Genet's recall, and sometime later, Rufus King and John Jay, probably on Hamilton's instigation, made public Genet's threat that he would appeal over the President's head to the people if he did not get his way. The patriotic reaction was swift and predictable. Genet was bitterly denounced and the weary President found himself lionized once again in town and country.[14]

Adams wrote, years later, of the intense opposition to Washington's policies in the capital. Perhaps somewhat exaggerated, he remembered:

Ten thousand people in the streets of Philadelphia, day after day, threatened to drag Washington out of his house, and effect a revolution in the government, or compel it to declare war in favor of the French Revolution and against England. The coolest and firmest minds, even among the Quakers in Philadelphia, have given their opinions to me, that nothing but the yellow fever, which removed Dr. Hutchinson and Jonathan Dickinson Sergeant from this world, could have saved the United States from a fatal revolution of government.[15]

To add to the confusion, when the plague swept through the city, the government was virtually forced to close down. Hamilton contracted yellow fever, and when Washington attempted to stay, his wife refused to leave without him. Finally he, too, departed, and the Federalist ministers memorialized the lessons—their God of revenge was responding to the excesses of the French Revolution and its hold on some Americans.

Thus, despite intense criticism, the President's policies prevailed. He had proven, as so many executives before and after him, that energy and dispatch, as Hamilton once noted, gave immense advantages. Through the tense spring and summer of 1793, Washington steadfastly insisted on maintaining a policy of neutrality and finally was successful.

In the beginning of 1794, though, the Republicans in the Senate sought to keep the controversy alive. The Senate, by a one-vote majority, demanded from the President copies of correspondence from Gouverneur Morris, the American Minister to France. Randolph, who had become Secretary of State on Jefferson's resignation, argued that the papers could not be withheld, but the rest of the cabinet disagreed. Washington apparently had the Secretary of State meet privately with James Madison and Justice James Wilson on the question.

Randolph came back and suggested that Washington deliver to the Senate that part of the dispatches the President thought it prudent to send. Randolph had argued that one had to distinguish between the Senate's "executive and its legislative capacities." A request in the first category could be refused in toto, since the Senate possessed executive powers only when reviewing presidential appointments and in the ratification of treaties. A request in its "legislative" capacity, however, would have to be complied with, although the president could reserve the right to exercise his discretion as to what is fit to be given to the Senate. Finally Washington sent the correspondence, except probably for one sensitive dispatch. As the divisiveness continued, the Republicans in the House, led by Madison, offered seven resolutions designed to lay more duties on British trade at the very time the administration was trying to avoid antagonizing that nation. The Federalists and Republicans debated the measures extensively and finally decided to postpone most matters until March.[16]

Meanwhile, in France, the radical Jacobins seized control of the faltering French republic, and they acceded to Washington's request to replace Genet. Indeed, they wanted him arrested and deported for trial back home. Even Genet recognized that the guillotine was probably his fate, and he in turn pleaded for asylum, which Washington granted. The once fiery Republican married Governor Clinton's daughter and lived peacefully out of the public eye until his death in 1834. The Genet affair was over, but the respite from controversy for the president was to be rather brief.

23

THE WHISKEY
INSURRECTION

We find a great majority of the people in this country have got the
canine madness against the government. . . .

Captain David Ford,
Autumn 1794

While the administration was closely watching the tense situation in Europe,
domestic dissension was increasing in the United States over the economic
program and the taxes levied to pay for it. In order to win the support of
a recalcitrant Congress, Hamilton had agreed to a variety of compromises
that greatly increased the new government's indebtedness. From 1790 to
1800, the payment on the interest of the national debt alone consumed more
than 40 percent of the federal government's revenue.

The main source of revenue to run the government was the tariff, which
brought in about $6 million a year. The tariff of 1789 was a compromise
between those who wanted a high protective policy aimed at fostering
American industry and commerce, and those who wanted to add on duties
just high enough to raise revenues for maintaining a modest administration.
The duty on molasses was reduced from previous levels and the ad valorem
charges on most items set at about 5 percent, although the duty on some
selected items reached 50 percent. In addition to the tariff, revenues were
raised through internal taxes, although the amount seldom reached $600,000
a year. The most controversial of these internal taxes was the excise tax on
whiskey, which ended up increasing the net price of a gallon by about 25
percent.[1]

The excise taxes were strongly attacked in the House, where the main
opponent was John Jackson of Georgia, who maintained that Hamilton's
economic plan favored the merchant class and the bankers at the expense
of the farmers. Madison and Jefferson, though, because of their part in

securing passage of the debt bill, remained generally quiet during the public debate, and the excise taxes passed.

From the time of its passage, the whiskey excise was vigorously denounced, especially in the frontier region of Pennsylvania. In opposing this tax, the frontiersmen continued a long and honored tradition that went back to colonial America and even to their English forebears. Americans, as a people, detested taxes, and their hatred of the Townshend Acts and the duties on tea and stamps was part of the national folklore. Across the ocean, the reaction was historically similar. The excise on liquor in 1626 created so much acrimony that the Parliament went on to declare it unconstitutional. In 1641, when a temporary excise tax was passed, a riot ensued in London and troops had to be called in to end the disturbances. The next year, when the rumor spread that the excise tax would be levied again, the leaders of the House of Commons bitterly assailed such false and scandalous talk. In 1734 the first minister publicly rejected the notion of an excise tax, concluding that he "would not be the minister who should carry out any measure of this sort." The defeat of the excise tax was greeted with bonfires and, appropriately enough, generous libations. Summarizing the sentiment of his fellow countrymen, Dr. Samuel Johnson, in his famed *Dictionary*, defined the excise tax as "a hateful tax levied upon commodities, and adjudged not by the common judges of property, but wretches hired by those to whom excise is paid."

The frontiersmen of western Pennsylvania and elsewhere may not have read Dr. Johnson, but they surely shared his opinion. For them, whiskey was as common as wine or beer was in continental Europe. Whiskey served a variety of purposes: it was a beverage at meals, a freely accepted article for barter, the measure of Western hospitality, an elixir to forget hardships, part of a soldier's ration, and a component often of the local minister's salary.

The frontier farmers had little cash and were unable to transport lumber, grain, and meat at reasonable cost across the mountains to market. Instead, they often turned rye into whiskey, which could be easily transported in bulk and sold at a profit. The excise on whiskey, then, was a direct burden on their livelihoods and a restriction on one of the few sources of cash they could generate. From their point of view, the federal government provided little protection on the frontier against the Indians, and yet it demanded taxes to run its administration way back in the East.

Many of these dissident farmers, though, were not the noble yeomen of democratic folklore. As the Frenchman Crèvecoeur observed in his travels, the western Pennsylvania settlers were uncouth, drunken, lazy, brutal, wasteful, and contentious, being "no better than carnivorous animals of a superior rank." They seldom paid any taxes and observed little in the way of law, and many of them drank all the whiskey they distilled without worrying about having a cash crop later. When the excise notice was put up on one site, which was near a sign with Washington's picture on it, the notice was promptly ripped down and the sign sprayed with bullets.

Back in the capital, Hamilton was receiving reports on the intense opposition to the whiskey tax, and he quickly told General Wayne to move his army in and crush the dissent. But Wayne, who at times was more cautious than his nickname, "Mad Anthony," would suggest, refused to move, arguing that "the army was raised to protect the people and not to oppress them." But Hamilton remained convinced that a show of strength was necessary to establish the pre-eminence of the new federal government. At first, he agreed to compromise on one of the problems created by the excise tax law. The original act required that any person accused of violating the statute had to travel to the nearest *federal* court for trial, which in Pennsylvania meant going to Philadelphia. On April 4, 1794, a bill was introduced in Congress to allow the state courts to handle such cases when the federal courts were more than fifty miles away; it passed, and in June the President signed it.

Even though the bill was recommended by Hamilton and seemed likely to pass, during the time the bill was being debated in Congress, the secretary insisted that the Philadelphia district court bring action against seventy-five distillers for violations that were a year old. The writs were not served until July, but the administration maintained that these individuals had to be tried under the provisions of the old law, and thus forced to come to Philadelphia. Hamilton, it seems, was clearly attempting to create a confrontation in order to mobilize the army and settle the question of federal power and authority. Indeed, in 1792, he had already argued to the President that it might be necessary, "if the processes of the courts are resisted, as is rather to be expected, to employ those means which in the last resort are put in the power of the Executive."

Washington, however, was less enamored with the idea of calling up troops and turned to his Attorney General, Edmund Randolph, for advice. Randolph counseled moderation, and the President, in 1792, issued a proclamation on the matter. At first, the controversy died down, but gradually through 1793 and the next year, violence increased and an excise agent in western Pennsylvania was attacked. When the news reached the capital, Washington met with his cabinet and with Supreme Court justice James Wilkinson, a strong Federalist supporter. The Militia Act of 1792 required that a federal judge had to verify that the judiciary was not able to operate in a region before the executive could mobilize troops and send them in. But Wilkinson was unwilling to certify that such a situation existed, and Washington had to try another course of action. The President decided instead to ask the officials of Pennsylvania to call up the state militia. But the governor was then Thomas Mifflin, an ardent Republican and a major critic of Washington during the Revolutionary War. On August 1 the President requested that Mifflin, the Secretary of State of Pennsylvania, and the state Attorney General meet with him to discuss the rising violence in the area.

The President argued that the rebels were a direct threat to law and order, and Randolph insisted that the state militia be mobilized. Hamilton interjected that the issue was "whether the government can maintain itself." The state officials, though, remained unimpressed by the presentation. Mifflin concluded that the state militiamen might refuse to turn out, since many of them opposed the excise taxes and were unwilling to march the long distance to confront their fellow citizens. Washington offered to take the criticism for the mobilization by publicly initiating a call for troops in the area. But the state officials were generally reluctant to support the administration's proposals.

After the meeting, Hamilton and Knox continued to press the President for a military solution, and they stressed the need for a 12,000-man army to move into the rebellious counties. But Randolph again counseled moderation, and he asked the President to issue another proclamation and send in a peace commission to the area. Washington concurred and a three-man delegation was sent out to the western counties to end the unrest.

As the delegates rode to the area, they reported back to Washington that there were rumors of violence and that the moderates were being intimidated by the radical elements. On receipt of those letters, the President met with Randolph and Hamilton, who was handling the army while Knox was in New England, to review the situation. Washington decided to ask his friend Governor Henry Lee to mobilize the Virginia militia, and he ordered the government to stockpile supplies in case the peace initiatives failed.

However, on August 28, the rebels unexpectedly agreed to recommend to their local township committee that it accept the federal government's terms. The delegates that Washington sent promised an amnesty for past offenses and a guarantee that future prosecutions would be in state courts; in return, they demanded an oath of allegiance to the federal government. The township committee at first vigorously opposed the terms, but finally the compromise was accepted thirty-four to twenty-three. Even though the majority of the committee was favorably disposed, a substantial group of resistors remained unsatisfied and the delegates noticed the ominous sight of nearly 1,000 packhorses moving down toward Maryland to procure military supplies. The delegates recommended to Washington that armed forces be sent into the area to deal with the continuing unrest.

Expecting trouble, Hamilton had carefully begun to orchestrate the Federalist press for the coming campaign; but when the news of the town meeting began to become known, the state militia and even some elements of the Republican press and party called for military action against the rebellious leaders. Soon after some of the oath signings were disrupted, the President issued a proclamation for military action, and by the end of September he and Hamilton were on the road to join the state militia units from New Jersey, Maryland, and Virginia, converging on Carlisle and Cumberland. Randolph bluntly told Washington that Hamilton should not come along on the march, since he was the symbol of this hated tax. But the President, in one of his few departures from sound judgment in the whole affair, disagreed and asked the delighted treasury secretary to join him.[2]

The great campaign was rather brief and one-sided. One New Jersey captain recorded in his diary that the militia first moved in and arrested an Irish schoolmaster who threatened to "blow the President's brains out if he attempted to lead the army. . . . " But by October 4 Washington had arrived safely in the area and was received by the Pennsylvania and New Jersey militia. The captain recorded that the President was "saluted by a Federal salute, and the ringing of bells; and every heart expanded with joy, except the whiskey boys." The captain recorded that the President met with a delegation led by William Findley, who had strenuously opposed the excise tax. He noted that

Washington received them coldly and told them he was determined to see the laws executed, if there was energy enough in the United States to do it; that what they said of the disposition of the people to return to order did not appear; that he was now at the head of one of the finest armies he had ever commanded, and that he would have as many more as he pleased, and shortly, that he was determined to march the army to the seat of the rebellion, and told them, if they met with the least resistance, he would not answer for the consequences. This stern reply seemed to discompose the old villain, and to please every Federalist.[3]

Findley, undeterred, urged the President personally to accompany the troops on their march, for the armed forces looked rather disorderly and seemed eager to punish the rebels. Washington had decided to place General Lee in charge, although before he left, he ordered a reorganization of the militia, having observed the same problems Findley cited. With Lee in command, Hamilton decided to remain and even took part in interrogating some suspects that were captured. As the army moved into the western counties, it encountered no real resistance. Findley later graciously remarked that the President was successful in reducing the rebels with such a measure of confidence that it prevented further disruption and gave the militia no cause for recriminations.

To some, especially Hamilton, the Whiskey Rebellion was an important opportunity to show that the federal government was a force to be reckoned with. The autumn campaign was a great chapter in the administration's history, and as late as 1797, Hamilton was arguing that criticism of Federalist policies led to violence and treason, as observed in the western counties of Pennsylvania. But to others, the Whiskey Rebellion was the first in a series of repressive steps by the new government that led to the Alien and Sedition Acts under Adams and the various violations of civil liberties under Jefferson. In that perspective, the whiskey rebels were kin to the men who refused to pay the Stamp Act duties and who dumped tea in Boston Harbor.

Of course taxes were inevitable and the excise tax on liquor was high for the times but not intolerable. Most of the public probably agreed, though, that the President had acted with due deliberation in a crisis that had been building for nearly three years. Hamilton was correct in one sense: the authority of the federal government finally was at stake.[4] Yet the rebels, in their own crude way, were also correct in their assessment. The administration was so concerned about the problems of bondholders, speculators, merchants, and bankers that it seemed to have little sensitivity to their problems. Hamilton's great state papers did more than establish a structure of strong national government. He quite consciously created a mosaic of privileges meant to bind the rich and well born to the new government. The government was successful in crushing the Whiskey Rebellion and in doing what Hamilton desired; it established a precedent for the use of federal force to carry out the law. Yet the vigor with which Hamilton acted and the satisfaction he enjoyed are a bit unsettling to even the most sympathetic observer. Washington shared in little of this; for him, it was a question of duty mixed with caution and regret. Like Anthony Wayne, he may have been more uneasy than he dared to admit about using an army against even ragtag elements of the citizenry. Perhaps it is just coincidence that Washington, after having ridden to western Pennsylvania, decided to return before that army went into the areas in question. Or it may be that the genuine hero of such battles as Princeton, Trenton, and Yorktown knew the difference between a real victory and a counterfeit one.

Washington publicly and privately stressed, however, the importance of the federal government's asserting its power to compel rebellious elements to obey the law. In a rare display of pointed criticism, he later attacked "self-created societies," meaning the Democratic–Republican clubs that the President felt had instigated the rebellion. The Senate quickly approved a resolution supporting the President's condemnation, but the House refused to concur. Madison called Washington's attack "perhaps the greatest error of his political life."[5] But the President went on to make his point by declaring January 1, 1795, a day of Thanksgiving. Federalist politicians, meanwhile, shrewdly used the rebellion to help them curtail Republican support in the 1794 elections. In the end, the trials of the rebels led to only two convictions, and on July 10 Washington issued a proclamation pardoning all those who were not then under indictment or sentence. Finally he ended up pardoning the two guilty rebels, who had been sentenced to death, noting that one was a simpleton and the other insane.

24

THE JAY TREATY

Such is the turbulence of human passions in party disputes.
George Washington,
July 27, 1795

While Washington tried to keep the new American republic neutral, the war in Europe continued and its consequences profoundly changed both the Old World and the New. In the end, though, the wars of ideology begun by revolutionary France and the wars of empire heralded by Napoleon resulted in the demise of the Spanish colonial system. The United States during Jefferson's presidency was to double its size as Napoleon gladly gave up the Louisiana Territory, and American leaders were soon after to proclaim confidently that European influence would no longer be expanded in this hemisphere.

But in 1794 Washington could not have known what would be the benevolent outcomes of a brutal European war that was destroying the old order and inflaming the hearts of many Americans. At first, the President had to contend with the increasing British violations of American rights. On June 3, 1793, the British ordered their naval commanders to seize all neutral ships bound for France that carried corn, flour, or meal. The Americans vigorously reaffirmed their traditional position of freedom of the seas, but the British retained the naval advantage and used it often indiscriminately. On November 6, 1793, the British extended their order to include confiscating the produce of any colony belonging to France; such a step soon led to confrontations with American ships trading in the Caribbean. Although the British, on January 8, 1794, modified this latter rule somewhat, their basic policies remained the same. Along with problems on the high seas, the administration received reports that the Governor General of Canada, Lord Dorchester, had told an Indian delegation that the British would soon be at war with the United States and that the Indians would then recover their lost lands.

To many Americans, especially Republicans, it was clear that the enemy remained the British. In response to British actions, Jefferson, before leaving his position as Secretary of State, proposed clear commercial ties with France and trade reprisals against England. Madison concurred, and in the House he introduced seven resolutions that specified discriminatory duties and tougher policies against British shipping. On March 26, 1794, the Congress, in an increasingly anti-British mood, passed a one-month embargo against foreign shipping. The measure was later extended for a second month, and the House went on to support mobilizing 80,000 militiamen and establishing a 25,000-man auxiliary army.

Then, when anti-British sentiment seemed most intense, the French increased their seizures of American ships bound for England. To gain American support, the British relaxed their orders-in-council and began to offer compensation for cargoes that had been confiscated earlier. Hammond, who had in vain urged his government to pursue moderation, was now told to foster amity with the Americans.

Faced with the possibilities of hostilities with the French and perhaps, if the occasion arose, the British, Federalist leaders tried to forestall any major confrontations. Obviously most of them wanted to ensure that some accommodation be reached with Britain, which Federalists viewed as America's natural ally and main trading partner. In the Senate, some of Washington's major supporters approached him with a plan to deal with British relations. With the approval of Robert Morris of Pennsylvania, Oliver Ellsworth of Connecticut and George Cabot and Caleb Strong, both of Massachusetts, decided to push for a special diplomatic mission to England. Ellsworth visited the President and urged that a special agent be sent to the West Indies to see if American shipping rights were being violated, and he also proposed that an envoy extraordinary be sent to England to require "satisfaction for the loss of our property and to adjust these points which menaced a war between the two countries."

The President seemed rather unenthusiastic at first, but as Ellsworth continued, Washington became more receptive. The President mentioned Hamilton as a possible envoy but quickly dismissed him, noting that he did not possess the confidence of the country. Instead, he considered Adams, Jefferson, or John Jay. When word got out that Washington was considering a special envoy, Republican leaders and even some Federalists criticized the proposal. While Hamilton's name was being argued over, the Secretary announced his support for Jay, and Washington quickly proposed the Chief Justice's name to the Senate and sent along a general outline of his intended mission. Some initial opposition emerged. Several of the senators argued that the American Minister to Great Britain, Thomas Pinckney, could just as well handle these negotiations. Others felt that a Supreme Court justice should not be involved in drafting a treaty that might come before the Court later for judicial review. In addition, a few senators did not believe that Jay would be sufficiently aggressive to win more concessions from the British.[1]

Although, in the past, the Senate was generally consulted about what the proposals would be, this time the Federalist leaders argued against providing the executive with any real guidelines.* When it was resolved that the upper house be provided with "the whole business, with which the proposed Envoy is to be charged," the majority voted down that request. Several Federalists, though, including Hamilton, Cabot, Ellsworth, and King, met secretly with Jay. Their exact instructions were not recorded, but it appears that Jay was given two binding conditions: he was not to negotiate any agreements that conflicted with American commitments to France and he could not agree to a treaty that barred American ships from entering the British West Indies. Jay was provided with other less important recommendations as well, but it was clear that he was expected to come home with an agreement that would guarantee peace between two nations. While the envoy was not supposed to depart from the American position of freedom of the seas, his supporters realized that he might have to compromise on that principle.[2]

Jay himself was no novice in the world of international diplomacy, and he had a long and distinguished career in American politics. Although of all the major figures of the Revolution and the Federalist period, probably John Jay is the most neglected today, in his own time, few men were as well known as he was. Jay was the eighth child of a Huguenot-descended father who was a merchant and shipper from New York City. In his youth, he was instructed in the classics and attended King's College (later Columbia), which was founded by a family friend, Dr. Samuel Johnson. Jay became a lawyer and turned his interests to politics, joining the New York moderates who were struggling to control the radical element of the colony. He became an articulate spokesman for those who wanted to avoid an open break with England, although in his *Address to the People of Great Britain*, he criticized the British ministry for both its violations of American liberties and its religious toleration of Canadian Catholics. As the revolutionary struggle became more intense, Jay joined with the more radical elements and was elected to several major committees, including one to write a new constitution for New York. Jay was later named Chief Justice of the Supreme Court in the province, and became also president of the Continental Con-

---

*The first treaty rejection in the new government occurred in 1789, when the Senate refused to deal with the pending Six Nations Treaty. The next incident occurred in 1794, when the Senate rejected General Putnam's pact with the Wabash and Illinois tribes, an agreement that the body had not been consulted on before negotiations began.

gress. When the war was not going well for Washington, Jay proved to be an important ally for the General against those who attempted to replace him. As the struggle dragged on, the Continental Congress, anxious to solicit European support, finally sent Jay as its Minister to Spain. Unable to accomplish much, he found that experience left him with rather strained feelings toward both Spain and France. When the war was coming to an end, Jay was named to the peace committee to negotiate the treaty, and still later, Congress named Jay its secretary of foreign affairs, electing him without his knowledge or consent.

When Jay returned from Europe, he found himself to be a rather well-respected figure in the colonies. By 1784 most of the major figures of the Revolutionary War had retired, were still in Europe, or were more concerned with local politics than with the new national government. Jay was one of the few leaders who operated on the national level after the war, and he proved to be a rather forceful Secretary whose views were widely respected by Congress. During the Confederation period, there was some concern in the new nation about the continuation of a British presence on the frontier posts and the uncertain status of navigation rights on the Mississippi. Jay's attempt to negotiate a settlement of the latter issues with Spanish Minister Gardoqui was unsuccessful, and James Monroe publicly criticized Jay for not pressing strongly enough for navigation rights. Although Jay was somewhat effective in his handling of his duties, he was acutely aware of the problems of the old Articles of Confederation. Although he was not sent by his state to the Constitutional Convention at Philadelphia, Jay played a role in the state ratifying convention and collaborated under a common pen name with Madison and Hamilton in defending the proposed Constitution.

After Washington took office, he asked Jay to continue as secretary until Jefferson returned and then offered Jay the position of the Chief Justice of the new Supreme Court. While on the bench, Jay continued to serve as an important confidential advisor to Washington and Hamilton, giving his advice on a variety of issues from diplomacy to appointments to executive prerogatives. However, when Hamilton (in 1790 and 1792) and the President and Jefferson (in 1793) asked the Court to give advisory opinions on political issues and not on specific cases before it, Jay, leading the Court, refused.[3]

With this extensive background in foreign affairs and the support of the President and leading Federalists, Jay left the United States determined to bring back a treaty to avoid war with Britain. Upon arriving in London, he was at first well received by the British government. At the request of Lord Grenville, the British Secretary of State for Foreign Affairs, Jay submitted a draft treaty and proposed compensation for the recent maritime seizures, evacuation of the western ports on June 1, 1795, a guarantee of the American boundaries promised in the Treaty of 1783, admittance of

American vessels of up to 100 tons to the British West Indies, and some trading concessions. Jay did not include any provision dealing with compensation for confiscated slaves or reimbursement of pre-war debts.

Grenville also avoided the question of the slaves and asked that in the future, the confiscating or sequestering of debts be prohibited. He also argued against tariff discriminations toward Britain and proposed that Britain be compensated for losses from privateers that had been outfitted in American ports. The Secretary also suggested that the British West Indies be opened to American ships up to seventy tons in size because these smaller ships did not generally engage in transatlantic trade, and thus could not compete with the British carriers. Grenville indicated that he was willing to evacuate the British posts on American soil by June 1, 1796, although he insisted that the British be allowed to trade with the Indians in American territory and that British Canadians be ensured free access to the Mississippi River.

Some historians have contended that Grenville's position in the negotiations hardened for several reasons. First, Hamilton was indiscreet enough to tell British Ambassador Hammond that the United States would not join the League of Armed Neutrality, the coalition of allied powers opposed to British hegemony in Europe. In addition, Grenville was annoyed at the news that the President had sent Francophile James Monroe to Paris as his Minister, and that Monroe was warmly received and had so obviously returned those sentiments.

The long diplomatic negotiations finally led to a treaty that was not well regarded either in the United States or in Britain. The questions of pre-Revolutionary debts, compensation for illegal maritime seizures, and settlement of boundaries between New England and Canada were referred to arbitration commissions. In addition, Jay was not successful in getting the British to accept the American principle that "free ships make free goods." Instead, the treaty incorporated the British rule of 1756 that naval stores, and even provisions, would be defined as contraband. The impressment of seamen was not mentioned, and thus not forbidden, under the terms of the treaty. The British did agree to evacuate the northwest posts by mid–1796, although while Jay was in Europe, the victories of General Wayne over the Indians had already destroyed British support in those territories. The British West Indies was opened, to a limited extent, to smaller American ships, but they could not carry molasses, sugar, coffee, cocoa, or cotton to the United States.

One of the major diplomatic results of the proposed Jay Treaty, though, was a sudden reevaluation of Spanish diplomacy in the Southwest. Faced with the conflict in Europe and the uncertain policies of his British allies, the Spanish leader Manuel de Godoy, late in the summer of 1794, signaled the United States that Spain was willing to end its hostility toward the American government. Calling himself the "Prince of Peace," de Godoy used his influence as the Queen's lover to move the Spanish government into a position of friendship with the United States. Washington responded by sending Thomas Pinckney, the regular American Minister to London, to Madrid as minister extraordinary and sole plenipotentiary to the court of Spain to cement the new turn toward amity.[4]

Although Jay had dispatched three separate copies of the treaty to Washington, only one reached Philadelphia and that arrived on March 7. After some wait, Washington called a special session of the Senate on June 8. There the Republicans launched what was to be a long and bitter challenge to the President. In the secret Senate debate, Aaron Burr proposed that the President reopen negotiations on seven major points. While his motion was killed twenty to ten, the Federalists realized that the treaty, which required two-thirds ratification, was in for some trouble. Then, on June 24, a Federalist Senator from South Carolina, Jacob Read, unexpectedly raised the issue of compensation for slaves. While the Federalist leaders quickly persuaded him to withdraw his motion, the Republicans picked up the touchy issue. After some debate, the motion was defeated fifteen to twelve.

The Republicans pushed for rejection and renegotiation, but the Federalists held firm and passed a motion by the bare minimum of twenty to ten to consent to all of the treaty except Article XII. The twenty who favored the treaty on June 8 were the same number who voted for it on June 24. Not one vote was altered on either side as a result of the debate. Party lines had formed on the issue, and wisely, Hamilton had advised the Federalist leadership to request a renegotiation of the ambiguous article that prohibited the reexport to Europe of certain commodities imported from the British West Indies. Washington seemed at first confused as to how to deal with the striking of Article XII, and he asked his cabinet whether the Senate expected the revision of Article XII to be submitted for assent before the treaty should be signed. Did not the Constitution permit the president to secure whatever adjustments were necessary, and then ratify without submitting the altered article? Secretary of the Treasury Oliver Wolcott and Secretary of War Timothy Pickering both responded that the President need not deliver the revised clause to the Senate. Randolph generally agreed. Washington, however, once again consulted the retired Hamilton.

While he waited for Hamilton's response, the President watched as opposition to the treaty mounted. The agreement on secrecy was soon broken after the Senate vote, when Benjamin Franklin Bache published a summary of the treaty in his newspaper, the *Aurora*. Steven Thomason Mason, a senator from Virginia, had given Bache a copy and the editor printed a large quantity for distribution in the New England and the Middle States; by the end of July the treaty was published as far south as Charleston and Savannah, and the public responses were rather negative.

Throughout New England, Republican partisans attacked the treaty, in some cases, even before they knew of its provisions. In New York, Jay, who had been easily elected governor, was now bitterly criticized, while Hamilton, attempting to address a crowd on the issue, was stoned. In Philadelphia major Republican leaders, such as the commonwealth Secretary Alexander J. Dallas and the Chief Justice Thomas McKean, joined with House Speaker Frederick Mühlenberg to denounce the treaty. At one rally, the opponents of the treaty impaled a copy of it on a pole and carried it to the French Ambassador, Pierre Adet, who discreetly did not respond. Hamilton, in disgust, concluded that "the cry against the treaty is like that against a mad dog." Contemporary observers claimed that Jay could have walked from one end of the country to the other in the dead of night by following the lights of his own burning effigies, and in Boston the walls surrounding the house of a prominent Federalist were chalked in large letters: "Damn John Jay! Damn everyone that won't damn John Jay! Damn everyone that won't put lights in his windows and sit up all night damning John Jay!!!" Philip Freneau attacked the treaty and its supporters in a parody:

> This Treaty in one page confines
> The sad result of base designs;
> The wretched purchase here behold
> Of traitors—who their country sold.
> Here, in their proper shape and mien,
> Fraud, perjury, and guilt are seen.
> And few, a chosen few, must know,
> The Mysteries that lurk below.

While the debate continued, Washington moved to find a replacement for Jay, who had resigned from the Court, and he chose an old Republican, John Rutledge, who had been a member of the Court before his retirement in 1791. To Washington, it was a responsible appointment, one that he made, in his own words, "without hesitating a moment." But in December 1795 the Senate, faced with the claims that Rutledge was eccentric in his behavior and a wrong-thinking partisan, refused to approve the appointment.

With the unsigned treaty on his desk, Washington received evidence that British cruisers were again seizing American ships bound for France. Randolph suggested that Hammond be informed that while the President would sign the treaty and not resubmit a revision of Article XII to the Senate, the British had first to cease their seizures of American ships.

In the midst of the controversy, Washington, in mid-July, decided to leave for Virginia, where the heat would be more bearable. While he was at Mount Vernon, news came of the meetings in Boston, New York, Philadelphia, and elsewhere opposing the treaty. A distraught Washington asked his cabinet to draft a reply to one important petition against the treaty made by the British selectmen. In his response of July 28, the President defensively reminded them that "in every act of my administration I have sought the happiness of my fellow citizens."[5] Predisposed at first toward the treaty, he was facing a landslide of opposition from all corners of the country. Then, to add to his problems, Washington received a strange letter from Pickering, posted July 31, that asked him to return quickly because of a "special reason."

Washington left his estate on August 6 and on August 11 arrived in the capital. The President immediately requested Pickering's presence, and while waiting for him, he had dinner with Randolph. When Pickering arrived, Washington left Randolph and stepped into the next room with the Secretary of War. The President inquired why he had written such a cryptic letter, and Pickering, pointing to the door, replied, "That man is a traitor!" The President learned that Pickering had received indirectly from the British Minister certain dispatches of the French envoy that were on route to his superiors in Paris. These documents supposedly confirmed that Randolph had asked the French ambassador for money and had intimated that American policy could be influenced by bribes. Pickering said that Wolcott would bring the letters later that evening. Washington's feelings were obviously mixed: outwardly he seemed calm and said, "Let us return to the other room to prevent any suspicion of the cause of our withdrawing." But the President had known Randolph for twenty years and his relationship to the Secretary was close, in some ways almost paternal. That night Washington read Pickering' translations of the dispatches and concluded that Randolph had indeed compromised himself.

On August 12 the President summoned all four cabinet members to his office, and after some discussion, he clearly indicated his intention to sign the treaty. For several days he worked with Randolph on the correspondence that was to accompany the ratification. In a rare departure from etiquette, the President even visited the Secretary at home, and only when the full ratification process was complete and all details were taken care of, did Washington move to deal with Randolph. On August 19 the President met with Pickering and Wolcott; later he had the Secretary of State join them. The President closely watched Randolph's reaction as he handed him the dispatches and asked for an explanation. Randolph began to answer coolly and then stopped and requested that he be allowed to answer in writing. The President agreed. Randolph, however, deeply resented the presence of the other two secretaries at his inquisition and resigned on August 19. He proceeded to write a bitter denunciation of Washington in a long pamphlet entitled "Vindication." Much later, when Washington received a copy of this pamphlet, he angrily denounced Randolph for plotting against him, attempting to use the French minister Fauchet to overturn his administration, and receiving money for that purpose, while "all this time I have had entire faith in him, and been led by that faith to pay deference to his representations to delay the certification of the British Treaty."

Randolph was not really guilty, as Washington and the others believed, but the circumstances of his resignation tended to cloud his case, and his attack on the President and Washington's dignified silence did not help to support his claim. There is some evidence that what troubled Washington was not the suspicion that Randolph was in the pay of foreign government—for that was most unlikely—but the conversations that were attributed to Randolph concerning the Whiskey Rebellion. Randolph was supposed to have indicated that the administration's response was dictated less by a concern for preserving law and order than by a crude attempt to establish the supremacy of the federal government over an easy target. Washington clearly came off as either a dupe or a fool, an impression surely not lost on the proud President.[6]

Whatever Washington's innermost thoughts were at the time, the consequences were the same: the President not only lost an old friend, but also eliminated the last Republican figure from his official family, as partisans were quick to notice. Thus Randolph became another victim of the heightened partisanship—an atmosphere that spread out from the capital and transformed events into explosive issues, breaking down once and for all much of the older politics of deference that characterized the early republic.

Still concerned about the treaty, Washington decided at first to follow Randolph's advice and sign it only after Britain withdrew its offensive order-in-council. But fearing treachery on Randolph's part, faced with increasing Republican agitation, and desperately trying to avoid war, Washington decided to sign the treaty rather than delay it until the British proved more sensitive to American interests. Later the revision of Article XII would be resubmitted to the Senate.

25

TROUBLES IN THE
HOUSE, 1796

... and a speedy death to General Washington.

A public toast by James Thomson Callender, 1795

If Washington had hoped that by signing the treaty he would still the controversy surrounding it, he was quite mistaken. Fervent Republican partisans unleashed an attack in the House of Representatives criticizing the President's judgment and challenging his executive prerogatives. By the end of the summer Washington was moving toward a confrontation with the House, while at the same time, he was finding it difficult to staff his major departments.

In mid–1793 his personal aide, Tobias Lear, had left his service, and at the end of that year, Jefferson had resigned. By the winter of 1794–1795 Knox was gone and so was Hamilton. After he fired Randolph, Washington had to find a new Secretary of State as well as a successor to Attorney General William Bradford, who died after a long illness. The President asked his Secretary of War, Timothy Pickering, to handle also the State Department for a while. After five persons refused the position at State, the President persuaded Pickering to accept the post and appointed James McHenry to the War Department in January 1796. Washington then recruited another scion of the talented Lee family in Virginia, Charles, to assume the Attorney General spot.

Thus, by 1796, the President was not only advised by a cabinet of distinctly less able men than before, but he was also becoming the focal point for the opposition attack. The Republican newspapers hastily criticized his foreign policy and even his once revered character and record of public service. Bache called the President "a malediction on departed virtue" and "the omnipotent director of a seraglio instead of the first magistrate of a free people." In Boston another critic wrote that Washington's "modesty is comfortable to his abilities." Even his war record was subject to discredit, as Washington's opponents maintained that he had entered the nation's service only because he was preoccupied with power and glory. The *Daily Gazette* in New York charged that the Virginian had in fact betrayed his troops in the Revolution, and the *Aurora* in Philadelphia found his military record filled with examples of ineptitude and concluded that Washington was simply ill-educated.

The *Aurora*'s attacks were the most pointed and the most personal. The President was sarcastically called "Saint Washington," a man who maintained "the secularism of a monk and the supercilious distance of a tyrant." The newspaper charged that Washington had overdrawn his salary account and had received more than the authorized amount. Washington had, over the years and with the approval of Congress, drawn an advance on that account but never more than a quarter's allotment. But the newspaper pursued the matter by wondering if, in the first term, he actually received more than what was due him. If so, he should now be impeached, the journal concluded. Back in New Jersey, Freneau added his own judgment that Washington acted like a monarch and was a person who "swallows adulation like a king and vomits offensive truths in your face." Washington bitterly remarked that he was being attacked "in such exaggerated and indecent terms as would scarcely be applied to Nero, a notorious defaulter, or even a common pick-pocket."

Republican political leaders had also been increasingly alienated from the President. Jefferson blamed all of Washington's problems on Hamilton's influence over him, and John Beckley informed Madison that the President's popularity was ebbing, since he was marked "in indelible character as the lead of a British faction." To lay the groundwork for their battle against the treaty in the House of Representatives, the Republicans tried to drum up support from the state legislatures. In Virginia they pushed through the legislature a series of proposed amendments to the U.S. Constitution that included provisions to increase popular control over the U.S. Senate, require treaties to be approved by a majority of House members, and prohibit federal judges, like Jay, from holding any other appointment while sitting on the bench. The legislatures of South Carolina, Kentucky, and Georgia passed similar resolutions, but nine other states voted them down.

When the House of Representatives convened, the Republicans anxiously awaited the President's request for appropriations to implement parts of the treaty. But Washington instead waited, deciding to let matters cool down. He blandly noted that since he had not yet received notice of British ratification, no appropriations were needed. When, in February, the request from the President was still not forthcoming, the Republican leaders in the House grew so resentful that they refused to adjourn as usual to pay their respects to the President on his birthday. Finally, on February 29, Washington declared the treaty in effect and the next day he laid it before Congress, but still he did not request funding.

By then the more radical Republicans abandoned Madison's cautious leadership and one of their number, Edward Livingston, challenged the executive by demanding that the President be directed to send to the House copies of Jay's instructions and all relevant correspondence on the matter. Madison attempted to contain the attack by introducing a resolution giving the President some discretion, but the House defeated his motion. During the debate, Uriah Tracy of Connecticut asked if the resolution in any way anticipated an impeachment against John Jay or the President. Livingston responded that his motion was offered "chiefly for the sake of information." But Congressmen John Nicholas of Virginia and John Swanwick of Pennsylvania returned to Tracy's point by advancing the possibility of discovering grounds for impeaching the President.[1]

The Republicans in the House were sure that they had the votes necessary to defeat any motion to implement provisions of the treaty. By then both parties were using the caucus as a way of establishing some discipline over members and nearly two-thirds of the Congressmen voted en bloc about 93 percent of the time. What the Republicans had not counted on was Washington's intransigence and the powerful pressures the Federalists could mobilize. First, the Federalists began to circulate petitions, especially in Virginia and Maryland, to counter Republican support. Then two major bank presidents in Philadelphia hinted none too discreetly that merchants and traders would have trouble getting discounts at their institutions if they did not support the Federalist petition drives. Madison wrote Jefferson that the insurance companies in Philadelphia and New York had stopped doing business in order to alarm the public into thinking that war would follow any rejection of the treaty's provisions. It was reported that underwriters in New York had notified other seaports that vessels would not be insured until the treaty provisions were fully in operation. The Federalist establishment showed all too well how Hamilton's alliance of political power and economic influence could be quickly and effectively mobilized.

The administration also unexpectedly benefited from the news that Thomas Pinckney had completed his negotiations with the Spanish. In February 1796 the President received a copy of that document and was delighted with the results. The terms were highly favorable to the United States' earlier positions and guaranteed unrestricted use of the Mississippi River, set the thirty-first parallel as the southwest boundary, pledged Spanish cooperation in curtailing Indian attacks on the frontier, and granted the right of tax-free deposits of goods in New Orleans for export. The Senate unanimously approved the Pinckney Treaty and the Federalists reminded the Representatives from the West that the same constitutional principles and diplomatic processes that produced that popular treaty applied to the Jay document as well. In the House the Federalist leader Theodore Sedgwick also celebrated the newly ratified Algiers Treaty, which committed the Dey of Algiers to releasing Americans held in captivity on the Barbary Coast and pledged an end to the attacks that had so plagued American shippers in the Mediterranean Sea. For a ransom of $800,000 and a yearly tribute of $24,000, the administration had bought peace in the region. It began to seem that the President's diplomacy was bearing some fruit after all.

The Federalists kept up the pressures; in the Senate they warned that if the House refused to appropriate money to fund the Jay Treaty, then they might defeat passage of several important pieces of legislation, including the federal city loan, the land office bill, and even the army appropriation. They strongly warned that war was in the wind if the Jay Treaty were repudiated. The Republicans responded that Britain already had enough problems in Europe and wanted no conflict with America.[2] During the debate, the House Republicans, on the offensive and supported by several Federalists and even friends of Washington, demanded more information on the treaty. One Republican from Massachusetts, Nathaniel Freeman, pointedly asked, "on what principle was it that the Representatives were placed at such an immense distance from the Executive that they could not approach him with decency and ask for information on a subject before them?" By a vote of sixty-two to thirty-seven, the full House agreed.

Washington found himself faced with a major political and constitutional problem. Even in dealing with the Senate, the President had been cautious about providing information to that body. When, for example, in January 1794, the Senate requested the full diplomatic correspondence of Gouverneur Morris in France, it appears that the President withheld one sensitive dispatch out of the forty available. In dealing with the House, however, the President was reminded by all the cabinet secretaries that the Constitution did not give to the House any role in foreign affairs, although Attorney General Lee counseled that some accommodation should be reached. In fact, at the Constitutional Convention, a proposal was made that the House should be involved in the treaty process, and that "no treaty shall be binding on the U.S. which is not ratified by a law." The Convention delegations rejected it eight to one, with one divided.

Further researching the question, Lee and Treasury Secretary Wolcott could not find in the government's records one instance in which Washington even inadvertently conceded such a role to the House of Representatives. Thus, after considerable deliberation, the President refused the request, concluding that the House did not have a part in the treaty process and noting, "A just regard to the Constitution and to the duty of my Office ... forbids a compliance with your request." Then he bluntly added, "It does not occur that the inspection of the papers ... can be relative to any proposal under the cognizance of the House of Representatives, except that of an impeachment, which the resolution has not expressed."[3]

The Republican leaders were astonished and angry at the President's refusal. Madison wrote Monroe that the advice and the message "were contrived in New York"—an obvious reference to Hamilton's supposed influence. Since the President had finally forwarded the Pinckney Treaty to the House with a request for funds to implement it, he then decided to nominate commissioners for the arbitration commission specified in the Jay Treaty as well. The Republicans in turn sought to bar any appropriations to implement the controversial agreement. This would be their response to Washington.

Fisher Ames of Massachusetts called the development "the most serious [crisis] I ever witnessed"; the new Chief Justice, Oliver Ellsworth, saw the House's proposed action "as unwarranted as it is dangerous"; and Hamilton forwarded a list of thirteen reasons why the President should resist legislative "usurpation." The Republicans, led by Madison, argued that it was a major constitutional question, and Albert Gallatin maintained that any treaty that challenged existing legislation, as the Jay agreement seemed to, required House approval.

The precise role of the House in foreign affairs was, and is, unclear. That body is not part of the official treaty approval mechanism, yet it is the beginning of the appropriation process. If a treaty requires some financial commitment, does the House, then, have in effect a veto that the Constitution does not formally grant? Jefferson recorded that he had previously discussed the issue with the President when he was Secretary of State, when another treaty issue arose. The Senate had informed the executive in that case that he should take the money from the Treasury or float a special loan, but that the executive need not go to the House for any appropriation. Washington, however, did not agree and relied on the general goodwill of the House, while he avoided admitting that that body should be granted specific consideration in foreign affairs. He told Jefferson that "he did not like throwing too much into democratic hands, that if they would not do what the Constitution called on them to do, the government would be at an end, and must *then assume another form*." Jefferson argued for some prior consultation of the House, but Washington "desired me to strike out the intimation that the seal would not be put till both Houses should have voted the money."[4] This exact issue then became a major point of contention again, when the Republicans in control of the House tried to prevent the Jay Treaty from being implemented.

In the debate, the Federalists realized that they needed a forceful spokesman in the House to present the administration's position and to capitalize on the popular fear that if the Jay Treaty was repudiated, war would occur with Britain. The ablest speaker they had was Fisher Ames, and he captivated the Representatives with his arguments on the issue. Ames was the son of a Dedham, Massachusetts, innkeeper, physician, and astronomer. At the age of twelve, the gifted boy was sent to Harvard College, where he quickly established himself as a scholar and a fine public speaker. He was deeply influenced by the classics, and later, in 1781, he was admitted to the bar. Ames became a major critic of the Articles of Confederation, and in his "Camillis" essays in 1787, he argued for significant changes. Elected to the Massachusetts ratifying convention, he strongly supported the Constitution and was seen as a powerful Federalist ally when he defeated Samuel Adams and entered the First Congress. Ames soon became a loyal supporter of Washington and Hamilton and a critic of what he called the "yawning listlessness" of his fellow congressmen. Replete with classic references, devoid of vanity, and recognized as an honest and fearless opponent, Ames was an impressive figure in the House.

In the debate on the Jay Treaty, he quickly argued for the sanctity of treaties and the need for the House to support efforts to bring a peaceful solution to the strained relationship. He pleaded in the best eighteenth-century oratorical style:

Will our government be able to temper and restrain the turbulence of such a crime? The government, alas! will be in no captivity to govern a divided people, and divided counsels! Shall we cherish the spirit of peace or show the energies of war? Shall we make our adversary afraid of our strength, or dispose him, by measure of resentment and broken faith, to respect our rights? Do gentlemen rely on the state of peace, because both nations will be worse disposed to keep it? Because injuries and insults still harder to endure, will be mutually offered?

In the gallery, Justice James Iredell remarked to John Adams, "My God! How great he is!" and the Vice-President, with tears in his eyes, replied, "It is divine."[5]

As the debate continued, the House, sitting as a Committee of the Whole, was clearly divided, and the body finally split forty-nine to forty-nine on whether to approve the request to fund the provisions of the treaty. The decision was up to Frederick Mühlenberg, the Committee's chair, a staunch Pennsylvania Republican and previously a vocal opponent of the treaty. Mühlenberg, however, voted against his own party and supported the President. A few days later he was stabbed by his own brother-in-law, a rabid Republican, and in the next election he was defeated.

The Republican leadership, which had counted on victory, now saw its carefully constructed campaign voted down. Madison lamented that it was a crippling defeat and concluded that "the name of the President and the alarm of war have had a greater effect than was apprehended on our side." Washington generally avoided public comment on the issue, but privately he accused the House of "striking at one, and boldly too, the fundamental principles of the Constitution." Somewhat defensively the President wrote to David Humphreys, "I am attacked for a steady opposition to every measure which has a tendency to disturb the peace and tranquility." But, he concluded, he would continue to render his country service, knowing that "I have not . . . been guilty of a willful error, however numerous they may have been from other causes."

The Republicans had thus forced Washington closer into the Federalist camp, but they had seriously misjudged the deep public affection the President had in the country and among many in their own ranks. Jefferson, observing the defeat in the House, simply said, "One man outweighs them all in influence over the people."[6]

As for the Jay Treaty, it did not provide Americans with the types of guarantees they wanted. But in the long run, the treaty did keep British markets open, and the value of U.S. exports to the Empire increased 300 percent in the period from 1795 to 1800, while trade with the British West Indies doubled during that time. American willingness to reach agreement with Britain certainly laid the groundwork for a Spanish settlement, one that was warmly applauded by Americans. Overall, Jay had done what Hamilton and the Federalist leadership advocated: he opened the trading lanes to Britain, which increased the general revenues that supported in turn the former secretary's financial structure. Most important, though, Jay had heeded Washington's concern to move the two countries away from possible war. The Republican position was an appealing one, but a short-sighted policy for a weak country with a token military and only the loosest ties of nationalism.

26

FRENCH IRE TO THE
END, 1796–1797

After bringing the country to the very brink of ruin, Washington has
fled from the gathering storm.

Aurora,
March 13, 1797

During the difficult controversy over the Jay Treaty, Washington, in despair, wrote Hamilton, "What am I to do for a Secretary of State?" Hamilton
had already sounded out Rufus King, who refused, and was forced to
conclude that "in fact, a first-rate character is not attainable. A second-rate
must be taken with good dispositions and barely decent qualifications. I
wish I could throw more light. 'Tis a sad omen for the government."

At first, the President had his Secretary of War, Pickering, take over the
State Department, but the burden proved too great, and Washington became
annoyed when matters that needed attention were forgotten or mishandled.
For example, in December 1795 Congress requested a report on the state
of the military, but none was forthcoming. Congressional leaders complained to the President that they were not given the information they
needed, and Washington in turn had to reprimand the harried Secretary.

Part of the problem was that Pickering's background was more administrative than policy making, and he had no real experience for the position
at State, where he ended up during Washington's second term. He came
from a well-established family in Salem, Massachusetts, and was a graduate
of Harvard College, continuing on to earn a master's degree, probably in
preparation for the ministry. Instead of pursuing that vocation, he turned
to the study of law and joined the local militia. In the late 1760s, when early
colonial resistance was starting, Pickering remained a Tory in his politics
and conservative in his sentiments. As the patriot cause grew more popular,
though, he tended to move toward the local leaders and served in a variety
of positions, including in the legislature. Pickering decided to stay in the

militia and became a colonel of the First Essex Regiment. Later, because of his caution, his troops arrived too late to intercept the British on their way to the Battle of Lexington.

During the war, he became an Adjutant General, a member of the Board of War, and, from 1780 to 1788, the Quartermaster of the Army. He was less a leader of men or a great strategist than he was a competent bureaucrat, at home in the structured world of the military. He remained convinced that the society around him was corrupt and only the regular army epitomized civic virtue. But the post-war military was a small service, and Pickering quit rather than "starve in public life," as he put it. He soon moved to Philadelphia and began an unprofitable business partnership. By 1784 Pickering was trying to become the new Quartermaster of the Army, but Congress appointed Henry Knox. Deeply disappointed, he moved to the Wilkes Barre area of Pennsylvania and became involved in some land disputes. By 1790 he wrote William Duer, Hamilton's Assistant Secretary and an old-time war acquaintance, and asked about the possibility of some government post that might soon open up. Pickering was eventually recommended for the postmaster general position, and while he waited for final approval, the administration sent him to negotiate a treaty with some tribes in the northern areas.

Pickering then became a minor figure in the new administration, a competent but unimaginative public servant who stood at the periphery of events while titans like Hamilton and Jefferson split the government into factions. However, as the years passed, low salaries and the desire of many political leaders to stay in their own state led many established figures to reject major posts in the federal government. In one sense, Washington desperately wanted to recruit and retain the very best people for these spots, but in another sense, he probably reflected how such independent spirits had contributed to his problems in the first place.[1]

With his new Secretary of State in place, Washington set the direction of foreign policy and left Pickering to implement those judgments and deal with the diplomatic corps in the capital. By then Genet had been replaced by Pierre Adet, who proved to be equally belligerent in his dealings with the American administration. He clearly presented the French government's view that the Jay Treaty was a violation of the earlier treaty that the United States and France had signed in 1778, when both supported freedom of the seas. Now, he argued, the administration watched as its loyal ally, France, went to war with its recent enemy and tacitly concurred in the royal navy's curtailments of non-belligerent shipping.

Adet presented his case to the public, and unlike his predecessor, he did not threaten to go over the President's head, but simply made his letter to Pickering available to the Republican press. The Minister announced that the Directory would adopt a more restrictive policy toward American vessels carrying provisions and naval stores to English ports. The French, he warned, would treat neutral nations in the same way as "they allow themselves to be treated by the British." Adet's objectives were, in some ways, similar to Genet's: he attempted to support secession on the western frontiers and tried to strengthen France's position in the Louisiana Territory. He even went further than the impulsive Genet by trying to influence American voters to support Thomas Jefferson for President. On November 15, 1796, he issued a public letter that recalled old Revolutionary allegiances, pleaded for a restoration of amiable relations, and aimed to sway the electors' meetings in December. Finally he concluded his plea by announcing that his mission to the United States had been suspended.[2]

Washington and Pickering attempted to reply to Adet's criticisms on several occasions. In the beginning of 1797, the President sent to the House a series of supporting documents that traced the history of Franco-American relations since the war in Europe began. As was customary, the House would publish and distribute these documents to interested parties. Once the record came out, critics were quiet for a while and Madison was moved to refer to the documents as "an overt patronage of the British cause."

The administration, though, found that not only was Adet a problem, but so were the British with their attacks on American ships and seamen. Despite the provisions of the Jay Treaty, English privateers were capturing American merchant vessels during the period from 1795 to 1796. Pickering's protests had sharply reduced the number of such incidents, but the Republicans continued to point out the British violations. The Republicans further pushed for some action to end British impressment of American seamen, and the Federalists had little choice but to join in the patriotic outrage.

The administration finally appointed an American agent in Great Britain to deal with the impressment issue, and Pickering sent Silas Talbot, an old Revolutionary War hero, to the Caribbean to check out the problem. After some investigation, Talbot found that there were fewer cases than had been charged and noted that British commanders were becoming more circumspect in their actions. The issue was deflected in time for the 1796 election, but as British desertions increased, the number of seizures and impressments rose again. Republicans devoted considerable space in their newspapers to these alleged British atrocities; and Adet pressed Pickering, claiming that American sailors were crucial to manning the British navy in the West Indies. Pickering tried to ignore Adet's charges, but the Minister used the Secretary's unresponsiveness as part of his public attack on the administration.

Troubled by these events, Washington was concerned that American policies were not being properly conveyed to the French Directory, and he decided to heed Hamilton's advice and recall James Monroe, who was a critic of the Jay Treaty. At first, the President tried to work out a compromise whereby Monroe would stay as Minister to France and a special envoy would be sent to settle disputes between the two nations. But Pickering, with Hamilton's concurrence, drafted the cabinet's reply, asserting that the President's proposal was "unconstitutional," since any such envoy had to be approved by the Senate, and the Congress was not in session. For good measure, Pickering reminded Washington that Monroe was in communication with the Republican leaders who were attacking him personally. Finally the President agreed to replace Monroe with Charles C. Pinckney, a reliable Southern Federalist. The French Directory, however, refused to receive the new ambassador, and he was ordered home in late January 1797, just after the election of John Adams.

In terms of domestic politics, the President issued on September 17, 1796, his farewell address, and his withdrawal turned the election into a real partisan contest. Adams had inherited a fractionalized coalition, and there were rumors that Hamilton was really maneuvering to get Thomas Pinckney of South Carolina elected. The Republicans rallied around Jefferson and focused their efforts on the key areas in the South and in the Middle States. The major battleground seemed to be in Pennsylvania, and the Republicans, under John Beckley, were rather organized, putting together a slate of highly visible leaders who could attract votes and lend support to Jeffersonian electors. Beckley publicized Adams' supposedly British leanings, and he may have asked Adet to issue the statement criticizing Federalist foreign policy. It is doubtful whether Adet's letter had any real effect, but the Jefferson slate carried fourteen out of fifteen electoral votes in the state, even though its plurality was only 125 votes out of 24,487 cast. It soon became apparent, however, that while Jefferson had captured the critical Pennsylvania delegation, his support was still not strong enough to overcome Adams' earlier lead elsewhere.[3]

As for Washington, he pursued his neutrality policy during the election and afterward. Even toward the end of his term, he found himself subject to some of the bitterest criticisms ever leveled against him during his long career in public life. In late 1796 Thomas Paine, the pen of the American Revolution, published a vehement attack on the President. Paine felt that Washington had done too little to get him out of a French jail, and he decided to accuse Washington of arrogance, fraud, and even the murder of French diplomats at Jumonville. He summed up his case, "The world will be puzzled to decide whether you are an apostate or an imposter; whether you have abandoned good principles, or whether you ever had any."[4] Was this to be the way posterity would remember him, Washington worried? Concerned as always about his reputation, the President collected voluminous records so that future generations might judge his stewardship favorably.

Some of his personal colleagues joined in the criticism of the President in a more private way. Jefferson wrote that there was a decline in Washington's powers by 1793—the period he and the President went their separate ways. Jefferson remarked that "his memory was already sensibly impaired by age. The firm tone of his mind, for which he had been re-markable, was beginning to relax. Its energy was abated; a listlessness of labor, a desire for tranquility had crept on him, and a willingness to let others act or even think for him." At that time, an indiscreet letter from Jefferson to Philip Mazzei was published in Paris and then in the United States. In it, Jefferson complained that the "Anglican, Monarchial and Aris-tocratical Party" controlled the government and indirectly attacked Wash-ington with the observation, "it would give you a fever were I to name to you the apostates who have gone over to these heresies, men who were Samsons in the field and Solomons in the Council, but who have had their heads shorn by the harlot, England."[5]

Elbridge Gerry, at the same time, criticized the president for not having established a broad basis of support for his policies, relying instead only on "the union of the funded, bank, commercial, Cincinnati and anti-revolu-tionary or monarchial interest."[6] Yet it is important to realize that after 1795, Washington lacked experienced advisors, faced major diplomatic and political problems, and insisted on assuming personal leadership in foreign policy. If he was on the slope of a decline, Washington surely must have drawn on extraordinary reserves, as he continually prevailed in that period.

There is no question that opposition to the Jay Treaty was intense in some quarters, and that the document did not seem favorable to American interests. When the President concurred in the treaty and refused to back down from the challenge in the House, criticisms in the capital grew more heated and quite personal. But Philadelphia was not the United States, and its cafes and boarding houses, its newspapers and caucuses did not reflect the general feeling of the nation as a whole. The appeal that Washington had from his long career of public service was so deep-rooted that the populace never came to share in Freneau's cynicism or the *Aurora*'s bitter-ness. Wherever the President went, there was a tremendous outpouring of support, and despite the diatribes of Randolph, Paine, and, later, Monroe, Washington's reputation was safe in the hearts of the citizenry. By the time of the election of 1796, Washington was closing out his public career with a thoughtful farewell to the nation. His Republican critics, and probably even some of his Federalist supporters, were glad that he had stepped down, but they all knew that if he had chosen to run again, the presidency would be easily his for the asking for the rest of his life.

When Adams' election was announced, Washington expressed satisfaction that his Federalist successor would preserve the United States "in peace and friendship with all the world." In January the President recorded with satisfaction that "all the diplomatic corps (except France) dined with me." He then turned his attention to raising some cash from his many debtors to help finance his move back to Mount Vernon. On his birthday, the last one he would celebrate in public life, some 1,200 persons turned out to honor him once again. But the *Aurora* would not give up; it published forged letters from 1777 that supposedly showed Washington guilty of still other crimes. The President had never answered these old charges, but this time he decided to write a response and deposit it in the State Department "as a testimony of the truth to the present generation and to posterity." Always posterity, always the fame and reputation that men brought up in the American classic tradition so coveted.[7]

On March 3 he held a dinner for department heads, foreign dignitaries, and others, toasting them "for the last time . . . as a public man." Then the next day the President walked to Congress for Adams' inauguration. Wearing a black suit, a powdered wig, and a military hat with a cockade, he approached the larger House chamber and was greeted with a tremendous ovation. Jefferson, the newly elected vice-president, followed. There, sitting on the elevated dais, Adams thought, "A solemn scene it was indeed, and it was made affecting to me by the presence of the General, whose countenance was as serene and unclouded as the day. He seemed to me to enjoy a triumph over me. Methought I heard him say, 'Ay! I am fairly out and you're fairly in! See which of us will be happier!' "[8]

The ceremony over, the first transition having been completed, Washington watched as President Adams walked out of the hall, and he motioned to Vice-President Jefferson that he should go next. But Jefferson deferred until Washington, ever mindful of protocol, insisted.

27

WASHINGTON AS
LEGEND

Did anyone ever see Washington nude?

Nathaniel Hawthorne

While Washington, in his own lifetime, reached heroic stature in the eyes of many, it was only after his passing that the process of true mythologizing took place. At the time of his death in December 1799, many eulogies were given and nearly 300 published. The image of Washington was quickly shaped by the publication of a biography written by an Episcopal minister, Mason Locke Weems. Weems traveled the countryside in his wagon, selling books after he played a tune on his fiddle. In his first venture into publication, he wrote in favor of early marriages and large families in a tract entitled *Matrimonial Tattoo Against Bachelors*, later reissued as *Hymen's Recruiting-Sergeant*. Seeing the obvious market for a Washington biography, Weems collected anecdotes, created others, invented conversations, and turned his work into a profitable enterprise. He wrote one publisher that his volume on Washington would not only promote morality and patriotism, but also make "a world of peace and popularity" for the author and publisher.

When in 1800 the biography was published, critics denounced the work as a "literary antic," but Weems' *The Life of Washington, the Great* went through nine printings and sold more than eight editions. It is from Weems that we have the famous cherry tree story and other anecdotes that have so charmed generations. Weems' account was followed by John Marshall's five-volume biography published from 1804 to 1807, which John Adams criticized as "a mausoleum, 100 feet square at the base and 200 feet high." Despite its cumbersome style, Marshall's study sold well for years and added to the image of Washington as a godlike hero. Those works were followed by Jared Sparks' biography in 1837 and Washington Irving's five-volume effort in the 1850s, both of which furthered the image of a sanitized figure.[1]

As the Revolution itself became romanticized and the new American nation witnessed a growth of self-conscious nationalism, Washington's role became paramount. This new patriotism was best epitomized by historian George Bancroft, who discerned the influence of God in American history and cast Washington as the instrument of such divine intervention. Beyond the nineteenth century and into the twentieth century, the Washington myth grew larger. By 1932 a special Bicentennial commission devoted itself, through a Madison Avenue-style exhibit, to further "Freedom's Myth." Stamps, coins, medals, pageants, pictures, all celebrated Washington's birthday; a special song was written by George M. Cohan, a new march composed by John Philip Sousa, and a well-known poem, written by Edwin Markham and titled "Man with a Hoe," portrayed Washington as a figure who "toiled with men until he flamed with God."

When Thackeray attempted in 1858 to portray Washington realistically in *The Virginians*, one American commentator warned that "Washington's character has come to us spotless, and must remain so." By 1880 Henry Adams, in his novel *Democracy*, had several of his characters explain what Washington meant to them, and their responses ranged from a Job-like figure to an illiterate, profane, and dull man. Thus, by the twentieth century, the outlines of Washington's life were known to all, but the personality of the man seemed lost. One English historian concluded that it is impossible to separate the man from the myth, for "the man isn't the monument; the monument is America." Yet, oddly enough, by so suppressing the real Washington, he has become boring and even a bit pompous to the posterity he so cared about. Abigail Adams, observing the beginnings of the mythological process, objected, "simple truth is his best, his greatest eulogy."

Part of the gap is due to the fact that the men who worked with Washington seldom wrote any systematic character sketches of the man. Hamilton, for example, gave the impression that Washington's main purpose in life was to foster his own plans. The Federalists used the Washington name in the late 1790s to solidify their shaky political base, and some bitter Republicans, after his death, were heard to toast, "George Washington—down to the 1787, and no farther." Even the muddling Timothy Pickering wrote that while Washington had moral integrity, his prudence was often the result of a lack of decisiveness and other deficiencies.

In order to rescue Washington from the Federalists, Jefferson, in his own inaugural address, graciously referred to his fellow Virginian as "our first and great revolutionary character . . . entitled to the first place in his country's love, and . . . the fairest page in the volume of faithful history." And it was Jefferson who, in his discerning way, penned in 1814 the best summary evaluation of the first President:

His mind was great and powerful, without being of the very first order; his penetration strong, though not so acute as that of a Newton, Bacon or Locke; and as far as he saw, no judgment was ever sounder. It was slow in operation, being so little aided by invention or imagination, but sure in conclusion.... Perhaps the strongest feature in his character was prudence, never acting until every circumstance, every consideration, was maturely weighed; refraining if he saw a doubt, but, when once decided, going through with his purpose whatever obstacles opposed. His integrity was most pure, his justice the most inflexible I have ever known, no motives of interest or consanguinity, of friendship or hatred, being able to bias his decision. He was, indeed, in every sense of the words, a wise, a good, and a great man.

His temper was naturally irritable and high-toned; but reflection and resolution had obtained a firm and habitual ascendancy over it. If, however, it broke its bounds, he was most tremendous in his wrath. In his expenses he was honorable, but exact; liberal in contributions to whatever promised utility; but frowning ... on ... all unworthy calls on his charity. His heart was not warm in its affections; but he exactly calculated every man's value, and gave him a solid esteem proportioned to it. His person ... was fine, his stature exactly what one would wish, his deportment easy, erect and noble; the best horseman of his age, and the most graceful figure that could be seen on horseback. Although in the circle of his friends, where he might be unreserved with safety, he took a free share in conversation, his colloquial talents were not above mediocrity, possessing neither copiousness of ideas, nor fluency of words. In public, when called on for a sudden opinion, he was unready, short and embarrassed. Yet he wrote readily, rather diffusely, in an easy and correct style. This he had acquired by conversation with the world, for his education was merely reading, writing, and common arithmetic, to which he added surveying at a later day. His time was employed in action chiefly, reading little, and that only in agriculture and English history.... His correspondence became necessarily extensive, and, with journalizing his agricultural proceedings, occupied most of his leisure hours within doors. On the whole, his character was, in its mass, perfect, in nothing bad, in a few points indifferent; and it may truly be said, that never did nature and fortune combine more perfectly to make man great, and to place him in the same constellation with whatever worthies have merited from man an everlasting remembrance. For his was the singular destiny and merit, of leading the armies of his country successfully through an arduous war, for the establishment of its independence; of conducting its councils through the birth of a government, new in its forms and principles until it had settled down into a quiet and orderly train; and of scrupulously obeying the laws through the whole of his career, civil and military, of which the history of the world furnishes no other example.... He has often declared to me that he considered our new constitution as an experiment on the practicability of republican government, and with what dose of liberty could man be trusted for his own good; that he was determined the experiment should have a fair trial, and would lose the last drop of his blood in support of it ... I do believe that General Washington had not a firm confidence in the durability of our government. He was naturally distrustful of men, and inclined to gloomy apprehensions; and I was ever persuaded that a belief that we must at length end in something like a British constitution, had some weight in adoption of the ceremonies of levees, birth-days, pompous meetings with Congress, and other forms of the same character, calculated to prepare us gradually for a change which he believed possible, and to let it come on us with as little shock as might be to the public mind.

These are my opinions of General Washington, which I would vouch at the judgment seat of God, having been formed on an acquaintance of thirty years... I felt on his death, with my countrymen, that "verily a great man hath fallen this day in Israel."[2]

Thus, to many people even in his own time, Washington assumed heroic proportions that put him beyond their reach. He was, after all, the leader of the Revolution and was compared with Moses, Samuel, Josiah, Fabius, and, of course, Cincinnatus. His bearing led some extravagant supporters to refer to him as the "godlike Washington" even when he was alive. Although Washington was not immune to bitter criticism during his time in office, after his death there was a nearly universal period of mourning that spread throughout the nation and most of Europe. Eulogies, commemorative poems, public demonstrations of grief were profuse. The most famous funeral oration was given by Henry "Light-Horse Harry" Lee of Virginia, who drew up the resolution introduced in Congress by John Marshall to commemorate the death of the first president: "First in war, first in peace, and first in the hearts of his country-men; he was second to none in the humble and endearing scenes of private life; pious, just, humane, temperate, and sincere; uniform, dignified, and commanding; his example was as edifying to all around him as were the effects of that example lasting."[3]

As the biographers reworked their material, Washington became idealized as a man of personal integrity and selfless patriotism. More emphasis was placed on his military glory than on his presidential service, and as the spirit of sectionalism grew in the 1840s and 1850s, he became a figure that both sides could praise. Lincoln's orations and Webster's speeches pointed to his nationalism, while Southern spokesmen reminded citizens of Washington's love of his state and his holding of slaves during his lifetime.[4]

Emerson, watching the development of the patriotic cult, noted that "every hero becomes a bore at least . . . "; but by the middle of the nineteenth century, the myth of George Washington was firmly entrenched. Used by partisan orators, needed by nationalist politicians, exploited by sentimental and commercial biographers, the reality of an intense, often impatient, honest patrician was lost. The cold, almost impassive figure, the frozen image of a stoic Roman warrior became memorialized, dwarfing the Virginian who loved to dance with beautiful women, enjoyed riding the finest mounts, and was prone to incredible fits of periodic energy before he would retreat into solitude and listlessness. Washington had struggled all of his life to master his vigorous impulses, to hold his temper, to control his emotions. He was never totally successful in curtailing that side of himself. Only in his death was he fully drained of such human passions and thus lost to posterity. He became the noble patriarch—a pale reflection of his full self, but an image that he would probably appreciate in spite of it all.[5]

EPILOGUE

Oh, my country! May peace be within thy walls, and prosperity within thy palaces.

> John Adams,
> December 28, 1800

With Washington's retirement, the mantle of executive leadership passed to his Federalist successor, John Adams. Although Adams barely won an electoral college majority over Thomas Jefferson, still many Republicans hailed the choice as an improvement over the previous administration. The editor Bache, who had so mercilessly attacked Washington, now called Adams a man of "incorruptible integrity" and "an admirer of republicanism." And Jefferson, who knew the new President well, once praised his civic virtue, concluding that Adams was "as disinterested as the God who made him."[1]

John Adams began his administration by adhering to the Federalist model of the presidency, continuing Washington's policies, and even keeping his cabinet in place. The latter decision was surely a misguided one, as it ended up leaving the major government positions in the hands of men more loyal to Hamilton than to the President himself. The Adams presidency inherited the uneasy neutrality policies of Washington, but the new President deliberately made overtures to the French regime, including sending a special commission to Paris to push for a modus vivendi—only to have those overtures rebuffed. Adams cautiously asked a reluctant Congress to approve an increase in military preparedness, and as the French government proved more intransigent, the President was pushed by some Federalist leaders into a more belligerent posture.[2]

In France the French Foreign Minister Talleyrand reminded the American envoys of Napoleon's victories and warned of the "power and violence of France," while he presented in turn a demand for bribes from the peace delegation. The U.S. government had paid such bribes before to the North African pirate states, but this time the price was too high, especially from a seeming ally. One of the American delegates, Charles Pinckney, blurted out, "It is no, no; not a sixpence." The exclamation became a slogan, and Federalists added to it the famous rejoinder, "Millions for defense; not one penny for tribute." The Old World had once again misjudged the New, and the world-weary cynicism of Talleyrand provided a convenient contrast to the pristine republicanism that marked the American self-image.[3]

Intense partisans of both parties in the United States used the confusion and the anxieties that grew up around the war in Europe to further their own ends. The Federalist party leaders, especially in New England, combined their hatred of French radicalism with a paranoid suspicion of Jefferson and the Republican party. They helped to generate local hysterias, and rumors spread of Irish, French, and even Bavarian plots to overthrow the federal government. In order to curtail the growing electoral influence of the opposition party, the Federalists in Congress pushed legislation to hamstring the Republican press and to abridge the liberties of foreigners—many of whom went on to join the Republican party.[4]

Many Republicans in turn insisted on continuing their policy of friendship toward France, even after common sense and political prudence should have told them to disassociate their sentiments from the new regime. Some of the more radical party leaders in the House of Representatives even sought to discredit Adams' foreign policy as they had sought to discredit Washington's—with the same result. When Adams was asked for copies of his instructions to the American commissioners in Paris, he quickly complied, sending those documents as well as a record of the French's insulting response. The public reaction to the so-called XYZ correspondence was predictably patriotic and vitriolic. Adams began picking up the tempo by handing out to visiting groups the black cockade, an old American Revolution decoration, to replace the tricolor hats worn by some admirers of the French government. It has been estimated that three-quarters of the nation's newspapers rallied behind the administration, and Henry Knox, watching the event, concluded admiringly, "The President shines like a God."[5]

Then the Federalist-controlled Congress, caught up in the patriotic fever, approved an increase in the size of the armed forces and the naming of a reluctant George Washington to be commander in chief in the field. The legislative branch also approved a series of new laws aimed at curtailing dissent and controlling aliens. On June 18, 1798, the President signed the Naturalization Act, and soon after the Alien Act, the Alien Enemy Act, and the Sedition Law, legislation designed to control foreigners, prolong the citizenship waiting period, and clamp down on criticism of the government. As for the President, Adams wrote in the summer of 1798 endless responses to formal addresses and town resolutions about the crisis, and he flayed away at the French Directory and their alleged domestic supporters. His own judgment was clear: "The finger of destiny writes on the wall the word: War."[6]

But the Congress was reluctant to go to war and, as usual, not disposed to raise taxes right away. Also, Adams was beginning to see the scheming hand of Hamilton making its way into control over the New Army, and the President started to procrastinate on the mobilization effort. He privately lamented later that "with all ministers against me, a great majority of the Senate and the House of Representatives, I was no more at liberty than a man in prison, chained to the floor and bound hand and foot."[7]

Adams also seemed genuinely uncomfortable with enforcing the Alien Acts and often acted as a break on arrests and deportations begun by his own cabinet officers. He had fewer problems, though, implementing the Sedition Act, as opposition press leaders, who had attacked the administration, were tried and convicted. The Republicans were clearly thrown on the defensive, with even the Vice-President being under informal surveillance. Jefferson and Madison secretly tried to induce friendly state legislatures to interpose themselves between the federal government and their citizens, but only Virginia and Kentucky would follow their clandestine proposals. The real relief in sight came, as Jefferson had predicted: "The disease of the imagination will pass over because the patients are essentially Republicans. Indeed the Doctor is now on his way to cure it, in the guise of the tax gatherer."[8]

Suppressing newspapers and deporting aliens were inexpensive exercises. But the raising up of an army was not, and Congress had to impose more taxes, duties, and customs on the people. Historically, Americans, as a people, both loved liberty and hated taxes, and sometimes it is difficult to find out which held the main allegiance in their hearts—indeed, the Revolution showed that the two could really be the same. The Federalist assault began to come undone because the populace did not want war, did not wish to pay for preparedness, and because Adams was concerned about the role of Hamilton in the grand strategy.

By early 1799 the President also began to receive some reports from Europe and from one of his envoys back from France that the attitudes of Napoleon and Talleyrand were changing toward America. Adams embarked on an abrupt peace initiative and ended up appointing another special commission to go to France in order to resolve the problems between the two republics.[9] When his cabinet opposed his decision, Adams decided to return from his home in Massachusetts and take command of his own administration. Finally, in the summer of 1800, the President demanded the resignations of his Secretaries of State, War, and Treasury. The peace mission was successful, but its results arrived too late to influence the presidential election. Adams was left in retirement with the consolation that the peace missions he sent to France were, in his words, "the most disinterested and meritorious actions of my life." He was correct in that flattering judgment.

The defeat of Adams and the confusingly tense, but pacific passing of power to the opposition party were extraordinary sights. Free people had created republics before, only to see them flounder during crisis and be consumed in domestic struggle. The election of 1800 completed the development of the early presidency—executive authority had been redefined, reasserted, and institutionalized, and executive power had passed without the clash of arms to a new faction, although rumblings were heard when it appeared that Jefferson might be cheated out of his due.

The Federalist model of the presidency, then, was a casualty in the destruction of the Federalist party, with its internal divisions between Hamilton and Adams, the extreme positions that characterized some of the New England partisans, the criticisms of the class-oriented economic policies of Hamilton's economic system, and the genuine disdain from many for the Alien and Sedition Acts and the philosophy behind them.

But Adams' defeat was probably not caused by Hamilton's schism or a major popular repudiation of his administration. A comparison of Adams' elections in 1796 and 1800 shows that the major factors in his defeat were the loss of New York's twelve electoral votes to the Jefferson–Burr ticket and the end of independent electors. In 1796 seventy-eight electoral votes were cast for candidates besides the four put forth by the parties for president and vice-president. By 1800 only one vote was cast outside that group of four—that ballot being for John Jay. Thus within four years, the Republicans had solidified the Virginia–New York alliance and party allegiances had firmed up considerably.

The Federalist model of the presidency was lost under the rising tide of a strong party system. With its pose above partisanship, its distance from congressional politics and intrigue, its conservative sense of public policy and public stewardship, the Federalist model was not attuned to the broader expanses of equalitarianism and democratic leadership that Jefferson and, more importantly, his lieutenants brought in. Republican gains in 1800 were even more apparent in Congress as the party carried both Houses.

As for Jefferson himself, he was no outsider to the Founding Fathers. Distrust him they might, but the Federalists had to admit that he was a genuine part of their Revolutionary past and surely much preferred to that dangerous "new man," that parvenu Burr. While Hamilton undercut Adams and characterized Jefferson as a "contemptible hypocrite," still he found Burr was "the most unfit and dangerous man in the country." And as President, Jefferson, with his exquisite love of the felicitous phrase and his sound political instinct, calmly struck the right tone of reconciliation in his inaugural address as he pronounced, "We are all Federalists, we are all Republicans. We have called men of the same brethren by different names."[10]

Still he moved quickly to lay aside much of the trappings of the Federalist model of the presidency. Jefferson abandoned the pomp, played down public appearances, and shrewdly used party leaders to control the Republican-dominated Congress. He urged a few prosecutions of Federalist editors at the state level, purged some obnoxious Federalist judges and officeholders, and preached about the "Revolution of 1800." But in the end, he left in place the Hamiltonian economic system, avoided excessive Francophile feelings, and abandoned his notion of limited government and a limited executive long enough to double the size of the United States with a stroke of the pen. The presidency under the Republicans would surely change, but Washington and the Federalists had created a new executive force that could be eclipsed at times by events and by the legislative branch, yet not undone.

The long historical trip from royal authority to indigenous institutions, from kings and ministers to popular governors and state ratifying conventions, had been complete. The presidency, more than any other political innovation, is a unique American contribution to the art and science of government. A powerful, quasi-defined executive, with its ambiguous historical roots, unsettled constitutional powers, and a popular political base, it remains unbeholden to parliamentary majorities, royal favor, or military cliques.

To appreciate the early development of this office, one can best look at the world in which these colonials-turned-Founding Fathers lived. That world, as today's, had few free peoples and few limited governments. By 1700 most of the old European states were being transformed into centralized monarchies that were extending their sway beyond that continent and into Africa and the Western Hemisphere. The Americas were prime colonies for exploitation, and the varied tribes of black Africa provided millions of slaves to work the plantations, the mines, and the estates of the New World. An estimated 9.3 million tribesmen were enslaved, and nearly 90 percent of them were destined for Brazil and the Caribbean areas alone. In the non-European world, the Moghuls controlled the Indian subcontinent, the Ottoman empire extended from North Africa throughout the Middle East and into the Balkans, the descendants of the Manchus ruled China, and the Tokugawa family had taken over the hereditary title of Shogun and ruled in the Japanese emperor's name.

And, of course, in Europe the eighteenth century marked the end of the feudal system and the rise of the great autocratic monarchs who sought to increase their centralized control over the armies, the tax collectors, and even the cultural achievements of their respective sovereign states. That trend is best epitomized by the rule of Louis XIV, who reigned from 1660 to 1715 and who created the new nation-state. In Prussia, Frederick William I began the same sort of centralization, and his successor, Frederick the Great, who ruled from 1740 to 1786, created a court that combined conservative militarism with the liberal rhetoric of the Enlightenment. In the nearby Hapsburg empire, Maria Theresa and then her son, Joseph, proceeded to extend the royal agenda of reform by fostering education, judicial revisions, religious toleration, limits on censorship, and agrarian advances.

Even in strange and distant Russia the mercurial Peter the Great sought to modernize the economy and the attitudes of that brooding land by emulating the West. As has happened so often in its history, Russia and its leaders proved to be more willing to learn new techniques than to foster a climate of liberty and political toleration. After Peter's death, a generation of intrigue resulted, and finally German-born Catherine the Great renewed in part his agenda, while she extended the power of the nobles over the exploited serfs.

As the monarchs and the nobility engaged in conflicts over the centralization of authority, the life of the vast majority of the common people was a dismal affair. In central and eastern Europe most peasants were still serfs, bound to the land and directly controlled by the lords of the manor. In western Europe, where the central regimes and independent cities were stronger, the feudal system of obligations was breaking down. But in most of these regions, a myriad of taxes, forced labor, and ceaseless levees were extremely burdensome, and the life of the peasantry in the early part of the century was indeed nasty, short, and brutish.

Still, great visible political changes were being accompanied, if not dictated, by subtler and equally far-reaching alterations in the demography and economy of Europe. Population grew dramatically as infant mortality dropped and hygiene improved; increased agricultural prosperity and productivity made larger urban centers possible; and the rudimentary outlines of an industrial order were beginning to develop. Britain, France, and, to a lesser extent, Spain, Portugal, and the Netherlands became major colonial empires, fired by economic lust, and fed by cheap slave labor and abundant commercial opportunity.

But despite the rhetoric and the legends of the "enlightened" princes, the monarchs of Europe were generally unsuccessful in advancing the celebrated causes of liberty and progress. Instead, they often left ruined experiments in centralized nation-states with swollen armies and inefficient bureaucracies. In Bohemia in 1775 a major peasant revolt ensued as the Hapsburg monarchy was unable to build support for its ambitious reforms. In Russia a strange Cossack, Emelyan Pugachev, gathered a large following when he claimed to be Peter III, the "redeemer Tsar." A frightened Catherine finally succeeded in crushing his army, but she became even more suspicious toward the alien land she uneasily ruled. In Poland the brief attempt at political reform, incorporated in the May Constitution, ended in 1793, when Russia and Prussia partitioned that nation once again. Even in England the strains of a far-flung empire and the changes brought by the new agriculture led to political and social unrest. John Wilkes, a member of Parliament, conducted for nearly a

decade a bitter crusade against the Crown's policies. Riots swept across England, and the masses of people were moved by the simple eloquence of the slogan "Wilkes and Liberty." The usually adaptable English upper classes dug in, and even the great Pitt was unable to reform the political system when he tried to abolish thirty-six "rotten" boroughs.[11]

Turmoil was in the air in the latter part of the eighteenth century, and nowhere did it wreak greater havoc than in the most powerful, the richest, and the most centralized nation-state, the France of the Bourbon kings. To curtail the power of the monarch, the aristocracy insisted on having the king call back the Estates General, last convened in 1614. That move in turn led to a torrent of protests and eventually the French Revolution, which disintegrated into aimless violence, political murder, and, eventually, the dictatorship of Napoleon.[12]

Thus, by the time of the Federalist presidencies, Europe was overtaken by war and by social repression. In Prussia, Frederick William II proceeded to undo the reforms of Frederick II, and in the Hapsburg Empire, Francis also turned away from political toleration and mobilized for war. By 1795 Prussia, Russia, and Austria liquidated the Polish state altogether, and within a year of that, Paul I replaced his mother, Catherine, as Tsar of Russia. He publicly disavowed her modest efforts at reform, and proved himself to be even more erratic and arbitrary than previous Tsars had dared. In England the fear of French revolutionaries led William Pitt the Younger to ask the House of Commons in 1794 to suspend the habeas corpus act, and he pushed through a treasonable practices bill to curtail criticism of the government and a seditious meeting bill to restrict public gatherings. In China the emperor's plan to wage "The Great Campaigns" proved to be too expensive and his chief minister presided over a crumbling military and civilian administration. In October 1795 the emperor abdicated and his minister committed suicide. Across the strait in Japan the reform shogunite of Matsudaira Sanaobu failed, and by 1793 he, too, was dismissed.[13]

The world of the early eighteenth century was often a picture of mercurial autocrats fighting for greater control over the nobility while they used the language of the philosophes of the Enlightenment. The feudal past was still instilled in much of the class structure of Europe, and some of the networks of privilege and influence that govern those nations to this day are residues of that history. To the Americans, freed from the scarcity of land and scornful of the claims of king, noble, and church, the rough seaboard cities and the primitive frontiers were Edens of freedom.

By the end of that century their confidence proved correct. The bogus age of the enlightened autocrats was clearly over, and the period of national wars of expansion and imperialism was beginning with a vengeance. France was a political contagion to all civilized nations, and in England even the Whigs led a frantic movement to curtail political liberty.

Put within these broad historical perspectives, the American experience

seems to be a moderate and restrained exercise. While the dialogue was surely heated and the political leadership given to paranoid excesses at times, still the new nation remained, in that charming image, a city on a hill, a near promised land of relative toleration and republican virtue. For all of their shortcomings, the Founding Fathers were true Enlightenment figures, more than the monarchs or the court and country philosophers of Europe. Befitting their heritage, American executives were responsible and sensible men of their age. Perhaps no greater compliment can be paid to them than to appreciate the sound and the fury of the world from whence they emerged, reminding us once again that the primary task of man on earth is to master himself.

NOTES

Part One: The Origins of Executive Authority

1. The Uncertain Heritage

1. American–British colonial relations are of central concern in the work of the so-called "imperialist school" of historians, especially Charles Andrews, George R. Beer, Lawrence Gipson, and Herbert Osgood. My main source is Beer's four volumes, especially *The Origins of the British Colonial System 1578–1600* (Gloucester, Mass.: Peter Smith, reprinted 1959). See also his *British Colonial Policy 1754–1765* (reprinted 1958); *The Old Colonial Systems 1660–1754*, volumes 1 and 2 (reprinted 1958). A shorter summary of Gipson's work is *The Coming of the Revolution* (New York: Harper and Row, 1962).

2. H. Trevor Colbourn, *The Lamp of Experience* (New York: W. W. Norton, 1965); Donald W. Hanson, *From Kingdom to Commonwealth* (Cambridge, Mass.: Harvard University Press, 1970); J. H. Plumb, *The Growth of Political Stability in England 1675–1725* (London: Macmillan, 1967); Gordon J. Schochet, *Patriarchalism in Political Thought* (New York: Basic Books, 1975); Edward O. Smith, Jr., *Crown and Commonwealth* (Philadelphia: Transactions of the American Philosophical Society, 1976), volume 66; Lewis Namier, *England in the Age of the American Revolution* (London: MacMillan, 1961); Ernest H. Kantorowicz, *The King's Two Bodies* (Princeton, N.J.: Princeton University Press, 1957).

3. Beer, *Origins of the British Colonial System* and his *Old Colonial Systems*, volume 1.

4. Jack Greene, *The Quest for Power* (New York: W. W. Norton, 1963); Bernard Bailyn, *The Origins of American Politics* (New York: Vintage Books, 1967); John F. Burns, *Controversies Between Royal Governors and Their Assemblies in the North American Colonies* (New York: Russell and Russell, reprinted 1969), see p. 7 on the 1692 law.

5. Caroline Robbins, *The Eighteenth Century Commonwealthmen* (Cambridge, Mass.: Harvard University Press, 1959); James K. Martin, *Men in Rebellion* (New Brunswick, N.J.: Rutgers University Press, 1973).

6. Bailyn, *Origins of American Politics* and his *Ideological Origins of the American Revolution* (Cambridge, Mass.: Harvard University Press, 1967); Trenchard and

Gordon's work can be read in *Cato's Letters*, four volumes in two (New York: Russell and Russell, reprinted 1969) and in a shorter, more readable selection, David L. Johnson, *The English Libertarian Heritage* (Indianapolis: Bobbs-Merrill Company, 1965).

7. Plumb, *Growth of Political Stability 1675–1725*; his "The World Beyond America at the Time of the Revolution," in his *Men and Centuries* (Boston: Houghton Mifflin, 1963); and Basil Williams, *The Whig Supremacy 1714–1760* (Oxford: Clarendon Press, 1939).

8. J. H. Plumb, *Sir Robert Walpole*, volumes 1 and 2 (Boston: Houghton Mifflin, 1961), which is also abridged in a one-volume edition; the Wolrige quote is in the latter edition, p. 177. For a critical view of the concept of a court party in the early seventeenth century, see Conrad Russell, *Parliaments and English Politics 1621–1629* (Oxford: Clarendon Press, 1979).

2. The Royal Prerogative

1. Colbourn, *The Lamp of Experience*; Gary Wills, *Inventing America* (Garden City: Doubleday, 1978); Caroline Robbins, "Algeron Sidney's *Discourses Concerning Government: Textbook of Revolution*," *William & Mary Quarterly*, 3rd series, 4 (July 1947), pp. 267–296; and Francis D. Wormuth, *The Royal Prerogative 1603–1649, A Study of English Political and Constitutional Ideas* (Ithaca, N.Y.: Cornell University Press, 1939).

2. John Locke, *Two Treatises on Civil Government* (New York: E. P. Dutton, 1953), chapter 14, pp. 199–203.

3. William Blackstone, *Commentaries on the Laws of England* (Chicago: Callahan and Co., 1899), Book 1, chapter 7, pp. 239–250 on the king's prerogative.

4. Blackstone discusses high treason in Book 4, chapter 6, and the personal immunity of the sovereign in Book 3, chapter 17. Also see D. L. Keir, *The Constitutional History of Great Britain 1485–1937* (London: Adams and Charles Black, 1938).

5. Baron de Montesquieu, *The Spirit of the Laws* (New York: Hafner, 1949), Book 11, part 6.

6. Lewis Namier, *The Structure of Politics at the Accession of George III* (New York: Macmillan, 1968); G. H. Guttridge, *English Whiggism and the American Revolution* (Berkeley: University of California Press, 1963).

3. The Provincial Governors

1. Charles M. Andrews, *The Colonial Background for the American Revolution* (New Haven, Conn.: Yale University Press, 1924).

2. Stephen Saunders Webb, *The Governors-General: The English Army and the Definition of the Empire 1569–1681* (Chapel Hill: University of North Carolina Press, 1979).

3. Leonard W. Labaree, *Royal Government in America* (New York: Frederick Ungar, reprinted 1958); Evarts B. Greene, *The Provincial Governor in the English Colonies of North America* (New York: Longmans, Green, 1898); and Burns, *Controversies Between Royal Governors and Their Assemblies*.

4. James A. Henretta, *"Salutary Neglect," Colonial Administration Under the Duke of Newcastle* (Princeton, N.J.: Princeton University Press, 1972).

5. Michael G. Kammen, *Rope of Sand* (Ithaca, N.Y.: Cornell University Press, 1968), pp. 103–104, and Franklin B. Wickwire, *British Subministers and Colonial America 1763–1783* (Princeton, N.J.: Princeton University Press, 1966).

6. Bernard Bailyn, *The Ordeal of Thomas Hutchinson* (Cambridge, Mass.: Harvard University Press, 1974), and the sketch in *Dictionary of American Biography*, edited by Dumas Malone (New York: Charles Scribner's Sons, 1946). Also of interest is John A. Schultz, *William Shirley* (Chapel Hill: University of North Carolina Press, 1961). Shirley's fifteen years (1741–1756) were ones of peace and stability.

7. Jonathan Trumbull, *John Trumbull: Governor of Connecticut 1769–1784* (Boston: Little, Brown, 1919), and Glynn Weaver, *Jonathan Trumbull* (Hartford: Connecticut Historical Society, 1956).

4. The War Governors

1. Margaret B. MacMillan, *The War Governors in the American Revolution* (New York: Columbia University Press, 1943), and Howard Zinn, *A People's History of the United States* (New York: Harper & Row, 1980), chapters 3, 4, and 5.

2. *The Works of John Adams*, edited by Charles Francis Adams, volume 4 (Freeport, Long Island: Books for Libraries Press, reprinted 1969); Charles Thach, *The Creation of the Presidency 1775–1789* (Baltimore: Johns Hopkins University Press, 1922).

3. *The Federalist*, edited by Jay Cooke (Cleveland: Meridian Books, 1961), see numbers 69 and 73, McLean edition numbers.

4. The various constitutions are compiled in *The Federal and State Constitutions*, edited by Francis N. Thorpe, seven volumes (Washington, D.C.: Government Printing Office, 1909). The Massachusetts constitution's executive article is in volume 3, pp. 1899–1903.

5. MacMillan, *War Governors*, passim.

6. E. Wilder Spaulding, *His Excellency George Clinton: Critic of the Constitution*, second edition (Port Washington, N.Y.: Ira J. Friedman, reprinted 1964). Clinton also served as governor from 1801 to 1804.

7. A more sympathetic view of Jefferson's governorship is presented in Dumas Malone, *Jefferson: The Virginian* (Boston: Little, Brown, 1948), chapters 22 through 25. Until his death, Jefferson was defending himself because of this incident; see Charles Royster, *Light Horse Harry Lee and the Legacy of the American Revolution* (New York: Alfred A. Knopf, 1981), chapter 6. Henry's governorship is covered in Henry Mayer, *A Son of Thunder: Patrick Henry and the American Republic* (New York: Franklin Watts, 1986).

5. Creating the Presidency

1. The literature on the Founding Fathers, especially on their motives, is rather extensive. I have found particularly useful Clinton Rossiter, *1787, The Grand Convention* (New York: Macmillan, 1966); Richard Hofstadter, *The American Political Tradition* (New York: Alfred A. Knopf, 1948), chapter 1; and John P. Roche, "The Founding Fathers: A Reform Caucus in Action," *American Political Science Review*, 60 (December 1961), pp. 799–816.

2. The standard source is *The Records of the Federal Convention 1787*, edited by Max Farrand, four volumes (New Haven, Conn.: Yale University Press, reprinted 1966). The account of the Convention given here follows Madison's notes. A convenient one-volume edition is *Notes of Delegates on the Federal Convention of 1787 Reported by James Madison*, introduction by Adrienne Koch (Athens: Ohio University Press, 1966). Hereafter cited as *Notes*. Quote on pp. 45–47.

3. *Notes*, p. 51.

4. *Notes*, pp. 60–79.

5. *Notes*, pp. 129–140.

6. Max Farrand, *The Framing of the Constitution of the United States* (New Haven, Conn.: Yale University Press, 1913), pp. 107–110, argues that the slavery issue was substantially less important than later generations believe. Catherine Drinker, *Miracle at Philadelphia* (Boston: Little, Brown, 1966), found the issue more significant.

7. *Notes*, pp. 411, 502–504.

8. *Notes*, p. 504.

9. *Notes*, pp. 306–307.

10. *Notes*, pp. 322–325.

11. *Notes*, p. 323.

12. *Notes*, pp. 330–331.

13. *Notes*, p. 335.

14. *Notes*, p. 421.

15. Rossiter, *1787*, p. 222.

16. *Notes*, p. 659.

6. The Ratification Controversy

1. Rossiter, *1787*, Ch. 13.

2. *The Federalist*. Jay's remarks are in number 64; Madison's in numbers 19, 20, 38, 39, 45, 48; Hamilton's in numbers 67 through 73.

3. Elbridge Gerry, *Observations on the New Constitutions and on the Federal and State Constitutions*, in *Pamphlets on the Constitution of the United States*, edited by Paul Leicester Ford (Brooklyn, N.Y.: Historical Printing Club, 1888), p. 9. Hereafter cited as Ford, *Pamphlets*.

4. Jonathan Jackson, *Thoughts Upon the Political Situation of the United States of America*... (Worcester, Mass.: Isaiah Thomas, 1788), p. 183; George Mason, *Objections to Proposed Federal Constitution*, reprinted in Ford, *Pamphlets*, pp. 327–332.

5. "Cato" (George Clinton), "Various Fears Concerning the Executive Department," reprinted in *The Anti-Federalist Papers*, edited by Morton Borden (Lansing: Michigan State University Press, 1965), p. 198. The titles in this volume are often Borden's and not the original authors'. On Jefferson's view see Robert A. Rutland, *The Ordeal of the Constitution* (Norman: University of Oklahoma Press, 1966), p. 188.

6. "Philadelphiensis" (Benjamin Workman), "The President as Military King," reprinted in Borden, *Anti-Federalist Papers*, pp. 407–409.

7. Rutland, *The Ordeal of the Constitution*, pp. 106–165, on criticism of the new document.

8. Alexander Conte Hanson, *Remarks on the Proposed Plan of a Federal Government*, reprinted in Ford, *Pamphlets*, pp. 228–233; Tench Coxe, *An Examination of the Con-*

stitution of the United States of America . . ., reprinted in Ford, *Pamphlets*, pp. 137–138.

9. *The Debates in the Several State Conventions on the Adoption of the Federal Constitution*, edited by Jonathan Elliot, second edition, five volumes (Philadelphia: J. B. Lippincott, 1896), especially volume 2.

10. Robert Dorithet Meade, *Patrick Henry: Practical Revolutionary* (Philadelphia: J. B. Lippincott, 1969), p. 360. Mayer, *A Son of Thunder*, also covers this controversy, viewing it as a prelude to the establishment of the Bill of Rights.

11. A longer treatment of the subject can be found in my "The Presidency and the Ratification Controversy," *Presidential Studies Quarterly*, 5 (Winter 1977), pp. 37–46.

Part Two: The Washington Administration

7. The Authentic American

1. Noemie Emery, *Alexander Hamilton* (New York: G. P. Putnam's Sons, 1982), p. 38.

2. On the dynamics of nationalism, see Seymour Martin Lipset, *The First New Nation* (New York: Basic Books, 1963), chapter 1.

3. Washington's early life and frustrations are the main themes of Noemie Emery's *Washington: A Biography* (New York: G. P. Putnam's Sons, 1976). See the quote on pp. 44–45. His English background is charted in *Burke's Presidential Families of the United States of America* (London: Burke's Peerage, Ltd., 1975). Washington's political attitudes are the subject of part of Catherine L. Albanese, *Sons of the Fathers: The Civil Religions of the American Revolution* (Philadelphia: Temple University Press, 1976), and Paul F. Boller, Jr., "George Washington and Religious Liberty," *William & Mary Quarterly*, 17, 3rd series (October 1960), pp. 486–506.

4. Emery, *Washington*, p. 67.

5. Emery, *Washington*, p. 94.

6. Emery, *Washington*, pp. 67–70, 113.

7. James Thomas Flexner, *George Washington: The Forge of Experience* (Boston: Little, Brown, 1965), p. 324.

8. Emery, *Washington*, p. 170.

9. Emery, *Washington*, p. 175.

10. Flexner, *Forge of Experience*, p. 341.

11. James Thomas Flexner, *George Washington in the American Revolution* (Boston: Little, Brown, 1967), p. 22.

12. Flexner, *American Revolution*, p. 83.

13. Flexner, *American Revolution*, p. 110.

14. Emery, *Washington*, pp. 285, 205.

15. Flexner, *American Revolution*, p. 189.

16. Flexner, *American Revolution*, part 5, and Douglas Southall Freeman, *George Washington: Victory with the Help of France*, volume 5 (New York: Charles Scribner's Sons, 1952), on the cabal and the conclusion of the war.

17. Flexner, *American Revolution*, p. 189.

18. Richard Kohn, *The Eagle and the Sword: The Federalists and the Creation of the*

Military Establishment in America, 1783–1802 (New York: Free Press, 1975), chapter 2.

8. Cincinnatus Returns

1. Classical imagery is explored in Richard M. Grummere, *The American Colonial Mind and the Classical Tradition* (Cambridge, Mass.: Harvard University Press, 1963), and James J. Walsh, *Education of the Founding Fathers of the Republic* (New York: Fordham University Press, 1935). See also Douglas Adair, "Fame and the Founding Fathers," in a volume with the same title, edited by Edmund P. Willis (Bethlehem, Pa.: Moravian College, 1967).

2. Douglas Southall Freeman, *George Washington: Patriot and President,* volume 6 (New York: Charles Scribner's Sons, 1954), p. 146.

3. George Washington, *Writings,* edited by John C. Fitzpatrick, 39 volumes (Washington, D.C.: Government Printing Office, 1931–44), volume 30, p. 119. Hereafter cited as *GW.*

4. Freeman, *Patriot and President,* pp. 156–57.

5. Deferential politics is discussed in Charles S. Sydnor, *Gentlemen Freeholders: Political Practices in Washington's Virginia* (Chapel Hill: University of North Carolina Press, 1952).

6. Joseph Nathan Kane, *Facts About the Presidents* (New York: Dell, 1960), pp. 3–24.

7. Freeman, *Patriot and President,* pp. 159–162.

8. Freeman, *Patriot and President,* p. 165.

9. *GW,* 30, pp. 285–286. See also Lewis R. Harley, *Life of Charles Thomson* (Philadelphia: George W. Jacobs, 1900).

9. The Grand Procession

1. *GW,* 30, pp. 290–296; Freeman, *Patriot and President,* vol. 6, is the best single account of the pre-inaugural period. Also of limited use is *The Diaries of George Washington,* edited by Donald Jackson and Dorothy Twohig (Charlottesville: University Press of Virginia, 1979), volume 5.

2. *GW,* 30, p. 287.

3. Freeman, *Patriot and President,* p. 169.

4. Freeman, *Patriot and President,* pp. 170–172.

5. James Thomas Flexner, *George Washington and the New Nation* (Boston: Little, Brown, 1969), p. 177, and Freeman, *Patriot and President,* pp. 175–176.

6. Freeman, *Patriot and President,* pp. 175–176.

7. Freeman, *Patriot and President,* p. 182.

10. The First Inauguration

1. Martha J. Lamb, *The Washington Inauguration* (New York and London: White and Allen, 1889); *An Account of the Inauguration of George Washington* (New York: Bankers Trust Co., 1939); Frank Monaghan, *Notes on the Inaugural Journey of George Washington* (New York: n.p., 1939); Rufus Wilmot Griswold, *The Republican Court*

or *American Society in the Days of Washington* (New York: Appleton, 1854); and Frank Fletcher Stephens, *The Transition Period 1788–1789 in the Government of the United States* (Columbia, Mo.: E. W. Stephens, 1909).

2. *Journal of William Maclay*, edited by Edgar S. Maclay (New York: D. Appleton, 1890), pp. 203.

3. Freeman, *Patriot and President*, vol. 6 describes the inaugural ceremony in detail. The documents surrounding that event are reprinted in James D. Richardson, *Messages and Papers of the Presidents 1789–1897* (Washington, D.C.: Government Printing Office, 1897), volume 1.

4. Freeman, *Patriot and President*, pp. 190–192.

5. Freeman, *Patriot and President*, pp. 194–197.

6. Freeman, *Patriot and President*, pp. 195.

7. Freeman, *Patriot and President*, pp. 197–198.

11. The Presidents Before Washington

1. Edmund C. Burnett, "Perquisites of the President of the Continental Congress," *American Historical Review*, 35 (October 1929), pp. 69–76.

2. Seymour Wemyss Smith, *John Hanson: Our First President* (New York: Brewer, Warren and Putnam, 1932).

3. Louise B. Dunbar, *Study of "Monarchial" Tendencies in the United States 1776–1801*, University of Illinois Studies in the Social Sciences, volume 10 (Urbana: University of Illinois, March 1922), pp. 1–164; Richard Krawel, "Prince Henry of Prussia and the Regency of the United States, 1786," *American Historical Review*, 17 (October 1911), pp. 44–51.

4. Jennings B. Sanders, *The Presidency of the Continental Congress 1774–1789*, second printing (Gloucester, Mass.: Peter Smith, 1971).

12. The Bureaucracy Before Washington

1. The best treatment of the growth of executive departments during the Confederation period is Jay Caesar Guggenheimer, "The Development of the Executive Departments," in *Essays in Constitutional History of the United States in the Formative Period, 1775–1789*, edited by J. Franklin Jameson (Boston: Houghton Mifflin, 1889), pp. 116–185. Also used is Lloyd Milton Short, *The Development of National Administrative Organization in the United States* (Baltimore: Johns Hopkins University Press, 1923); James Hart, *The American Presidency in Action, 1789* (New York: Macmillan, 1948); Leonard White, *The Federalists* (New York: Macmillan, 1956); Charles C. Thach, *The Creation of the Presidency, 1775–1789* (Baltimore: Johns Hopkins University Press, 1923).

2. Leonard White, *The Federalists* (New York: Macmillan, 1956); Freeman, *Patriot and President*, vol. 6, p. 220; and Carl E. Prince, *The Federalists and the Origins of the U.S. Civil Service* (New York: New York University Press, 1977).

13. The Removal Debate

1. Hart, *The Presidency in Action, 1789*, and Thach, *Creation of the American Presidency*, chapter 6, summarizes the debate that is contained in Joseph Gales, compiler,

The Debates and Proceedings in the Congress of the United States (Washington, D.C.: Gales and Seaton, 1834), hereafter cited as *The Annals*.

2. Thach, *Creation of the American Presidency*, pp. 147–148.

3. Hart, *Presidency in Action, 1789*, p. 183.

4. Thach, *Creation of the American Presidency*, p. 152.

5. Hart, *Presidency in Action, 1789*, p. 166.

6. The view that Chief Justice Taft in the *Meyers* decision misunderstood the conclusion of the congressional removal debate is expressed by Edward S. Corwin, "The President's Removal Power Under the Constitution," which has been published in its revised form in *Selected Essays on Constitutional Law: Book 4, Administrative Law*, edited by Douglas B. Maggs (Chicago: The Foundation Press, 1938), pp. 1467–1518. The Judiciary Act of 1789 provided for the appointment of an attorney general, marshals, and district attorneys. It made no reference to tenure or removal of the first two categories of officials, but it did indicate that the marshals were "removable from office at pleasure." The marshal of each district could appoint deputies who would be removable at pleasure by the district judge or circuit court. Here Congress was regulating the tenure of inferior officers whose appointment was not vested in the president (Hart, *Presidency in Action*, p. 193). Another act put the postmaster general under the authority of the president. Whether in these cases the president, in the absence of any legislation, could remove inferior officers or just department heads is unclear. However, if he controlled the department heads, then the question usually became moot.

14. His Highness, the President

1. Forrest McDonald, *The Presidency of George Washington* (New York: W. W. Norton, 1975), pp. 28–31, speculates on the significance of such pretensions. The debate over titles is related in the *Journal of William Maclay*. Freeman, *Patriot and President*, vol. 6, p. 253, describes Washington's dinners, and Flexner, *New Nation, 1783–1793* (Boston: Little, Brown, 1969), chapter 16, outlines the social obligations of the new president.

2. McDonald, *Washington*, pp. 30–31.

3. Freeman, *Patriot and President*, p. 200.

4. Freeman, *Patriot and President*, p. 201.

5. Marvin Kitman's irreverent *George Washington's Expense Account* (New York: Ballantine Books, 1970), presents a detailed list of the general's Revolutionary War expenses.

6. Flexner, *New Nation*, p. 198.

7. Flexner, *New Nation*, pp. 200–201.

8. Rufus W. Griswold, *The Republican Court or American Society in the Days of Washington* (New York: Appleton, 1854).

15. The Debt Assumption Deal

1. McDonald, *Washington*, pp. 50–59. Indispensable to an understanding of Hamilton's reports on credit and the bank are the notes that accompany his *Papers of Alexander Hamilton*, edited by Harold C. Syrett and Jacob E. Cooke (New York: Columbia University Press, 1961), volume 6. Hereafter cited as *AH*.

2. Robert Hendrickson, *Hamilton II* (New York: Mason-Charter, 1976), pp. 33–34.

3. John Miller, *The Federalist Era* (New York: Harper and Row, 1960), pp. 40–41.

4. The single best explanation of the Hamiltonian program is McDonald's clear and concise treatment in *The Presidency of George Washington*, especially chapters 3 and 4, which I have followed closely, and Broadus Mitchell, *Alexander Hamilton, the National Adventure: 1788–1804* (New York: Macmillan, 1962). Miller, *Federalist Era*, chapter 3; Bray Hammond, *Banks and Politics in America from Revolution to Civil War* (Princeton, N.J.: Princeton University Press, 1957); John T. Holdsworth, *First Bank of the United States* (Washington, D.C.: National Monetary Commission, 1910); Gerald Stourzh, *Alexander Hamilton and Idea of Republican Government* (Stanford University Press, 1970); and Whitney K. Bates, "Northern Speculators and Southern State Debts: 1790," *William & Mary Quarterly*, 19, 3rd series (January 1962), pp. 30–48, are also of use. The speculation about Madison's motives is presented in Forrest McDonald, *Alexander Hamilton* (New York: W. W. Norton, 1979), p. 175.

5. *The Complete Anas of Thomas Jefferson*, edited by Franklin B. Sawvel (New York: The Roundtable Press, 1903), pp. 33–34. On p. 106, for February 16, 1793, Jefferson did note that "there is reason to believe that the rejection of the late additional Assumption by the Senate, was effected by the President through Lear, operating on Langdon. Beckley knows this." Jefferson provides additional insights in his *Writings*, edited by Paul Leicester Ford, 10 volumes (New York: Putnam, 1892–1899), volume 5, pp. 168, 187–189; 6, pp. 172–173; 1, pp. 154–168, which contains the above account. Hereafter cited as *TJ*. The most comprehensive collection of Jefferson's works is still unfinished, *The Papers of Thomas Jefferson*, edited by Julian Boyd (Princeton, N.J.: Princeton University Press, 1950—). Also see *GW*, 31, pp. 67, 84.

6. Freeman, *Patriot and President*, p. 264.

16. The Establishment of the Bank

1. Margaret Woodbury, "Public Opinion in Philadelphia, 1789–1801," *Smith College Studies in History*, 5, October 1919 to July 1920. (Northampton, Mass.: Smith College, 1920), pp. 1–138.

2. *GW*, 33, p. 488; 37, p. 250; 31, pp. 215–16. Noble Cunningham, *The Jeffersonian Republicans, 1789–1801* (Chapel Hill: University of North Carolina Press, 1957), chapter 1; Miller, *Federalist Era*, chapters 4–5.

3. Flexner, *New Nation*, pp. 281–282.

4. McDonald, *Washington*, pp. 76–77.

5. McDonald, *Alexander Hamilton*, p. 203.

6. Flexner, *New Nation*, p. 291.

7. Details of the Bank proposal are in Mitchell's *Alexander Hamilton*, volume 2, which provides a good summary of the Bank proposal and the debate that followed. Hamilton's response is contained in *AH*, 7, pp. 57–58, 97–134. Also of interest is Curtis P. Nettels, *The Emergence of a National Economy 1775–1815* (New York: Holt, Rinehart and Winston, 1962), and Miller, *Federalist Era*, pp. 60–63.

17. Washington as Administrator

1. Thomas A. Bailey, *Presidential Greatness* (New York: Appleton-Century-Crofts, 1966), p. 268.

2. Emery, *Hamilton*, pp. 71–73; Hendrickson, *Hamilton I 1757–1789*, chapter 14.

3. Flexner, *New Nation*, pp. 52–54.

4. Some brief references to Washington's staff are in Freeman, *Patriot and President*, and Flexner, *New Nation*, and can be found in the indexes under the staff members' names used in this narrative. That information has been supplemented by sketches of Lear and Humphreys in the *Dictionary of American Biography*, and Stephen Decatur, Jr., *Private Affairs of George Washington from the Records and Accounts of Tobias Lear, Esquire, His Secretary* (Boston: Houghton Mifflin, 1933), and Richard Rush, *Washington in Domestic Life* (Philadelphia: J. B. Lippincott, 1857).

5. *The Diary of George Washington*, edited by Benson J. Lossing (Richmond, Va.: Press of the Historical Society, 1861).

6. White, *Federalists*, p. 35. See also Lynton K. Caldwell, *Administrative Theories of Hamilton and Jefferson* (Chicago: University of Chicago Press, 1944).

7. Miller, *Federalist Era*, p. 31.

8. Prince, *Federalists and the Origins of the U.S. Civil Service*, passim.

9. General background on the position is in White, *Federalists*, chapters 15 and 16.

10. Miller, *Federalist Era*, pp. 234–241.

11. Forrest McDonald, *The Presidency of Thomas Jefferson* (Lawrence: University Press of Kansas, 1976), chapter 2.

12. Prince, *Federalists and the Origins of the U.S. Civil Service*, p. 116; Julius Goebel, *The History of the Supreme Court: Antecedents and Beginnings to 1801*, volume 1 (New York: Macmillan, 1971), and Gaillard Hunt, "Office Seeking," *American Historical Review*, 1 (January 1896), pp. 270–283.

13. Jonathan Daniels, *The Ordeal of Ambition: Jefferson, Hamilton, Burr* (Garden City, N.Y.: Doubleday, 1970), p. 129.

14. Prince, *Federalists and the Origin of Civil Service*, chapters 10 and 11.

18. The Tribes and the Long Knives

1. The basic outline of Knox's career is given in two biographies: North Callahan, *Henry Knox, General Washington's General* (New York: Rinehart and Co., 1958), and Noah Brooks, *Henry Knox: A Soldier of the Revolution* (New York: G. P. Putnam's Sons, 1900). His revisions of the army are detailed in Kohn, *Eagle and Sword*.

2. Freeman, *Patriot and President*, pp. 221–224.

3. The relationship between the Indians and British and Spanish presences on the frontier is explored in John S. Bassett, *The Federalist System 1789–1801* (New York: Cooper Square Publisher, reprinted 1968), chapters 4 and 5; Frederick Jackson Turner, *The Significance of Sections in American History* (New York: Peter Smith, 1950), especially the chapters on Genet's diplomacy and French policy in the Mississippi region; and Samuel Flagg Bemis, *A Diplomatic History of the United States* (New York: Holt, Reinhart and Winston, 1965).

4. The Indian–frontiersmen conflict is detailed in George D. Hanson, *Sixty Years of Indian Affairs* (Chapel Hill: University of North Carolina Press, 1941); Jennings Wise, *The Red Man in the New World Drama*, edited and revised by Vine Deloria, Jr. (New York: Macmillan, 1971); Reginald Horsman, *The Frontier in the Formative Years 1783–1815* (New York: Holt, Rinehart and Winston, 1970) and his *Expansion and American Indian Policy 1783–1812* (Lansing: Michigan State University Press, 1967); Payson J. Trent, *The National Land System 1785–1820* (New York: E. B. Trent, 1910); Donald L. McMurry, "The Indian Policy of the Federalist Government and the Economic Development of the Southwest," *Tennessee Historical Society*, 1 and 2 (March and June 1915), pp. 21–39, 106–119; and A. L. Crabb, "George Washington and the Chickasaw Nation, 1795," *Mississippi Valley Historical Review*, 19 (December 1932), pp. 404–407.

5. Flexner, *New Nation*, pp. 262–265.

6. Freeman, *Patriot and President*, pp. 272–289.

7. Washington's reaction to the St. Clair disaster is in Katherine C. Turner, *Red Man Calling on the Great White Father* (Norman: University of Oklahoma Press, 1951), pp. 304, which also goes into some of the personal contacts the president had with the chiefs. John W. Caughey, *McGillivray of the Creeks* (Norman: University of Oklahoma Press, 1938), tells of his subject's complex role with federal authorities. The wars on the frontier are detailed in Randolph C. Downes, *Council Fires on the Upper Ohio* (Pittsburgh: University of Pittsburgh Press, 1940).

8. *TJ*, 1, p. 189.

9. *Anthony Wayne: A Name in Arms: The Wayne-Knox-Pickering-McHenry Correspondence*, edited by Richard C. Knopf (Pittsburgh: University of Pittsburgh Press, 1960), contains the dispatches between Wayne and the first three Secretaries of War. The best treatment of the relationship between frontier problems and the growth of the country is in Kohn's *Eagle and Sword*, chapter 6. Important discussions are outlined in *TJ*, 1, pp. 189–190; *GW*, 32, pp. 62–63.

10. Wise, *Red Man*, pp. 159–172.

11. Dumas Malone, *Jefferson and the Ordeal of Liberty* (Boston: Little, Brown, 1962), pp. 104–106, on some of the confusion of the period.

12. Bernard W. Sheehan, *Seeds of Extinction* (New York: W. W. Norton, 1973).

19. Fathering the Parties

1. Joseph Charles, *The Origins of the American Party System* (Williamsburg, Va.: Institute of Early American History and Culture, 1956); William N. Chambers, *Political Parties in a New Nation* (New York: Oxford University Press, 1963).

2. Jackson Turner Main, *Political Parties Before the Constitution* (New York: W. W. Norton, 1973); H. James Henderson, *Party Politics in the Continental Congress* (New York: McGraw-Hill, 1974), and his "The First Party System," in *Perspectives on Early American History*, edited by Alden T. Vaughan and George Athan Billias (New York: Harper and Row, 1973), pp. 325–374.

3. Sydnor, *Gentlemen Freeholders: Political Practices in Washington's Virginia*, discusses the notion of deference. Good studies of state political systems and federal issues are Homer C. Hockett, "Western Influences on Political Parties to 1825," *Ohio State University Bulletin*, 22 (August 1917), number 3; Ulrich B. Phillips, "The South Carolina Federalists," *American Historical Review*, 14 (April and July 1909),

pp. 529–543, 731–743; Gilbert Lycam, "Alexander Hamilton and the North Carolina Federalists," *North Carolina Historical Review*, 25 (October 1948), pp. 442–465; Norman K. Risjord, "The Virginia Federalists," *Journal of Southern History*, 33 (November 1967), pp. 468–517; Richard J. Purchell, *Connecticut in Transition 1775–1818* (Middletown, Conn.: Wesleyan University Press, 1963; original edition, 1918); Lisle A. Rose, *Prologue to Democracy: The Federalists in the South, 1789–1800* (Lexington: University of Kentucky Press, 1968). Also of interest is Russell J. Ferguson, *Early Western Pennsylvania Politics* (Pittsburgh: University of Pittsburgh Press, 1938), and Edward Channing, "Washington and Parties, 1789–1797," *Proceedings of Massachusetts Historical Society*, 47 (October 1913—June 1914) (Boston: John Wilson and Son, 1914), pp. 35–44.

4. Bernard Fay, "Early Party Machinery in the United States," *Pennsylvania Magazine of History and Biography*, 60 (October 1936), pp. 375–390; George D. Leutscher, *Early Political Machinery in the United States* (Philadelphia: n.p., 1903); and Richard McCormick, *The Second Party System* (New York: W. W. Norton, 1966).

5. The importance of these issues differed throughout the country, but by 1790 the major points of contention were the growth of federal authority, the settlement of the West, the Hamilton economic policy, and Washington's foreign policy. See Rudolph Bell, *Party and Faction in American Politics: The House of Representatives* (Westport, Conn.: Greenwood Press, 1973); Mary P. Ryan, "Party Formation in the United States Congress, 1789–1796: A Quantitative Analysis," *William & Mary Quarterly*, 3rd series, 28 (October 1971), pp. 523–542.

6. The standard work on the societies is Eugene Perry Link, *Democratic Republican Societies 1790–1800* (New York: Columbia University Press, 1942), which also shows the growth of post offices as an index of communications. The increase of newspapers is chartered in Donald Stewart, *The Opposition Press in the Federalist Period* (Albany: State University of New York Press, 1969).

7. Cunningham, *Jeffersonian Republicans*, pp. 62–64.

8. Charles, *Origins*, part 1.

20. A Falling Out of Sons

1. Flexner, *New Nation*, pp. 233–234.

2. Freeman, *Patriot and President*, p. 349; Flexner, *New Nation*, chapters 27 through 30.

3. Nathan Schachner, *The Founding Fathers* (New York: A. S. Barnes, 1954), chapter 13.

4. *TJ*, 1, pp. 154–168.

5. Cunningham, *Jeffersonian Republicans*, pp. 10–12.

6. Cunningham, *Jeffersonian Republicans*, pp. 14–19.

21. The Fires of Factionalism, 1792

1. Dumas Malone, *Jefferson and the Rights of Man* (Boston: Little, Brown, 1951), pp. 395–397.

2. A sense of the controversies of the period can be gotten from *GW*, 32, pp. 130–135; *TJ*, 6, pp. 100–104; *AH*, 12, pp. 347–350. Flexner, *New Nation*, pp. 355–356.

3. Flexner, *New Nation*, p. 357.

4. Miller, *Federalist Era*, pp. 96–97.

5. Cunningham, *Jeffersonian Republicans*, pp. 25–28.

6. Freeman, *Patriot and President*, pp. 369–370.

7. Cunningham, *Jeffersonian Republicans*, chapters 3, 4, and 5.

8. Hendrickson, *Hamilton II*, speculates that Burr was probably connected to the initial approach of the Reynolds couple to Hamilton.

9. Alfred Steinberg, *The First Ten* (Garden City, N.Y.: Doubleday, 1967), pp. 40–41.

10. Flexner, *New Nation*, pp. 362–363.

11. Flexner, *New Nation*, p. 366.

12. Flexner, *New Nation*, pp. 360–362.

13. Hendrickson, *Hamilton II*, p. 194; Monroe's observations are in Cunningham, *Jeffersonian Republicans*, p. 47.

22. Toward Neutrality

1. *GW*, 32, pp. 419–420, 430–431; *AH*, 14, pp. 308–310, 328, 367–396; *TJ*, 1, p. 27; 6, pp. 218–231. Bemis, *Diplomatic History of the United States*, chapters 5 and 6; and Bassett, *Federalist System*, chapters 4 and 5.

2. Steinberg, *First Ten*, surveys these developments.

3. Frederick Jackson Turner, "The Origins of Genet's Projected Attack on Louisiana and the Floridas," in his *Significance of Sections in American History*, pp. 52–85.

4. Flexner, *New Nation*, p. 253, on Lafayette, and Miller, *Federalist Era*, p. 126, on the French and liberty.

5. Jefferson, *Works*, 6, pp. 153–155.

6. C. D. Hazen, *Contemporary American Opinion of the French Revolution* (Baltimore: Johns Hopkins University Press, 1897); Barlow's ode is on pp. 225–226.

7. Douglas Southall Freeman (completed by J. A. Carroll and M. W. Ashworth), *George Washington: First in Peace*, volume 7 (New York: Charles Scribner's Sons, 1957).

8. *TJ*, 6, p. 315.

9. Freeman, *First in Peace*, p. 52.

10. John J. Reardon, *Edmund Randolph* (New York: Macmillan, 1974), chapter 16; and Charles Marion Thomas, *American Neutrality in 1793* (New York: Columbia University Press, 1931); and *TJ*, 6, pp. 244–246.

11. Miller, *Federalist Era*, pp. 130–132.

12. The debate can be found in *AH*, volumes 14 and 15; and *The Writings of James Madison*, edited by Gaillard Hunt (New York: G. P. Putnam's Sons, 1900–1910), volume 6.

13. Miller, *Federalist Era*, p. 138.

14. Harry Ammon, "The Genet Mission and the Development of American Political Parties," *Journal of American History* 52 (March 1966), pp. 725–741; Frank Monaghan, *John Jay* (Indianapolis: Bobbs-Merrill, 1935), passim; Miller, *Federalist Era*, chapter 8.

15. Leland Baldwin, *Whiskey Rebellion: The Story of an Uprising* (Pittsburgh: University of Pittsburgh Press, 1935), pp. 90–97.

16. Reardon, *Edmund Randolph*, pp. 253–254.

23. The Whiskey Insurrection

1. Miller, *Federalist Era*, p. 15.

2. Baldwin, *Whiskey Rebellion*, passim; also see Jacob E. Cooke, "The Whiskey Insurrection: A Re-evaluation," *Pennsylvania History*, 30 (July 1963), number 3, pp. 316–346, and David O. Whitlea, "The Economic Inquiry into the Whiskey Rebellion of 1794," *Agricultural History*, 49 (July 1975), pp. 491–504; the more critical observation from Crèvecoeur is in Forrest Mcdonald, *Alexander Hamilton*, p. 297.

3. Captain David Ford, *Journal of an Expedition Made in the Autumn of 1794* (n.p.: n.d.), Princeton University Library.

4. Kohn, *Eagle and Sword*, chapter 8.

5. *GW*, 32, pp. 149–152; 33, pp. 464, 475–476, 506–507, 520–523; 34, pp. 3, 16–18, 28–37, 98; 35, pp. 325–326. *AH*, 12, p. 413. William Miller, "The Democratic Societies and the Whiskey Insurrection," *Pennsylvania Magazine of History and Biography*, 62 (July 1938), pp. 324–359. Also of interest is William D. Barber, " '*Among the Most Techy Articles of Civil Police*': Federal Taxation and the Adoption of the Whiskey Excise," *William & Mary Quarterly*, 25, 3rd series (January 1968), pp. 58–84.

24. The Jay Treaty

1. Bemis, *A Diplomatic History of the United States*, chapters 6 and 7; Alexander De Conde, *Entangling Alliance* (Durham, N.C.: Duke University Press, 1958); Felix Gilbert, *To the Farewell Address* (Princeton, N.J.: Princeton University Press, 1961); Bradford Perkins, *The First Rapprochement* (Berkeley: University of California Press, 1967), chapter 3; and A. L. Burt, *The United States, Great Britain and British North America* (New York: Russell and Russell, 1961), chapter 8.

2. Ralston Hayden, *The Senate and Treaties 1789–1817* (New York: Macmillan, 1920), chapter 4.

3. *GW*, 33, pp. 320–321. See also Monaghan, *John Jay*, and Richard B. Morris, *John Jay, The Nation and the Court* (Boston: Boston University Press, 1967).

4. *GW*, 34, pp. 212–213, 224–228, 237–240. Samuel Flagg Bemis, *The Jay Treaty* (New Haven, Conn.: Yale University Press, 1923); Arthur P. Whitaker, "Godoy's Knowledge of the Terms of Jay's Treaty," *American Historical Review*, 35 (July 1930), pp. 804–810.

5. McDonald, *Washington*, chapter 8, and Miller, *Federalist Era*, chapter 10.

6. *GW*, 34, pp. 280, 266, 316–317, 277, 321, 339–342, 343–345; 33, pp. 343–346, 424. Monroe D. Conway, *Edmund Randolph* (New York: G. P. Putnam's Sons, 1888); Reardon, *Edmund Randolph*, chapters 21 and 22; Irving Brant, "Edmund Randolph, Not Guilty," *William & Mary Quarterly*, 3rd series, 7 (April 1950), pp. 179–198; and Mary K. Bonsteal Tachau, "George Washington and the Reputation of Edmund Randolph," *Journal of American History*, 73 (June 1986), pp. 15–34.

25. Troubles in the House, 1796

1. Bemis, *Jay Treaty*, and De Conde, *Entangling Alliance*, cover, in passing, this period; the House debate and the allusion to impeachment is in *The Annals* of the Fourth Congress, pp. 427–451.

2. Jerald A. Combs, *The Jay Treaty* (Berkeley: University of California Press, 1970).

3. *GW*, 33, pp. 414–415, 420–422; 34, pp. 140, 218; 35, pp. 30, 32, 2–5, 9. Freeman, *First in Peace*, pp. 354–355 and passim. See also W. Taylor Reveley III, *War Powers of the President and Congress*, p. 88; a similar problem is recorded in Jimmy Carter, *Keeping Faith* (New York: Bantam Books, 1982), pp. 180–185.

4. *The Anas of Thomas Jefferson*, pp. 73–74.

5. Winfred E. A. Bernard, *Fisher Ames* (Chapel Hill: University of North Carolina Press, 1965), and *Works of Fisher Ames*, edited by Seth Ames, volume 2 (New York: Da Capo, reprinted 1969).

6. Combs, *Jay Treaty*, p. 178.

26. French Ire to the End, 1796–1797

1. *GW*, 35, pp. 255–256, 300, 358–359, covers some of the president's reactions during this strained period. Gerard H. Clarfield, *Timothy Pickering and American Diplomacy 1795–1800* (Columbia: University of Missouri Press, 1969), chapters 1 and 2.

2. Miller, *Federalist Era*, chapter 12.

3. Clarfield, *Timothy Pickering*, chapters 3 and 4.

4. James Thomas Flexner, *George Washington: Anguish and Farewell* (Boston: Little, Brown, 1972), pp. 324–325; Eugene Perry Link, *Democratic–Republican Societies, 1790–1800*, summarizes some of these criticisms.

5. Flexner, *Anguish and Farewell*, p. 382.

6. Freeman, *First in Peace*, chapter 15.

7. Freeman, *First in Peace*, pp. 435–436.

8. Freeman, *First in Peace*, p. 437.

27. Washington as Legend

1. Mason Weems, *The Life of Washington*, edited by Marcus Cunliffe (Cambridge, Mass.: Belkap Press of Harvard University Press, 1962), reprint of the ninth edition of the original; John Marshall, *The Life of George Washington* (Fredericksburg, Va.: The Citizens' Guilds of Washington's Boyhood Home, 1926); Washington Irving, *Life of George Washington* (New York: AMS Press, 1973), reprint of the 1890 edition.

2. *TJ*, 9, pp. 446–457.

3. Freeman, *First in Peace*, p. 651.

4. William Alfred Bryan, *George Washington in American Literature 1775–1865* (New York: Columbia University Press, 1952); Bernard Mayo, *Myths and Men* (Athens: University of Georgia Press, 1959); and Marcus Cunliffe, *George Washington, Man and Monument* (New York: Mentor Books, 1960).

5. Robert P. Hay, "George Washington: American Moses," *American Quarterly*,

21 (Winter 1969), pp. 780–791; Mary W. Smith, "Contemporary Songs and Verses About Washington," *New England Quarterly*, 5 (April 1932), pp. 281–292; Louis M. Miner, *"Our Rude Forefathers": American Political Verse, 1783–1788* (Cedar Rapids, Iowa: The Torch Press, 1937), and Albanese, *Sons of the Fathers.*

Epilogue

1. Peter Shaw, *The Character of John Adams* (Chapel Hill: University of North Carolina Press, 1976); John R. Howe, Jr., *The Changing Political Thought of John Adams* (Princeton, N.J.: Princeton University Press, 1966); Page Smith, "The Election of 1796," *History of American Presidential Elections 1789–1986*, edited by Arthur M. Schlesinger, Jr., Fred L. Israel, and William P. Hansen (New York: Chelsea House Publishers, 1971), pp. 59–80; Page Smith, *John Adams*, two volumes (Garden City, N.Y.: Doubleday, 1962). The role of Hamilton is disputed in McDonald, *Hamilton*, p. 438.

2. *The Works of John Adams*, volume 1, p. 483, Richardson, *Messages and Papers of the Presidency*, volume 1, pp. 233–239, and Ralph Adams Brown, *The Presidency of John Adams* (Lawrence: University Press of Kansas, 1978), chapter 3. Also of use is McDonald, *Hamilton*, pp. 331–332; Alexander De Conde, *The Quasi War* (New York: Charles Scribner's Sons, 1966), pp. 16–17; Kohn, *Eagle and Sword*, pp. 193–218; John R. Rowe, Jr., "Republican Thought and the Political Violence of the 1790s," *American Quarterly*, 19 (Summer 1967), pp. 147–165; J. Wendell Knox, *Conspiracy in American Politics 1787–1815* (New York: Arno Press, reprinted 1972); Marshall Smelser, "The Federalist Period as an Age of Passion," *American Quarterly*, 10 (Winter 1958), pp. 391–419; his "The Jacobin Phrenzy: Federalism and the Menace of Liberty, Equality and Fraternity," *Review of Politics*, 13 (October 1951), pp. 457–482; and his, "The Jacobin Phrenzy: The Menace of Monarchy, Plutocracy and Anglophilia, 1789–1798," *Review of Politics*, 22 (January 1959), pp. 239–258.

3. Crane Brinton, *The Lives of Talleyrand* (New York: W. W. Norton, 1936); De Conde, *The Quasi War*, chapter 2; Eugene F. Kramer, "John Adams, Elbridge Gerry and the Origins of the XYZ Affair," *Essex Institute Historical Collection*, 94 (1958), pp. 57–68; Arthur B. Darling, *Our Rising Empire* (New Haven, Conn.: Yale University Press, 1940); Marvin R. Zahniser, *Charles Cotesworth Pinckney: Founding Father* (Chapel Hill: University of North Carolina Press, 1967), chapters 6 and 7; Clarfield, *Timothy Pickering and American Diplomacy*, chapter 8.

4. Brown, *Presidency of John Adams*, pp. 45–46; Miller, *Federalist Era*, chapters 12 and 13; James A. James, "French Opinion as a Factor in Preventing War Between France and the United States 1795–1800," *American Historical Review*, 30 (October 1924), pp. 44–55, and Samuel Flagg Bemis, *John Quincy Adams and the Foundations of American Foreign Policy* (New York: Alfred A. Knopf, 1969), chapters 3 through 5.

5. Kohn, *Eagle and Sword*, p. 211; Knox, *Conspiracy*, chapter 4; Smelser, "The Jacobin Phrenzy," both articles cited above.

6. De Conde, *The Quasi War*, p. 89.

7. Kohn, *Eagle and Sword*, pp. 224–225; William J. Murphy, Jr., "John Adams: The Politics of the Additional Army, 1798–1800," *New England Quarterly*, 52 (June 1979), pp. 234–249; Brown, *The Presidency of John Adams*, chapter 6; Peter B. Hill,

William Vans Murray: Federalist Diplomat (Syracuse, N.Y.: Syracuse University Press, 1971).

8. James Martin Smith, *Freedom's Fetters* (Ithaca, N.Y.: Cornell University Press, 1956), pp. 24, 85–92, 106, 166, 184, 187; John Miller, *Crisis in Freedom* (Boston: Little, Brown, 1951), pp. 134–135; Adrienne Koch and Harry Ammon, "Virginia and Kentucky Resolutions," *William & Mary Quarterly*, 3rd series, 5 (April 1948), pp. 145–176; and James Morton Smith, "Grass Roots Origins of Kentucky Resolution," *William & Mary Quarterly*, 3rd series, 27 (April 1970), pp. 221–245.

9. Brown, *Presidency of John Adams*, chapter 1; Gerald Clarfield, "John Adams: The Marketplace and American Foreign Policy," *New England Quarterly*, 52 (September 1979), pp. 345–357; De Conde, *The Quasi War*, chapters 4 through 6; Robert Ernst, *Rufus King* (Chapel Hill: University of North Carolina Press, 1968), chapters 13 and 14; Bemis, *John Quincy Adams*, chapter 5; Frederick B. Tolles, *George Logan of Philadelphia* (New York: Oxford University Press, 1953), chapters 8 through 10; and *The Works of John Adams*, volume 8, passim.

10. Cunningham, *Jeffersonian Republicans*, chapter 7; Miller, *Federalist Era*, chapter 14; Manning J. Dauer, *The Adams Federalists* (Baltimore: Johns Hopkins University Press, 1968), chapters 14 through 16.

11. Isser Woloch, *Eighteenth Century Europe* (New York: W. W. Norton, 1982).

12. R. R. Palmer, *The Age of the Democratic Revolution*, two volumes (Princeton, N.J.: Princeton University Press, 1959 and 1964).

13. Richard B. Morris and Graham N. Irwin, *Harper Encyclopedia of The Modern World* (New York: Harper and Row, 1967), and Peter Gay, *The Columbia History of the World* (New York: Harper and Row, 1972), part 4, are good summaries that coordinate various regional events in this era.

BIBLIOGRAPHICAL ESSAY

I have tried, where possible, in the notes to group references in such a way that I could limit the number of pages taken up by those sources, but still acknowledge my considerable debt to those major monographs and articles. Primary sources are also cited in that way for the specialist interested in following the thoughts and statements of the major principals involved in this period. There has been a considerable growth in the secondary literature on the origins of the American Revolution and the conditions of eighteen-century English political life. Of use is Bernard Bailyn, *The Origins of American Politics* (New York: Vintage Books, 1967), his *Ideological Origins of the American Revolution* (Cambridge, Mass.: Harvard University Press, 1967), and Caroline Robbins, *The Eighteenth-Century Commonwealthmen* (Cambridge, Mass.: Harvard University Press, 1959). A broader interpretation of the British imperial system is provided by several historians; the most extensively used in this study is the four volumes by George R. Beer, *The Origins of the British Colonial System 1578–1600* (Gloucester, Mass.: Peter Smith, reprinted 1959), his *British Colonial Policy 1754–1765* (1958), and his *The Old Colonial Systems 1660–1754*, volumes 1 and 2 (1958).

British notions of royal authority and political leadership are explored in J. H. Plumb, *The Growth of Political Stability in England 1675–1725* (London: MacMillan, 1967); Lewis Namier, *England in the Age of the American Revolution* (London: MacMillan, 1961); and Basil Williams, *The Whig Supremacy 1714–1760* (Oxford: Clarendon Press, 1939). The best biography of Robert Walpole's life is J. H. Plumb, *Sir Robert Walpole*, two volumes (Boston: Houghton Mifflin, 1961). I have used Blackstone and Locke as two authorities on royal power and authority in the period before the gestation of the American Revolution. Although the English realities were quite different, both writers were well known in the colonies and highly influential on the American colonial mind.

The other manifestation of executive authority before the Revolution was the royal or provincial governors. I have profited from Stephen Saunders Webb, *The Governors-General: The English Army and the Definition of the Empire 1569–1681* (Chapel Hill: University of North Carolina Press, 1979), and Leonard W. Labaree, *Royal Government in America* (New York: Frederick Ungar, reprinted 1958). An older study has proven most useful: Evarts B. Greene, *The Provincial Governor in the English Colonies of North America* (New York: Longmans, Green, 1898). The contrast between Thomas Hutchinson and Jonathan Trumbull illustrates how some royal officials adapted and most did not to the patriot cause. The best biographies are Bernard Bailyn, *The Ordeal of Thomas Hutchinson* (Cambridge, Mass.: Harvard University Press, 1974), and Glynn Weaver, *Jonathan Trumbull* (Hartford: Connecticut Historical Society, 1956).

The development of an indigenous American executive is covered in Margaret B. MacMillan, *The War Governors in the American Revolution* (New York: Columbia University Press, 1943). The most successful state governor of the period was George Clinton, and a useful study is E. Wilder Spaulding, *His Excellency George Clinton: Critic of the Constitution*, second edition (Port Washington, N.Y.: Ira J. Freedman, reprinted 1964). The various state constitutions are compiled in Francis N. Thorpe, ed., *The Federal and State Constitutions*, seven volumes (Washington, D.C.: Government Printing Office, 1909). Also of importance is an older survey of executive authority: Charles Thach, *The Creation of the Presidency 1775–1789* (Baltimore: Johns Hopkins University Press, 1922).

The debates on the presidency in the Constitutional Convention are referred to in Clinton Rossiter's lucid *1787, The Grand Convention* (New York: Macmillan, 1966), and Catherine Drinker's fast-paced account, *Miracle at Philadelphia* (Boston: Little, Brown, 1966). The standard reference remains *The Records of the Federal Convention 1787*, edited by Max Farrand, four volumes (New Haven, Conn.: Yale University Press, reprinted 1966). I have surveyed the pamphlet literature and the state ratifying conventions in my "The Presidency and the Ratification Controversy," *Presidential Studies Quarterly*, 5 (Winter 1977), pp. 37–46. The major volume on that period is Robert A. Rutland, *The Ordeal of the Constitution* (Norman: University of Oklahoma Press, 1966).

Washington's position on the development of the early presidency is central. The major multivolume biographies of his life and career are Douglas Southall Freeman, *George Washington*, especially volume 6 (New York: Charles Scribner's Sons, 1954) and volume 7 finished up by his associates, John Alexander Carroll and Mary Wells Ashworth (New York: Charles Scribner's Sons, 1957), and James Thomas Flexner, *George Washington*, four volumes (Boston: Little, Brown, 1965–1969). The governmental apparatus before Washington's administration has received little attention. The best treatments are somewhat dated: Frank Fletcher Stephens, *The Transition Period 1788–1789 in the Government of the United States* (Columbia, Mo: E. W. Stephens, 1909); Jennings B. Sanders, *The Presidency of the Continental Congress 1774–1789* (Gloucester, Mass.: Peter Smith, 1971); Jay Caesar Guggenheimer, "The Development of the Executive Departments," in *Essays in Constitutional History of the United States in the Formative Period, 1775–1789*, edited by J. Franklin Jameson (Boston: Houghton Mifflin, 1889), and James Hart, *The American Presidency in Action 1789* (New York: Macmillan, 1948).

The best single account of the Washington administration is Forrest McDonald's *The Presidency of George Washington* (New York: W. W. Norton, 1975), which is especially valuable in understanding the debt assumption crisis. John Miller, *The Federalist Era* (New York: Harper and Row, 1960), is a useful survey of the period that covers the major outlines of foreign and domestic controversies faced by Washington and Adams. Alexander Hamilton's state papers are especially important; see *Papers of Alexander Hamilton*, edited by Harold C. Syrett and Jacob E. Cooke (New

York: Columbia University Press, 1961—). His brilliant career is covered in Broadus Mitchell, *Alexander Hamilton, the National Adventure: 1788–1804* (New York: Macmillan, 1962); also of use is the little cited, but rather interesting Robert Hendrickson, *Hamilton*, two volumes (New York: Mason-Charter, 1976).

Noteworthy monographs on administrative history of the period include Leonard White, *The Federalists* (New York: Macmillan, 1956), and Carl E. Prince, *The Federalists and the Origins of the U.S. Civil Service* (New York: New York University Press, 1977). The establishment of the Bank of the United States and the rise of a party opposition is covered in some of the previous surveys of the period as well as in Noble Cunningham, *The Jeffersonian Republicans, 1789–1801* (Chapel Hill: University of North Carolina Press, 1957), and Bray Hammond, *Banks and Politics in America from Revolution to Civil War* (Princeton, N.J.: Princeton University Press, 1957).

The Indian wars and diplomatic negotiations with the first administration are generally overlooked aspects of the Washington years. One notable exception that was published after this manuscript was completed is Wiley Sword, *President Washington's Indian War* (Norman: University of Oklahoma Press, 1985). Very useful is Richard H. Kohn, *Eagle and Sword: The Federalists and the Creation of the Military Establishment in America* (New York: Free Press, 1975). Other important works are Reginald Horsman, *The Frontier in the Formative Years 1783–1815* (New York: Holt, Rinehart, and Winston, 1970), and George D. Hanson, *Sixty Years of Indian Affairs* (Chapel Hill: University of North Carolina Press, 1941).

Foreign policy in the administration is surveyed in various volumes, especially Thomas A. Bailey, *A Diplomatic History of the American People* (Englewood Cliffs, N.J.: Prentice-Hall, 1980). Charles Marion Thomas, *American Neutrality in 1793* (New York: Columbia University Press, 1931), is still useful, as is Alexander De Conde, *Entangling Alliance* (Durham, N.C.: Duke University Press, 1958), and Bradford Perkins, *The First Rapprochement* (Berkeley: University of California Press, 1967). Samuel Flagg Bemis, *The Jay Treaty* (New Haven, Conn.: Yale University Press, 1923), remains a valuable study of the controversial foreign policy pact. Equally valuable is Jerald A. Combs, *The Jay Treaty* (Berkeley: University of California Press, 1970). The management of the latter period's foreign policy is in Gerald H. Clarfield, *Timothy Pickering and American Diplomacy 1795–1800* (Columbia: University of Missouri Press, 1969).

The place of Washington in the American imagination is a powerful but disjointed one. One volume published after this manuscript was completed is rather interesting in tracing the Cincinnatus image: George Wills, *Cincinnatus* (New York: Doubleday, 1984). In a different vein, William Alfred Bryan, *George Washington in American Literature 1775–1865* (New York: Columbia University Press, 1952), traces the legend in the arts. Also important are the English perspective of Marcus Cunliffe, *George Washington, Man and Monument* (New York: Mentor Books, 1960), and a broader view, Catherine Albanese, *Sons of the Fathers: Civil Religion of the American Revolution* (Philadelphia: Temple University Press, 1977).

Good treatments of Adams' presidency are Peter Shaw, *The Character of John Adams* (Chapel Hill: University of North Carolina Press, 1976); Ralph Adams Brown, *The Presidency of John Adams* (Lawrence: University Press of Kansas, 1978);

James Martin Smith, *Freedom's Fetters* (Ithaca, N.Y.: Cornell University Press, 1956); Stephen G. Kurtz, *The Presidency of John Adams* (Philadelphia: University of Pennsylvania Press, 1957); and Manning Dauer, *The Adams Federalists* (Baltimore: Johns Hopkins University Press, 1958).

INDEX

Index

About the Author

MICHAEL P. RICCARDS is President of St. John's College, Sante Fe, New Mexico. He has previously been Provost and Professor of Political Science at Hunter College (CUNY) and Dean of Arts and Science at the University of Massachusetts at Boston. He holds a Ph.D. from Rutgers University, has been a Fulbright Fellow to Japan, a National Endowment for the Humanities Fellow at Princeton University, and a Henry Huntington Fellow. He is the author of *The Making of the American Citizenry: An Introduction to Political Socialization* and co-editor of *Reflections in American Political Thought: From Past to Present.*